SAS® System for Regression

Second Edition

SAS Institute Inc.
SAS Campus Drive
Cary, NC 27513

Contents

Acknowledgments

We would like to acknowledge several persons at SAS Institute whose efforts have contributed to the completion of this book. First of all, we are grateful to Jim Goodnight who originally encouraged us to write this book. Several persons reviewed the chapters and contributed many useful comments. The reviewers were Jim Ashton, Jenny Kendall, Charles Lin, Eddie Routten, Warren Sarle, and Mike Stockstill.

The work of several persons has influenced our writing. In particular, we acknowledge Professors Walt Harvey of Ohio State University, Ron Hocking of Texas A&M University, Bill Sanders of the University of Tennessee, and Shayle Searle of Cornell University.

Finally, we thank the students at Texas A&M University and the University of Florida whose research projects provided the ideas and data for many of the examples.

About the Authors

Rudolf J. Freund, Ph.D.

Rudolf J. Freund is a professor of statistics in the Department of Statistics at Texas A&M University, where he served as associate director and cofounder of the Institute of Statistics from 1962 to 1977. He received an M.A. degree in economics from the University of Chicago in 1951 and a Ph.D. in statistics at North Carolina State University in 1955. He was associate professor of statistics at Virginia Polytechnic Institute from 1955 until 1962 and was also the first director of the computing center for that university.

Dr. Freund is coauthor (with Paul D. Minton) of *Regression Methods* and *SAS System for Linear Models, Third Edition* (with Ramon Littell), and is currently writing (with William J. Wilson) a textbook on statistical methods for publication in 1991. He has also written a course supplement, *Learning Statistics with the SAS System*.

Currently, Freund teaches basic statistical methods and regression analysis courses for graduate students.

Ramon C. Littell, Ph.D.

Dr. Ramon C. Littell has the rank of professor of statistics at the University of Florida in Gainesville. He received his graduate training at Oklahoma State University earning an M.S. degree in mathematics in 1966 and a Ph.D. degree in statistics in 1970. Dr. Littell teaches graduate courses in linear models, a course in matrix algebra for statisticians, and courses in statistical methods.

Freund and Littell, both SAS users since 1972 and former SUGI chairmen, were closely associated with the Southern Regional Project that funded continued SAS development at North Carolina State University. In addition to their university positions, both authors publish widely in statistical and applied journals, consult in industry, and serve as Consulting Statisticians to their state Agricultural Experiment Stations. They are both fellows of the American Statistical Association.

Using This Book

Purpose

Most statistical analyses are based on linear models, and most analyses of linear models can be performed by three SAS procedures: REG, ANOVA, and GLM. Unlike statistical packages that need different programs for each type of analysis, these procedures provide the power and flexibility for almost all linear model analyses.

To use these procedures properly, you should understand the statistics you need for the analysis and know how to instruct the procedures to carry out the computations. *SAS System for Regression, Second Edition* was written to make it easier for you to apply these procedures to your data analysis problems. In this book, a wide variety of data is used to illustrate the basic kinds of regression models that can be analyzed with these SAS procedures.

Audience

SAS System for Regression is intended to assist data analysts who use SAS/STAT and SAS/ETS software to perform data analysis using regression analysis. This book assumes you are familiar with basic SAS System concepts such as creating SAS data sets with the DATA step and manipulating SAS data sets with the procedures in base SAS software.

Prerequisites

The following table summarizes the SAS System concepts that you need to understand in order to use SAS/STAT software.

You need to know how to	Refer to
invoke the SAS System at your site	instructions provided by the SAS Software Consultant at your site
use base SAS software	*SAS Language and Procedures: Introduction, Version 6, First Edition* for a brief introduction, or *SAS Language and Procedures: Usage, Version 6, First Edition* for a more thorough introduction
create and read SAS data sets	*SAS Language: Reference, Version 6, First Edition*

(Continued)

(*Continued*)

You need to know how to	Refer to
use SAS/STAT software	*SAS/STAT User's Guide, Version 6, Fourth Edition, Volume 1* and *Volume 2*
use SAS/ETS software	*SAS/ETS User's Guide, Version 6, First Edition*

Although this book contains some explanation of statistical methods, it is not intended as a text for these methods. The reader should have a working knowledge of the statistical concepts discussed in this book.

How to Use This Book

The following sections provide an overview of the information contained in this book and how it is organized.

Organization

SAS System for Regression represents an introduction to regression analysis as performed by the SAS System. In addition to the most current programming conventions for both Version 5 and Version 6 of the SAS System, this volume contains information about new features and capabilities of several SAS procedures. Here is a summary of the information contained in each chapter:

Chapter 1, "Regression Concepts"
   covers three topics: the terminology and notation used in regression analysis; an overview of matrix notation and the IML procedure; and an overview of regression procedures available in the SAS System.

Chapter 2, "Using the REG Procedure"
   introduces regression analysis, using PROC REG with a single independent variable. The statistics on the printed output are discussed in detail. Next, a regression is performed using the same data but with several independent variables. The MODEL statement options P, CLM, and CLI are used and explained. The NOINT option, which is controversial, is used and discussed. This option is also misused in an example to point out the dangers of forcing the regression response to pass through the origin when this situation is unreasonable or unlikely. Output data sets are created using the statistics generated with PROC REG.

Chapter 3, "Observations"
   discusses the assumptions behind the regression analysis and illustrates how the data analyst assesses violations of assumptions. This chapter discusses outliers, or those observations that do not appear to fit the model; these can bias parameter estimates and make your regression analysis less useful. This chapter also discusses ways to identify the influence (or leverage) of specific observations. Studentized residuals are used to identify large residuals. Examples are shown using residuals that are plotted using the PLOT and GPLOT procedures. In addition, this chapter discusses ways to detect specification errors and assess the fit of the model, ways to check the distribution of the errors for nonnormality, ways to check for

heteroscedasticity, or nonconstant variances of errors, and ways to detect correlation between errors.

Chapter 4, "Multicollinearity: Detection and Remedial Measures"
discusses the existence of multicollinearity (correlation among several independent variables) and measures you can use to detect multicollinearity and ways to alleviate the effects of it. Variance inflation factors are used to determine the variables involved. Multivariate techniques are used to study the structure of multicollinearity. Included in this chapter are discussions of principal components regression and variable selection, including stepwise regression techniques.

Chapter 5, "Polynomial Models"
gives examples of linear regression methods to estimate parameters of models that cannot be described by straight lines. The discussion of polynomial models, models in which the dependent variable is related to functions of the powers of one or more independent variables, begins by using one independent variable. Then examples are given using several variables. Response surface plots are used to illustrate the nature of the estimated response curve.

Chapter 6, "Special Applications of Linear Models"
covers some special applications of the linear model, including log-linear (multiplicative) models, spline functions with known knots, and the use of indicator variables.

Chapter 7, "Nonlinear Models"
covers special relationships that cannot be addressed by linear models or adaptations of linear models. Topics discussed include fitting nonlinear models, fitting nonlinear growth curves, and fitting splines with unknown knots, and a summary of the estimating algorithms available with the NLIN procedure.

Appendix, "Example Code," provides a summary of SAS code used in the examples.

Conventions

This section covers the conventions this book uses, including typographical conventions, syntax conventions, and conventions used in presenting output.

Typographical Conventions

This book uses several type styles. The following list summarizes style conventions:

roman	is the basic type style used for most text.
UPPERCASE ROMAN	is used for references in text to SAS language elements.

italic	is used in margin notes to provide cautionary information, in text to define terms, and in formulas.
bold	is used in headings, in text to indicate very important points, and in formulas to indicate matrices and vectors.
bold italic	is used in headings to refer to syntax elements that you supply.
`monospace`	is used to show examples of programming code. In most cases, this book uses lowercase type for SAS code. You can enter your own SAS code in lowercase, uppercase, or a mixture of the two. The SAS System changes your variable names to uppercase, but character variable values remain in lowercase if you have entered them that way. Enter the case for titles, notes, and footnotes exactly as you want them to appear in your output.

Syntax Conventions

Syntax conventions are used to show the basic format of a SAS statement. This book uses the following conventions for syntax:

UPPERCASE BOLD	indicates the names of functions and statements. These must be spelled as shown.
UPPERCASE ROMAN	indicates elements that must be spelled as shown.
italic	indicates elements (such as variable names) that you supply. In some cases, the procedure accepts a limited set of values, such as values between 0 and 1 for an option that provides probability values. In other cases, the procedure accepts any value you supply, such as the name of a data set.
<arguments in angle brackets>	are optional. Multiple arguments within one set of angle brackets means that if you use one argument, you must use all arguments.
arguments not in angle brackets	are required.
| (vertical bar)	indicates a choice of one of the items from a group. Items separated by bars are either mutually exclusive or aliases.
. . . (ellipsis)	indicates items that can be repeated indefinitely.

The following example illustrates these points:

TEST *'label'equation* <, . . . ,*equation*>;

TEST is in bold uppercase because it is a SAS statement. *label* and *equation* are in italic because you supply the values. In this TEST statement, a *label* and at least one *equation* is required. Additional *equation* specifications are optional. Commas must appear between each *equation*.

Conventions for Output

All SAS code in the book was run through Release 6.06 of the SAS System under the MVS operating system.

Because of differences in software versions, size options, and graphics devices, your graphics or numerical output may not be identical to what appears in this book.

Additional Documentation

The *Publications Catalog*, published twice a year, gives detailed information on the many publications available from SAS Institute. To obtain a free catalog, please send your request to the following address:

> SAS Institute Inc.
> Book Sales Department
> SAS Campus Drive
> Cary, NC 27513

SAS Series in Statistical Applications

SAS System for Regression is one in a series of statistical applications guides developed by SAS Institute. Each book in the SAS series in statistical applications covers a well-defined statistical topic by describing and illustrating relevant SAS procedures.

Other books currently available include

☐ *SAS System for Linear Models, Third Edition* (order #A56140) provides information about features and capabilities of the GLM, ANOVA, REG, MEANS, TTEST, and NESTED procedures. Topics include regression; balanced analysis of variance, including a discussion of the use of multiple-comparison procedures and nested designs; analysis-of-variance models of less-than-full rank; analysis of unbalanced data; analysis of covariance; multivariate linear models; and univariate and multivariate repeated-measures analysis of variance.

☐ *SAS System for Forecasting Time Series, 1986 Edition* (order #A5629) describes how SAS/ETS software can be used to perform univariate and multivariate time-series analyses. Early chapters introduce linear regression and autoregression using simple models. Later chapters discuss the ARIMA model and its special applications, state space modeling, spectral analysis, and cross-spectral analysis. The SAS procedures ARIMA, STATESPACE, and SPECTRA are featured, with mention of the simpler procedures FORECAST, AUTOREG, and X11.

☐ *SAS System for Elementary Statistical Analysis* (order #A5619) teaches you how to perform a variety of data analysis tasks and interpret your results. Written in tutorial style, the guide provides the essential information you need, without overwhelming you with extraneous details. This approach makes the book a ready guide for the business user and an excellent tool for teaching fundamental statistical concepts. Topics include comparing two or more groups, simple regression and basic diagnostics, as well as basic DATA steps.

This series is designed to aid data analysts who use the SAS System and students in statistics courses who want to see more practical applications of the methods discussed in textbooks, lectures, and primary SAS statistical documentation. These manuals are intended to supplement the references you are using now; they will not take the place of a good statistics book and should be used with appropriate SAS user's guides.

Documentation for Other SAS Software

You will find these other books helpful when using SAS/STAT and SAS/ETS software.

□ *SAS Language and Procedures: Introduction, Version 6, First Edition* (order #56074) provides information if you are unfamiliar with the SAS System or any other programming language.

□ *SAS Language and Procedures: Usage, Version 6, First Edition* (order #A56075) provides task-oriented examples of the major features of base SAS software.

□ *SAS Language: Reference, Version 6, First Edition* (order #A56076) provides detailed reference information about SAS language statements, functions, formats, and informats; the SAS Display Manager System; the SAS Text Editor; or any other element of base SAS software except for procedures.

□ The *SAS/STAT User's Guide, Version 6, Fourth Edition, Volume 1* and *Volume 2* (order #A56045) provides reference and usage material for SAS/STAT software.

□ The *SAS/ETS User's Guide, Version 6, First Edition* (order #A5849) provides reference and usage material for SAS/ETS software.

Chapter 1 Regression Concepts

1.1 Statistical Background

Multiple linear regression is a means to express the idea that a response variable, y, varies with a set of independent variables $x_1, x_2, \ldots, x_m$. The variability that y exhibits has two components: a systematic part and a random part. The systematic variation of y can be modeled as a function of the x variables. The model relating y to $x_1, x_2, \ldots, x_m$ is called the *regression equation*. The random part takes into account the fact that the model does not exactly describe the behavior of the response.

Formally, multiple linear regression fits a response variable y to a function of regressor variables and parameters. The general linear regression model has the form:

$$y = \beta_0 + \beta_1 x_1 + \beta_2 x_2 + \ldots + \beta_m x_m + \varepsilon$$

where

y is the response, or dependent, variable

$\beta_0, \beta_1, \ldots, \beta_m$ are unknown parameters

$x_1, x_2, \ldots, x_m$ are the regressor, or independent, variables

ε is a random error term.

Least squares is a technique used to estimate the parameters. The goal is to find estimates of the parameters $\beta_0, \beta_1, \ldots, \beta_m$ that minimize the sum of the squared differences between the actual y values and the values of y predicted by the equation. These estimates are called the *least-squares estimates* and the quantity minimized is called the *error sum of squares*.

Typically, you use regression analysis to do the following:

□ obtain the least-squares estimates of the parameters

□ estimate the variance of the error term

□ estimate the standard error of the parameter estimates

□ test hypotheses about the parameters

□ calculate predicted values using the estimated equation

□ evaluate the fit or lack of fit of the model.

The classical linear model assumes that the responses, y, are sampled from several populations. These populations are determined by the corresponding values of x_1, x_2, . . . , x_m. As the investigator, you select the values of the x's; they are not random. However, the response values are random. You select the values of the x's to meet your experimental needs, carry out the experiment with the set values of the x's, and measure the responses. Often, though, you cannot control the actual values of the independent variables. In these cases, you should at least be able to assume that they are fixed with respect to the response variable.

In addition, you must assume that

1. the form of the model is correct; that is, all important independent variables are included and the functional form is appropriate

2. the expected values of the errors are zero

3. the variances of the errors (and thus the response variable) are constant across observations

4. the errors are uncorrelated

5. for hypothesis testing, the errors are normally distributed.

1.1.1 Terminology and Notation

The principle of least squares is applied to a set of n observed values of y and the associated x_j to obtain estimates $\hat{\beta}_0$, $\hat{\beta}_1$, . . . , $\hat{\beta}_m$ of the respective parameters β_0, β_1, . . . , β_m. These estimates are then used to construct the fitted model, or estimating equation

$$\hat{y} = \hat{\beta}_0 + \hat{\beta}_1 x_1 + \ldots + \hat{\beta}_m x_m \quad .$$

Many regression computations are illustrated conveniently in matrix notation. Let y_i, x_{ij}, and ε_i denote the values of y, x_j, and ε, respectively, in the ith observation. The **Y** vector, the **X** matrix, and the ε vector can be defined as follows:

$$\mathbf{Y} = \begin{bmatrix} y_1 \\ . \\ . \\ . \\ y_n \end{bmatrix}, \mathbf{X} = \begin{bmatrix} 1 & x_{11} & \ldots & x_{1m} \\ . & . & & . \\ . & . & & . \\ . & . & & . \\ 1 & x_{n1} & \ldots & x_{nm} \end{bmatrix}, \varepsilon = \begin{bmatrix} \varepsilon_1 \\ . \\ . \\ . \\ \varepsilon_n \end{bmatrix}$$

Then the model in matrix notation is

$$\mathbf{Y} = \mathbf{X}\boldsymbol{\beta} + \boldsymbol{\varepsilon}$$

where $\boldsymbol{\beta}' = (\beta_0, \beta_1, \dots, \beta_m)$ is the parameter vector.

The vector of least-squares estimates is $\hat{\boldsymbol{\beta}}' = (\hat{\beta}_0, \hat{\beta}_1, \dots, \hat{\beta}_m)$ and is obtained by solving the set of normal equations (NE)

$$\mathbf{X}'\mathbf{X}\boldsymbol{\beta} = \mathbf{X}'\mathbf{Y} \quad .$$

Assuming that $\mathbf{X}'\mathbf{X}$ is of full rank (nonsingular), there is a unique solution to the normal equations given by

$$\hat{\boldsymbol{\beta}} = (\mathbf{X}'\mathbf{X})^{-1} \mathbf{X}'\mathbf{Y} \quad .$$

The matrix $(\mathbf{X}'\mathbf{X})^{-1}$ is very useful in regression analysis and is often denoted as follows:

$$(\mathbf{X}'\mathbf{X})^{-1} = \mathbf{C} = \begin{bmatrix} c_{00} & c_{01} & \cdots & c_{0m} \\ c_{10} & c_{11} & \cdots & c_{1m} \\ \cdot & \cdot & & \cdot \\ \cdot & \cdot & & \cdot \\ \cdot & \cdot & & \cdot \\ c_{m0} & c_{m1} & \cdots & c_{mm} \end{bmatrix}$$

1.1.2 Partitioning the Sums of Squares

A basic identity results from least squares, specifically,

$$\Sigma(y - \bar{y})^2 = \Sigma(\bar{y} - \hat{y})^2 + \Sigma(y - \hat{y})^2 \quad .$$

This identity shows that the total sum of squared deviations from the mean, $\Sigma(y - \bar{y})^2$, is equal to the sum of squared differences between the mean and the predicted values, $\Sigma(\bar{y} - \hat{y})^2$, plus the sum of squared deviations from the observed y's to the regression line, $\Sigma(y - \hat{y})^2$. These two parts are called the sum of squares due to regression (or model) and the residual (or error) sum of squares. Thus,

Corrected Total SS = Model SS + Residual SS .

Corrected Total SS always has the same value for a given set of data, regardless of the model that is used; however, partitioning into Model SS and Residual SS depends on the model. Generally, the addition of a new x variable to a model increases the Model SS and, correspondingly, reduces the Residual SS. The residual, or error, sum of squares is computed as follows:

$$\begin{aligned} \text{Residual SS} &= \mathbf{Y}'(\mathbf{I} - \mathbf{X}(\mathbf{X}'\mathbf{X})^{-1}\mathbf{X}')\mathbf{Y} \\ &= \mathbf{Y}'\mathbf{Y} - \mathbf{Y}'\mathbf{X}(\mathbf{X}'\mathbf{X})^{-1}\mathbf{X}'\mathbf{Y} \\ &= \mathbf{Y}'\mathbf{Y} - \hat{\boldsymbol{\beta}}'\mathbf{X}'\mathbf{Y} \quad . \end{aligned}$$

The error, or residual, mean square

$$s^2 = \text{MSE} = (\text{Residual SS}) / (n - m - 1)$$

is an unbiased estimate of σ^2, the variance of the ε's.

Sums of squares, including the different sums of squares computed by any regression procedure such as the REG and GLM procedures, can be expressed conceptually as the difference between the regression sums of squares for two models, called complete and reduced models, respectively. This approach relates a given SS to the comparison of two regression models.

For example, denote as SS_1 the regression sum of squares for a complete model with $m=5$ variables:

$$y = \beta_0 + \beta_1 x_1 + \beta_2 x_2 + \beta_3 x_3 + \beta_4 x_4 + \beta_5 x_5 + \varepsilon \quad .$$

Denote the regression sum of squares for a reduced model not containing x_4 and x_5 as SS_2:

$$y = \beta_0 + \beta_1 x_1 + \beta_2 x_2 + \beta_3 x_3 + \varepsilon \quad .$$

Reduction notation can be used to represent the difference between regression sums of squares for the two models:

$$R(\beta_4, \beta_5 \mid \beta_0, \beta_1, \beta_2, \beta_3) = \text{Model SS}_1 - \text{Model SS}_2 \quad .$$

The difference or reduction in error $R(\beta_4, \beta_5 \mid \beta_0, \beta_1, \beta_2, \beta_3)$ indicates the increase in regression sums of squares due to the addition of β_4 and β_5 to the reduced model. It follows that

$$R(\beta_4, \beta_5 \mid \beta_0, \beta_1, \beta_2, \beta_3) = \text{Residual SS}_2 - \text{Residual SS}_1$$

that is, the decrease in error sum of squares due to the addition of β_4 and β_5 to the reduced model. The expression

$$R(\beta_4, \beta_5 \mid \beta_0, \beta_1, \beta_2, \beta_3)$$

is also commonly referred to in the following ways:

□ the sums of squares due to β_4 and β_5 (or x_4 and x_5) adjusted for $\beta_0, \beta_1, \beta_2, \beta_3$ (or the intercept and x_1, x_2, x_3)

□ the sums of squares due to fitting x_4 and x_5 after fitting the intercept and x_1, x_2, x_3

□ the effects of x_4 and x_5 above and beyond or partialing the effects of the intercept and x_1, x_2, x_3.

1.1.3 Hypothesis Testing

Inferences about model parameters are highly dependent on the other parameters in the model under consideration. Therefore, in hypothesis testing, it is important to emphasize the parameters for which inferences have been adjusted. For example, $R(\beta_3 \mid \beta_0, \beta_1, \beta_2)$ and $R(\beta_3 \mid \beta_0, \beta_1)$ may measure entirely different concepts. Similarly, a test of H_0: $\beta_3 = 0$ versus H_1: $\beta_3 \neq 0$ may have one result for the model

$$y = \beta_0 + \beta_1 x_1 + \beta_3 x_3 + \varepsilon$$

and another for the model

$$y = \beta_0 + \beta_1 x_1 + \beta_2 x_2 + \beta_3 x_3 + \varepsilon \quad .$$

Differences reflect actual dependencies among variables in the model rather than inconsistencies in statistical methodology.

Statistical inferences can also be made in terms of linear functions of the parameters of the form

$$H_0: \mathbf{L}\boldsymbol{\beta}: \ell_0\beta_0 + \ell_1\beta_1 + \ldots + \ell_m\beta_m = 0$$

where the ℓ_i are arbitrary constants chosen to correspond to a specified hypothesis. Such functions are estimated by the corresponding linear function

$$\mathbf{L}\hat{\boldsymbol{\beta}} = \ell_0\hat{\beta}_0 + \ell_1\hat{\beta}_1 + \ldots + \ell_m\hat{\beta}_m$$

of the least-squares estimates $\hat{\boldsymbol{\beta}}$. The variance of $\mathbf{L}\hat{\boldsymbol{\beta}}$ is

$$V(\mathbf{L}\hat{\boldsymbol{\beta}}) = (\mathbf{L}(\mathbf{X}'\mathbf{X})^{-1}\mathbf{L}')\sigma^2 \quad .$$

A t test or F test is used to test H_0: $(\mathbf{L}\boldsymbol{\beta}) = 0$. The denominator is usually the residual mean square (MSE). Because the variance of the estimated function is based on statistics computed for the entire model, the test of the hypothesis is made in the presence of all model parameters. Confidence intervals can be constructed to correspond to these tests, which can be generalized to simultaneous tests of several linear functions.

Simultaneous inference about a set of linear functions $\mathbf{L}_1\boldsymbol{\beta}, \ldots, \mathbf{L}_k\boldsymbol{\beta}$ is performed in a related manner. For notational convenience, let $\mathbf{L}$ denote the matrix whose rows are $\mathbf{L}_1, \ldots, \mathbf{L}_k$:

$$\mathbf{L} = \begin{bmatrix} \mathbf{L}_1 \\ \cdot \\ \cdot \\ \cdot \\ \mathbf{L}_k \end{bmatrix}$$

Then the sum of squares

$$\mathrm{SS}(\mathbf{L}\boldsymbol{\beta} = 0) = (\mathbf{L}\hat{\boldsymbol{\beta}})'(\mathbf{L}(\mathbf{X}'\mathbf{X})^{-1}\mathbf{L}')^{-1}(\mathbf{L}\hat{\boldsymbol{\beta}})$$

is associated with the null hypothesis

$$H_0: \mathbf{L}_1\boldsymbol{\beta} = \ldots = \mathbf{L}_k\boldsymbol{\beta} = 0 \quad .$$

A test of H_0 is provided by the F statistic

$$F = (SS(\mathbf{L}\beta = 0) \,/\, k) \,/\, MSE \quad .$$

Three common types of statistical inferences are

□ a test that all parameters $(\beta_1, \beta_2, \ldots, \beta_m)$ are zero. The test compares the fit of the complete model to that using only the mean:

$$F = (\text{Model SS} \,/\, m) \,/\, MSE$$

where

$$\text{Model SS} = R(\beta_1, \beta_2, \ldots, \beta_m \mid \beta_0) \quad .^*$$

The F statistic has $(m, n-m-1)$ degrees of freedom.

□ a test that the parameters in a subset are zero. The problem is to compare the fit of the complete model

$$y = \beta_0 + \beta_1 x_1 + \ldots + \beta_g x_g + \beta_{g+1} x_{g+1} + \ldots + \beta_m x_m + \varepsilon$$

to the fit of the reduced model

$$y = \beta_0 + \beta_1 x_1 + \ldots + \beta_g x_g + \varepsilon \quad .$$

An F statistic is used to perform the test

$$F = (R(\beta_{g+1}, \ldots, \beta_m \mid \beta_0, \beta_1, \ldots, \beta_g) \,/\, (m - g)) \,/\, MSE \quad .$$

Note that an arbitrary reordering of variables produces a test for any desired subset of parameters. If the subset contains only one parameter, β_m, the test is

$$F = (R(\beta_m \mid \beta_0, \beta_1, \ldots, \beta_{m-1}) \,/\, 1) \,/\, MSE$$
$$= (\text{partial SS due to } \beta_m) \,/\, MSE$$

which is equivalent to the t test

$$t = \hat{\beta}_m \,/\, s_{\hat{\beta}m} = \hat{\beta}_m \,/\, \sqrt{c_{mm} MSE} \quad .$$

The corresponding $(1-\alpha)$ confidence interval about β_m is

$$\hat{\beta}_m \pm t_{\alpha/2} \sqrt{c_{mm} MSE} \quad .$$

□ estimation of a subpopulation mean corresponding to a specific x. For a given set of x values described by a vector $\mathbf{x}$, the estimated population mean is

$$E(y_\mathbf{x}) = \hat{\beta}_0 + \hat{\beta}_1 \mathbf{x}_1 + \ldots + \hat{\beta}_m \mathbf{x}_m = \mathbf{x}'\hat{\boldsymbol{\beta}} \quad .$$

---

* R $(\beta_0, \beta_1, \ldots, \beta_m)$ is rarely used. For more information, see the NOINT option in Section 2.4.5.

The vector $\mathbf{x}$ is constant; hence, the variance of $E(y_\mathbf{x})$ is

$$V(E(y_\mathbf{x})) = \mathbf{x}'(\mathbf{X}'\mathbf{X})^{-1}\mathbf{x}\sigma^2 \quad .$$

This equation is useful for computing confidence intervals. A related inference concerns a future single value of *y* corresponding to a specified *x*. The relevant variance estimate is

$$V(y_\mathbf{x}) = (1 + \mathbf{x}'(\mathbf{X}'\mathbf{X})^{-1}\mathbf{x})\sigma^2 \quad .$$

1.1.4 Using the Generalized Inverse

Many applications of regression procedures involve an $\mathbf{X}'\mathbf{X}$ matrix that is not of full rank and has no unique inverse. PROC GLM and PROC REG compute a generalized inverse $(\mathbf{X}'\mathbf{X})^-$ and use it to compute a regression estimate

$$\mathbf{b} = (\mathbf{X}'\mathbf{X})^-\mathbf{X}'\mathbf{Y} \quad .$$

A generalized inverse of a matrix $\mathbf{A}$ is any matrix $\mathbf{G}$ such that $\mathbf{AGA}=\mathbf{A}$. Note that this also identifies the inverse of a full-rank matrix.

If $\mathbf{X}'\mathbf{X}$ is not of full rank, then an infinite number of generalized inverses exist. Different generalized inverses lead to different solutions to the normal equations that have different expected values; that is, $E(\mathbf{b})=(\mathbf{X}'\mathbf{X})^-\mathbf{X}'\mathbf{X}\boldsymbol{\beta}$ depends on the particular generalized inverse used to obtain $\mathbf{b}$. Therefore, it is important to understand what is being estimated by the solution.

Fortunately, not all computations in regression analysis depend on the particular solution obtained. For example, the error sum of squares is invariant with respect to $(\mathbf{X}'\mathbf{X})^-$ and is given by

$$\text{SSE} = \mathbf{Y}'(1 - \mathbf{X}(\mathbf{X}'\mathbf{X})^-\mathbf{X}')\mathbf{Y} \quad .$$

Hence, the model sum of squares also does not depend on the particular generalized inverse obtained.

The generalized inverse has played a major role in the presentation of the theory of linear statistical models, notably in the work of Graybill (1976) and Searle (1971). In a theoretical setting it is often possible, and even desirable, to avoid specifying a particular generalized inverse. To apply the generalized inverse to statistical data using computer programs, a generalized inverse must actually be calculated. Therefore, it is necessary to declare the specific generalized inverse being computed. For example, consider an $\mathbf{X}'\mathbf{X}$ matrix of rank *k* that can be partitioned as

$$\mathbf{X}'\mathbf{X} = \begin{bmatrix} \mathbf{A}_{11} & \mathbf{A}_{12} \\ \mathbf{A}_{21} & \mathbf{A}_{22} \end{bmatrix}$$

where A_{11} is $k \times k$ and of rank k. Then A_{11}^{-1} exists, and a generalized inverse of $X'X$ is

$$(X'X)^{-} = \begin{bmatrix} A_{11}^{-1} & \varphi_{12} \\ \varphi_{21} & \varphi_{22} \end{bmatrix}$$

where each φ_{ij} is a matrix of zeros of the same dimension as A_{ij}.

This approach to obtaining a generalized inverse, the method used by PROC GLM and PROC REG, can be extended indefinitely by partitioning a singular matrix into several sets of matrices as illustrated above. Note that the resulting solution to the normal equations, $b = (X'X)^{-}X'Y$, has zeros in the positions corresponding to the rows filled with zeros in $(X'X)^{-}$. This is the solution printed by these procedures, and it is regarded as providing a biased estimate of β.

However, because b is not unique, a linear function, Lb, and its variance are generally not unique either. However, a class of linear functions called *estimable functions* exists, and they have the following properties:

□   The vector L is a linear combination of rows of X.

□ Lb and its variance are invariant through all possible generalized inverses. In other words, Lb is unique and is an unbiased estimate of $L\beta$.

Analogous to the full-rank case, the variance of an estimable function Lb is given by

$$V(Lb) = (L(X'X)^{-}L')\sigma^2 \quad .$$

This expression is used for statistical inference. For example, a test of H_0: $L\beta = 0$ is given by the t test

$$t = Lb \, / \, \sqrt{(L(X'X)^{-}L')MSE} \quad .$$

Simultaneous inferences on a set of estimable functions are performed in an analogous manner.

1.2 Performing a Regression with the IML Procedure

As you will see in Section 1.3, "Regression with the SAS System," and in greater detail in subsequent chapters, the SAS System provides a flexible array of procedures for performing regression analyses. You can also perform these analyses by direct application of the matrix formulas presented in the previous section using the IML procedure. PROC IML is most frequently used for the custom programming of methods too specialized or too new to be packaged into the standard regression procedures. It is also useful as an instructional tool for illustrating linear model and other methodologies.

The following example illustrates a regression analysis performed by PROC IML. This example is not intended to serve as a tutorial in the use of PROC IML. If you need more information on PROC IML, refer to *SAS/IML Software: Usage and Reference, Version 6, First Edition.*

The example for this section is also used in Chapter 2, "Using the REG Procedure," to illustrate PROC REG. The data set is described, and the data are presented in Section 2.1, "Introduction." For this presentation, the variable CPM is the dependent variable y, and the variables UTL, SPA, ALF, and ASL are the independent variables x_1, x_2, x_3, and x_4, respectively. Comment statements are used in the SAS program to explain the individual steps in the analysis.

```
/* Invoke PROC IML and create the x and y matrices using the   */
/* variables UTL, SPA, ALF, and CPM from the SAS data set AIR. */

proc iml;
   use air;
   read all var {'utl' 'spa' 'alf' 'asl'} into x;
   read all var {'cpm'} into y;

/* Define the number of observations (N) and the number of     */
/* variables (M) as the number of rows and columns of X. Add a */
/* column of ones for the intercept variable to the X matrix.  */

   n=nrow(x);     /* number of observations */
   m=ncol(x);     /* number of variables    */
   x=j(n,1,1)||x; /* add column of ones to X */

/* Compute C, the inverse of X'X and the vector of     */
/* coefficient estimates BHAT.                         */

   c=inv(x'*x);
   bhat=c*x'*y;

/* Compute SSE, the residual sum of squares, and MSE, the     */
/* residual mean square (variance estimate).                  */

   sse= y'*y-bhat'*x'*y;
   dfe= n-m-1;
   mse=sse/dfe;

/* The test for the model can be restated as a test for the    */
/* linear function Lβ where L is the matrix.                   */

   l={0 1 0 0 0,
      0 0 1 0 0,
      0 0 0 1 0,
      0 0 0 0 1};

/* Compute SSMODEL and MSMODEL and the corresponding F ratio.  */

   ssmodel=(l*bhat)'*inv(l*c*l')*(l*bhat);
   msmodel=ssmodel/m;
   f=(ssmodel/m)/mse;
```

```
/* Concatenate results into one matrix.                              */

   source=(m||ssmodel||msmodel||f)//(dfe||sse||mse||{.});

/* Compute                                                           */
/* SEB   vector of standard errors of the estimated coefficients     */
/* T     matrix containing the t statistic for testing that each     */
/*       coefficient is zero                                         */
/* PROBT significance level of test                                  */
/* STATS matrix which contains as its columns the coefficient        */
/*       estimates, their standard errors, and the t statistics.     */

   seb=sqrt(vecdiag(c)#mse);
   t=bhat/seb;
   probt=1-probf(t#t,1,dfe);
   stats=bhat||seb||t||probt;

/* Compute                                                           */
/* YHAT   predicted values                                           */
/* RESID  residual values                                            */
/* OBS    matrix containing as its columns the actual, predicted,    */
/*        and residual values, respectively.                         */

   yhat=x*bhat;
   resid=y-yhat;
   obs=y||yhat||resid;

/* Print the matrices containing the desired results.                */

   print 'Regression Results',
   source (|colname={DF SS MS F} rowname={MODEL ERROR}
   format=8.4|),,
   'Parameter Estimates',
   stats (|colname={BHAT SEB T PROBT} rowname={INT UTL SPA ALF ASL}
   format=8.4|) ,,,
   'RESIDUALS', obs (| colname={Y YHAT RESID} format=8.3|) ;
```

The results of this sample program are shown in Output 1.1.

Output 1.1
Output Produced by PROC IML

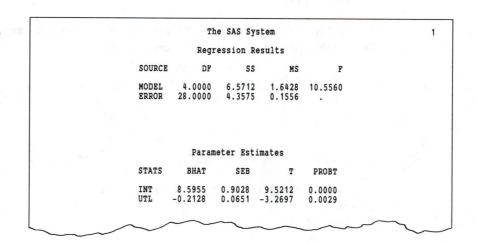

```
                        The SAS System                          1
                      Regression Results

            SOURCE      DF        SS        MS        F

            MODEL   4.0000    6.5712    1.6428   10.5560
            ERROR  28.0000    4.3575    0.1556    .




                      Parameter Estimates

            STATS     BHAT       SEB        T     PROBT

            INT     8.5955    0.9028    9.5212    0.0000
            UTL    -0.2128    0.0651   -3.2697    0.0029
```

```
            SPA    -4.9503   1.2170   -4.0678   0.0004
            ALF    -7.2114   1.3206   -5.4608   0.0000
            ASL     0.3328   0.1813    1.8351   0.0771



                         RESIDUALS

                OBS      Y       YHAT     RESID

                        2.258    2.574   -0.316
                        2.275    2.136    0.139
                        2.341    3.440   -1.099
                        2.357    2.424   -0.067
                        2.363    2.563   -0.200
                        2.404    2.879   -0.475
                        2.425    2.290    0.135
                        2.711    2.765   -0.054
                        2.743    3.367   -0.624
                        2.780    2.873   -0.093
                        2.833    2.636    0.197
                        2.846    3.183   -0.337
                        2.906    3.190   -0.284
                        2.954    2.932    0.022
                        2.962    2.975   -0.013
                        2.971    3.019   -0.048
                        3.044    3.324   -0.280
                        3.096    2.752    0.344
                        3.140    3.094    0.046
                        3.306    3.569   -0.263
                        3.306    2.748    0.558
                        3.311    3.483   -0.172
                        3.313    3.237    0.076
                        3.392    3.443   -0.051
                        3.437    3.520   -0.083
                        3.462    3.245    0.217
                        3.527    3.149    0.378
                        3.689    3.644    0.045
```

```
          The SAS System                              2

                        3.760    3.488    0.272
                        3.856    3.565    0.291
                        3.959    3.520    0.439
                        4.024    3.158    0.866
                        4.737    4.302    0.435
```

When you use PROC IML, all results are in the form of matrices. Each matrix is identified by its name, and its elements are identified by row and column indices. You may find it necessary to refer to the program to identify specific elements.

The results of this analysis are discussed thoroughly in Chapter 2; therefore, in this section only the results that can be compared with those from PROC REG (shown in Output 2.5) are identified.

The first section of statistics printed corresponds to overall model statistics produced by PROC REG. Included here are the degrees of freedom, sums of squares, and mean square for the model and for the error. The *F* statistic tests the significance of the entire model, which includes the independent variables UTL, SPA, ALF, and ASL.

The matrix **STATS** contains the information on the parameter estimates. Rows correspond to parameters (intercept and independent variables UTL, SPA, ALF, ASL respectively), and columns correspond to the different statistics. The first column contains the coefficient estimates (from matrix **BHAT**), the second contains the standard errors of the estimates (from matrix **SEB**), and the third contains the *t* statistics (from matrix **T**). The final column (**PROBT**) contains the probability associated with the *t* statistic.

The matrix **OBS** contains the information on observations. The rows correspond to the observations. Column one contains the original *y* values (matrix **Y**), column two contains the predicted values (from matrix **YHAT**), and column three contains the residuals (from matrix **RESID**).

The results achieved by using PROC IML agree with those from PROC REG, as shown in Output 2.5. Because PROC IML is most frequently used for the custom programming of new or specialized methods, the standard regression procedures are more efficient with respect to both programming time and computing time. For this reason, you should try to use these procedures whenever possible. In addition, the output produced with the standard regression procedures is designed to present analysis results more clearly than the printed matrices produced with PROC IML. See Section 1.3 for an overview of standard regression procedures.

1.3   Regression with the SAS System

This section reviews the following SAS/STAT software procedures that are used for regression analysis:

CALIS	ORTHOREG
CATMOD	PROBIT
GLM	REG
LIFEREG	RSREG
LOGISTIC	TRANSREG
NLIN	

PROC REG provides the most general analysis capabilities; the other procedures give more specialized analyses. This section also briefly mentions several procedures in SAS/ETS software.

Many SAS/STAT procedures, each with special features, perform regression analysis. The following procedures perform at least one type of regression analysis:

CALIS   fits systems of linear structural equations with latent variables and path analysis.

CATMOD   analyzes data that can be represented by a contingency table. PROC CATMOD fits linear models to functions of response frequencies and can be used for loglinear models and logistic regression.

GLM   uses the method of least squares to fit general linear models. In addition to many other analyses, PROC GLM can perform simple, multiple, polynomial, and weighted regression, as well as analysis of variance and analysis of covariance. PROC GLM has many of the same input/output capabilities as PROC REG but does not provide as many diagnostic tools or allow interactive changes in the model or data.

LIFEREG   fits parametric models to failure-time data that may be right-, left-, or interval-censored. These types of models are commonly used in survival analysis.

LOGISTIC	fits logistic regression models. PROC LOGISTIC can perform stepwise regressions as well as compute regression diagnostics.
NLIN	fits nonlinear regression models. Several different iterative methods are available.
ORTHOREG	performs regression using the Gentleman-Givens computational method. For ill-conditioned data, PROC ORTHOREG can produce more accurate parameter estimates than other procedures such as PROC GLM and PROC REG.
PROBIT	performs probit regression as well as logistic regression and ordinal logistic regression. PROC PROBIT is useful when the dependent variable is either dichotomous or polychotomous and the independent variables are continuous.
REG	performs linear regression with many diagnostic capabilities, selects models using one of nine selection methods, produces scatter plots of raw data and statistics, highlights scatter plots to identify particular observations, and allows interactive changes in both the regression model and the data used to fit the model.
	PROC REG provides options for special estimates, outlier and specification error detection (row diagnostics), collinearity statistics (column diagnostics), and tests of linear functions of parameter estimates. It can perform restricted least-squares estimation and multivariate tests. It can also produce SAS data sets containing the parameter estimates and most of the statistics produced by the procedure.
RSREG	builds quadratic response-surface regression models. PROC RSREG analyzes the fitted response surface to determine the factor levels of optimum response and performs a ridge analysis to search for the region of optimum response.
TRANSREG	obtains optimal linear and nonlinear transformations of variables using alternating least squares. PROC TRANSREG creates an output data set containing the transformed variables.

    Several SAS/ETS procedures also perform regression. The procedures listed below are documented in the *SAS/ETS User's Guide, Version 6, First Edition*:

AUTOREG	implements regression models using time-series data where the errors are autocorrelated.
MODEL	handles nonlinear simultaneous systems of equations, such as econometric models.
PDLREG	performs regression analysis with polynomial distributed lags.
SYSLIN	handles linear simultaneous systems of equations, such as econometric models.

    Finally, if a regression method cannot be performed by any of the SAS procedures above, SAS/IML software provides an interactive matrix language than can be used. See Section 4.5.1 "Incomplete Principal Component Regression," for more information. Some SAS System users may also find PROC IML an excellent instructional tool.

Chapter **2** Using the REG Procedure

2.1 Introduction

As indicated in Section 1.3, "Regression with the SAS System," PROC REG is the primary SAS procedure for performing the computations for a statistical analysis of data based on a linear regression model. The basic statements for performing such an analysis are

```
proc reg;
   model list of dependent variables = list of independent variables
   / model options;
```

This chapter provides instructions on the use of PROC REG for performing regression analysis. Included are instructions for employing some of the more frequently used options, producing data sets for further analysis, and utilizing the interactive features available for this procedure. Subsequent chapters deal with procedures for more specialized analyses and models.

The data for the example in this chapter concern factors considered to be influential in determining the cost of providing air service. The goal is to develop a model for estimating the cost per passenger mile so that the major factors in determining that cost can be isolated. The source of the data is a Civil Aeronautics

Board report, "Aircraft Operation Costs and Performance Report," August, 1972. The variables are

CPM   cost per passenger mile (cents)

UTL   average hours per day use of aircraft

ASL   average length of nonstop legs of flights (1000 miles)

SPA   average number of seats per aircraft (100 seats)

ALF   average load factor (% of seats occupied by passengers).

Data have been collected for thirty-three US airlines with average nonstop lengths of flights greater than 800 miles.

An additional indicator variable, TYPE, has been constructed. This variable has value zero for airlines with ASL<1200 miles, and unity for airlines with ASL≥1200 miles. This variable may be constructed in the DATA step with a set of IF-THEN statements. Alternately, you can use the Boolean operator as follows:

```
type=(asl>=1.200);
```

which assigns the value one to the variable TYPE if the condition in the parentheses is true and zero otherwise. This variable is used in Section 2.8, "Predicting to a Different Set of Data." The data appear in Output 2.1.

Output 2.1
Airline Costs Data

```
                              The SAS System                        1

       OBS    ALF     UTL     ASL      SPA     TYPE     CPM

         1   0.287    8.09   1.528    0.3522     1     3.306
         2   0.349    9.56   2.189    0.3279     1     3.527
         3   0.362   10.80   1.518    0.1356     1     3.959
         4   0.378    5.65   0.821    0.1290     0     4.737
         5   0.381   10.20   1.692    0.3007     1     3.096
         6   0.394    7.94   0.949    0.1488     0     3.689
         7   0.397   13.30   3.607    0.3390     1     2.357
         8   0.400    8.42   1.495    0.3597     1     2.833
         9   0.405    9.57   0.863    0.1390     0     3.313
        10   0.409    9.00   0.845    0.1390     0     3.044
        11   0.410    9.62   0.840    0.1390     0     2.846
        12   0.412    7.91   1.350    0.1920     1     2.341
        13   0.417    8.83   2.377    0.3287     1     2.780
        14   0.422    8.35   1.031    0.1365     0     3.392
        15   0.425   10.60   2.780    0.1282     1     3.856
        16   0.426    7.52   0.975    0.2025     0     3.462
        17   0.434    8.36   1.912    0.3148     1     2.711
        18   0.439    8.43   1.584    0.1607     1     2.743
        19   0.452    7.55   1.164    0.1270     0     3.760
        20   0.455    7.70   1.236    0.1221     1     3.311
        21   0.466    9.38   1.123    0.1481     0     2.404
        22   0.476    8.91   0.961    0.1236     0     2.962
        23   0.476    7.27   1.416    0.1145     1     3.437
        24   0.478    8.71   1.392    0.1148     1     2.906
        25   0.486    8.29   0.877    0.1060     0     3.140
        26   0.488    9.50   2.515    0.3546     1     2.275
        27   0.495    8.44   0.871    0.1186     0     2.954
        28   0.504    9.47   1.408    0.1345     1     3.306
        29   0.535   10.80   1.576    0.1361     1     2.425
        30   0.539    6.84   1.008    0.1150     0     2.971
        31   0.541    6.31   0.823    0.0943     0     4.024
        32   0.582    8.48   1.963    0.1381     1     2.363
        33   0.591    7.87   1.790    0.1375     1     2.258
```

2.2 A Model with One Independent Variable

A regression with a single independent variable is known as a simple linear regression model. Since such a model is easy to visualize, it is presented here to introduce several aspects of regression analysis you can perform with the SAS System. This model is illustrated using the single variable ALF, the average load factor, to estimate the cost per passenger mile, CPM. In terms of the example, the model is

$$CPM = \beta_0 + \beta_1(ALF) + \varepsilon \quad .$$

In this model, β_1 is the effect on the per passenger cost of a one unit (percentage point) increase in the load factor. For this example, you expect this coefficient to be negative. The coefficient β_0, the intercept, is the cost per passenger mile if the load factor is zero. Since a zero load factor is not possible, the value of this coefficient is not useful, but the term is needed to fully specify the regression line. The term ε represents the random error and accounts for variation in costs due to factors other than variation in ALF.

In the case of a regression with one independent variable, it is instructive to plot the observed variables. You can produce such a plot with the following SAS statements:

```
proc plot data=air;
    plot cpm*alf / hpos=30 vpos=25;
run;
```

Output 2.2 shows the resulting plot.

Output 2.2
Plot of Cost against Load Factor

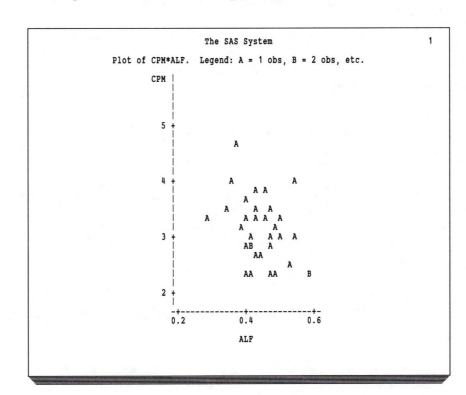

The plot shows the expected tendency for lower costs (CPM) with higher load factors (ALF). However, the relationship is not very strong. This suggests that there may be other factors affecting CPM as you will see in Section 2.3, "A Model with Several Independent Variables."

The SAS statements required for analyzing this model are

```
proc reg data = air;
    model cpm = alf;
run;
```

The PROC statement invokes the REG procedure, and DATA=AIR tells the SAS System to use the data set AIR. (The SAS System applies the called procedure to the most recently created data set if DATA=*data set name* is not specified in the PROC statement.) In the remainder of this book, the data set name is not always specified under the assumption that the appropriate data set was the last one created; however, specifying the data set is strongly recommended.

The MODEL statement contains the equation CPM=ALF, which corresponds to the desired model. The left-hand side specifies the dependent variable (CPM), and the right-hand side specifies the independent variable (in this case ALF). The intercept term is not specified because PROC REG automatically assumes that it is to be estimated (unless the NOINT option is used, see Section 2.4.5, "Regression through the Origin: the NOINT Option"). Also, no term is specified in the MODEL statement corresponding to the error term ε. PROC REG will produce ordinary least-squares estimates of the parameters (β_0 and β_1 in this example), which are optimal if the errors are independent and have equal variances. Methods for checking these assumptions and some suggestions for alternate methodologies are presented in Chapter 3, "Observations."

The output from PROC REG appears in Output 2.3. The bold numbers in Output 2.3 have been added to key the descriptions that follow.

Output 2.3
Results for Regression with One Independent Variable

```
                                    The SAS System                              1
1
Model: MODEL1
Dependent Variable: CPM

                              Analysis of Variance

                          3 Sum of     4 Mean        5
   2 Source     2 DF        Squares       Square       F Value      Prob>F

      Model        1       1.52682      1.52682        5.034       0.0321
      Error       31       9.40185      0.30329
      C Total     32      10.92867

       6 Root MSE       0.55071    7 R-square      0.1397
         Dep Mean       3.10570      Adj R-sq      0.1120
         C.V.          17.73237

                              Parameter Estimates

                 9 Parameter   10 Standard  11 T for H0:
   8 Variable  DF   Estimate         Error   Parameter=0      Prob > |T|

      INTERCEP   1    4.560547    0.65545893        6.958       0.0001
      ALF        1   -3.263548    1.45452657       -2.244       0.0321
```

1. The first two lines identify the model. Since PROC REG may have many models in one execution of the procedure (see Section 2.5.2, "Changing the Model"), each model is sequentially numbered.* Since a model may have several dependent variables, the second line identifies the dependent variable.

2. These two columns give the sources of variation and degrees of freedom associated with the sums of squares discussed in number 3 below.

3. The regression sum of squares (called MODEL SS, see Section 1.1.2, "Partitioning the Sums of Squares") is 1.5268, and the residual sum of squares (called ERROR SS, see Section 1.1.2) is 9.4109. The sum of these two is the TOTAL SS of 10.9287, the corrected total sum of squares. This illustrates the basic identity in regression analysis that CTOTAL SS= MODEL SS+ERROR SS, which says that variation among the observed values of the dependent variable can be attributed to two sources: (1) variation that is due to changes in the independent variable and (2) variation that is not due to changes in the independent variable. If the model is correctly specified, this latter variation is random variation.

4. Mean squares are computed by dividing the sums of squares by their respective degrees of freedom. The MS for error (MSE) is an unbiased estimate of σ^2, the variance of ε, if the model has been correctly specified.

5. The value of the F statistic, 5.034, is the ratio of the model mean square divided by the error mean square. For the general multiple regression case, it is used to test the composite hypothesis that all coefficients except the intercept are zero. In this case, the hypothesis is $\beta_1=0$. The p value (which follows the F statistic) of 0.0321 indicates that there is about a 0.032 chance of obtaining an F value this large or larger if, in fact, $\beta_1=0$. Thus, there is reasonable evidence to state that $\beta_1 \neq 0$.

6. ROOT MSE=0.5507 is the square root of the error mean square. It estimates the standard deviation of ε. DEP MEAN=3.106 is the mean of CPM.** C.V.=17.73 is the coefficient of variation. This is a measure of relative variation and is the ratio of ROOT MSE to the DEP MEAN, expressed as a percentage. In this example, the error standard deviation is 17.73% of the overall mean value of CPM. The coefficient is sometimes used as a standard to gauge the relative magnitude of the random error.

7. R-SQUARE=0.1397 is the square of the multiple correlation coefficient. For a one variable regression it is equivalent to the square of the correlation between the dependent and independent variable. Equivalently, since the predicted values are a linear function of the independent variable, it is also the square of the correlation between the dependent variable and its predicted values. Finally, it is also the ratio of MODEL SS divided by TOTAL SS, and thereby represents the fraction of total variation in the values of CPM explained by, or due to, the linear relationship to ALF (see number 3 above).

---

* You may specify your own model identification by preceeding the MODEL statement with a label followed by a colon. This is useful if a number of different models are being analyzed.

** All of these descriptive statistics are based on the number of observations used in the analysis, which will not be the same as the total number of observations in the data set if there are missing values. See Section 2.5.2 for a discussion of how PROC REG handles missing values.

ADJ R-SQUARE is an alternative to R-SQUARE, which is discussed in Section 2.3.

8. The Variable column identifies the regression coefficients. The label INTERCEP identifies β_0 and the other coefficients are identified by their respective variable names. In this case, the only coefficient is that for ALF.

9. The values in the Parameter Estimate column are the estimated coefficients. The estimate of the intercept, β_0, is 4.561, and the estimate of the coefficient, β_1, is -3.264. These give the fitted model

$$\widehat{\text{CPM}} = 4.561 - (3.264)(\text{ALF}),$$

where the caret ($\hat{\ }$) over CPM indicates that it is an estimated value. This expression can be used to estimate the average passenger mile cost for a given average load factor. The coefficient, -3.264, shows that on the average cost is decreased by 3.264 cents for each percentage point increase in the average load factor. Following sections show how to print and plot such estimates and their standard errors and confidence intervals.

10. The estimated standard errors of the coefficient estimates are given in the Standard Error column. These are 0.655 and 1.454, respectively, and may be used to construct confidence intervals for these model parameters. For example, a 95% confidence interval for β_1 is computed as

$$(-3.264 \pm 2.042*1.455)$$

where 2.042 is the 0.05 level two tail value of the t distribution for 30 degrees of freedom (used to approximate 31 degrees of freedom needed here).* The resulting interval is from -0.293 to -6.235. Thus, with 95% confidence, you can state that the interval (-0.293 and -6.235) includes the true change in cost due to a one percentage point increase in ALF.

11. The t statistics, used for testing the individual null hypotheses that each coefficient is zero, are given in the column labeled T for HO: Parameter=0. These quantities are simply the parameter estimates divided by their standard errors. The next column, labeled Prob> | T | , gives the p value for the two tailed test. For example, the p value of 0.0321 for ALF states that if you reject H$_0$: (ALF=0), there is a 0.0321 chance of erroneous rejection. Note that for this one variable model, this is the same as that for the F test of the model. Because the intercept has no practical value in this example, the p value for this parameter is not useful.

---

*   The exact value can be obtained by the TINV function available as a DATA step function.

2.3   A Model with Several Independent Variables

The same example is used throughout this chapter for illustrating the use of PROC REG in a model with several independent variables. This section presents the results obtained from a model for relating cost per passenger mile to all the variables in the data except for TYPE (see Output 2.1).

As you will see later, examining relationships among individual pairs of variables is not often useful in establishing the basis for a multiple regression model. Nevertheless, you may want to examine pairwise correlations among all variables in the model to compare these results obtained by using all variables simultaneously in a regression model. In addition, you may want to have some information about the nature of the variables in the model. The correlations as well as some simple statistics are obtained with the statements:

```
proc corr;
    var alf utl asl spa cpm;
    run;
```

The output from these statements appears in Output 2.4.*

Output 2.4
Correlations
among Airline
Cost Variables

```
                              The SAS System                              1
                           Correlation Analysis

            5 'VAR' Variables:  ALF      UTL      ASL      SPA      CPM


                             Simple Statistics

    Variable      N       Mean      Std Dev        Sum      Minimum     Maximum

    ALF          33     0.4458     0.0669      14.7110      0.2870      0.5910
    UTL          33     8.7173     1.4490     287.6700      5.6500     13.3000
    ASL          33     1.4691     0.6500      48.4790      0.8210      3.6070
    SPA          33     0.1836     0.0897       6.0581      0.0943      0.3597
    CPM          33     3.1057     0.5844     102.4880      2.2580      4.7370


        Pearson Correlation Coefficients / Prob > |R| under Ho: Rho=0 / N = 33

                  ALF          UTL          ASL          SPA          CPM

    ALF        1.00000     -0.20538     -0.08719     -0.49490     -0.37378
               0.0          0.2515       0.6295       0.0034       0.0321

    UTL       -0.20538      1.00000      0.62842      0.32442     -0.37197
               0.2515       0.0          0.0001       0.0655       0.0330

    ASL       -0.08719      0.62842      1.00000      0.60710     -0.35078
               0.6295       0.0001       0.0          0.0002       0.0453

    SPA       -0.49490      0.32442      0.60710      1.00000     -0.29758
               0.0034       0.0655       0.0002       0.0          0.0926

    CPM       -0.37378     -0.37197     -0.35078     -0.29758      1.00000
               0.0321       0.0330       0.0453       0.0926       0.0
```

---

*   PROC CORR is a comprehensive SAS procedure for computing various types of correlation and covariance statistics. Only the simplest options are used here. For more details see Chapter 15, "The CORR Procedure," in the *SAS Procedures Guide, Version 6, Third Edition.*

The upper portion of the output reports the mean, standard deviation, and other statistics for the specified variables. The correlation coefficients appear as a matrix in the lower portion of the output. Each row and column heading corresponds to a variable in the VAR (or VARIABLES) list. For a given row and column there are two numbers: the upper number is the estimated correlation coefficient between the row variable and the column variable and the lower number is the significance probability (p value) for testing the null hypothesis that the corresponding population correlation is zero.

An interesting feature of the CORR procedure is that each individual correlation coefficient is computed from all available pairs of values. If there are missing values, the number of such pairs is given for each pair below the p value. This feature can be very useful for detecting the existence of missing values.*

Examining the correlations, you can, for example, see that the estimated correlation between ALF and SPA is -0.4949, and is significantly different from zero at the $p=0.0034$ level. In other words, this tests provides evidence of a negative relationship between the average size of planes and the load factor.

The correlations between the dependent variable, CPM, and the four independent variables are of particular interest. All of these correlations are negative, and all, except for that with SPA, are significantly different from zero ($p<0.05$). This suggests that each of these three factors can be useful, by itself, in estimating the cost of providing air service.**

In terms of the example, the model for estimating CPM using the four cost factors is:

$$\text{CPM} = \beta_0 + (\beta_1)(\text{ALF}) + (\beta_2)(\text{UTL}) + (\beta_3)(\text{ASL}) + (\beta_4)(\text{SPA}) + \varepsilon \quad .$$

To fit this model, use the following statements:

```
proc reg;
     model cpm = alf utl asl spa;
run;
```

The results appear in Output 2.5.

Output 2.5
PROC REG with
CPM and Four
Independent
Variables

```
                              The SAS System                            1

Model: MODEL1
Dependent Variable: CPM

                         Analysis of Variance

                              Sum of        Mean
        Source        DF     Squares       Square    ❶ F Value    Prob>F

        Model          4     6.57115      1.64279      10.556     0.0001
        Error         28     4.35752      0.15563
        C Total       32    10.92867
```

---

* You can use the NOMISS option in the PROC CORR statement to get correlations that correspond to what PROC REG uses (see Section 2.5.2).

** Note that the correlation between CPM and ALF is the square root of the R-SQUARE value and the p value is the same as for the regression between these variables (Output 2.2).

```
           Root MSE       0.39449  2 R-square      0.6013
           Dep Mean       3.10570    Adj R-sq      0.5443
           C.V.          12.70228

                          Parameter Estimates
                          3            4           5
                       Parameter    Standard    T for H0:
           Variable DF  Estimate      Error    Parameter=0   Prob > |T|

           INTERCEP  1   8.595525   0.90277548     9.521       0.0001
           ALF       1  -7.211373   1.32056295    -5.461       0.0001
           UTL       1  -0.212816   0.06508642    -3.270       0.0029
           ASL       1   0.332769   0.18133342     1.835       0.0771
           SPA       1  -4.950301   1.21695241    -4.068       0.0004
```

The upper portion of the output, as in Output 2.3, contains the partitioning of the sums of squares and the corresponding mean squares. Other items in the output associated with the numbers in boldface are explained as follows:

1. The *F* value of 10.556 is used to test the null hypothesis

    $$H_0 : \beta_1 = \beta_2 = \beta_3 = \beta_4 = 0 \quad .$$

    The associated *p* value of 0.0001 leads to the rejection of this hypothesis and indicates that at least one of the coefficients is not zero.*

2. R-SQUARE=0.6013 tells you that a major portion of the variation of CPM is explained by variation in the independent variables in the model. Note that this R-SQUARE value is much larger than that for ALF alone (see Output 2.3). The statistic ADJ R-SQ=0.5443 is an alternative to R-SQUARE that is adjusted for the number of parameters in the model according to the formula:

    $$\text{ADJ R-SQ} = 1 - (1 - \text{R-SQUARE}) * [(n-1)/(n-m-1)]$$

    where *n* is the number of observations in the data set, and *m* is the number of regression parameters in the model excluding the intercept. This adjustment provides for measuring the reduction in the mean square (rather than sum of squares) due to the regression. It is used to overcome an objection to R-SQUARE as a measure of goodness of fit of the model, namely that R-SQUARE can be driven to one (suggesting a perfect fit) simply by adding superfluous variables to the model with no real improvement in the fit. This is not the case with ADJ R-SQ, which tends to stabilize to a certain value when an adequate set of variables is included in the model. When *m/n* is small, say less than 0.05, the adjustment almost vanishes. This adjustment is also purported by some authors (Rawlings 1988, Section 7.5) to permit the comparison of regression models based on different sets of data, although its value for this purpose is not uniformly agreed upon. ADJ R-SQ can have values less than zero.

---

* All tests in PROC REG are constructed with the principle of holding constant all paramters not mentioned in the hypothesis. Thus, this hypothesis holds constant the intercept, a fact that is usually assumed. See the discussion of Type I and Type II sums of squares in Section 2.4.2, "SS1 and SS2: Two Types of Sums of Squares."

3. Rounding the values of the parameter estimates provides the equation for the fitted model

$$\widehat{CPM} = 8.596 - (7.211)(ALF) - (0.213)(UTL) + (0.333)(ASL) - (4.950)(SPA) \quad .$$

Thus, for example, a one unit (percent) increase in the average load factor, (ALF), is associated with a decreased cost of 7.211 cents per passenger mile, holding constant all other factors.*

4. The estimated standard errors of the parameter estimates are useful for constructing confidence intervals as illustrated in Section 2.2, "A Model with One Independent Variable." Remember, however, to use the degrees of freedom for MSE.

5. The *t* statistics are used for testing hypotheses about the individual parameters. It is important that you clearly understand the interpretation of these tests. This can be explained in terms of comparing the fit of full and reduced models (Section 1.1.2, "Partitioning the Sums of Squares"). The full model for all of these tests contains all the variables on the right-hand side of the MODEL statement. The reduced model contains all these variables except the one being tested. Thus the *t* statistic of -5.461 for testing the null hypothesis that $\beta_1 = 0$ (there is no effect due to ALF) is actually testing whether the full four-variable model fits the data better than the reduced three-variable model containing only UTL, ASL, and SPA. In other words, the test indicates whether there is variation in CPM due to ALF that is not due to UTL, ASL, and SPA. The *p* value for this test is 0.0001 indicating quite clearly that there is an effect due to ALF. By contrast, the corresponding *p* value for ALF in the regression where it is the only variable was only 0.0321. Note that for UTL and SPA the *p* value for the parameter in the multiple variable model is smaller than that for the corresponding correlation (see Output 2.4), while for ASL the reverse is true. This type of phenomenon is the result of correlations among the independent variables. This is more fully discussed in the presentation of the Type I and Type II sums of squares (see Section 2.4.2), and in greater detail in Chapter 4, "Multicollinearity: Detection and Remedial Measures."

2.4 Various MODEL Statement Options

This section presents a number of MODEL statement options that produce additional results and modify the regression model. Although these options provide useful results, not all are useful for all analyses and should only be requested if needed.

---

* This coefficient is quite different from that obtained in the one variable regression (see Output 2.2). This is why simple two-variable plots or correlations are often not useful in trying to determine the effects of individual variables in a multiple regression model.

2.4.1 The P, CLM, and CLI Options

One of the most common objectives of regression analysis is to compute predicted values

$$\hat{y} = \hat{\beta}_0 + \hat{\beta}_1 x_1 + \ldots + \hat{\beta}_m x_m$$

as well as their standard errors for some selected values of $x_1, \ldots, x_m$. This can be done in several ways with PROC REG. The most direct way to obtain these values is to use the P and CLM options (which need not be used together) in the MODEL statement as follows:

```
proc reg data = air;
    model cpm = alf utl asl spa / p clm ;
    id alf;
run;
```

The results of these computations are printed below the basic PROC REG output (see Output 2.5), and are shown in Output 2.6. The specific items in Output 2.6 are identified by numbers in boldface.

Output 2.6
Computing
Predicted Values

```
                            The SAS System                              1
                                          4        5          6
                      2 Dep Var 3 Predict  Std Err  Lower95%   Upper95%
   Obs    1 ALF          CPM       Value   Predict    Mean       Mean

     1       0.287      3.3060    3.5692    0.206    3.1477     3.9906
     2       0.349      3.5270    3.1495    0.146    2.8504     3.4485
     3       0.362      3.9590    3.5205    0.183    3.1450     3.8960
     4       0.378      4.7370    4.3018    0.217    3.8580     4.7457
     5       0.381      3.0960    2.7518    0.146    2.4525     3.0510
     6       0.394      3.6890    3.6437    0.113    3.4129     3.8745
     7       0.397      2.3570    2.4243    0.260    1.8908     2.9578
     8       0.4        2.8330    2.6359    0.193    2.2413     3.0305
     9       0.405      3.3130    3.2374    0.144    2.9417     3.5331
    10       0.409      3.0440    3.3238    0.124    3.0704     3.5773
    11       0.41       2.8460    3.1830    0.148    2.8792     3.4868
    12       0.412      2.3410    3.4398    0.093    3.2488     3.6309
    13       0.417      2.7800    2.8730    0.152    2.5618     3.1843
    14       0.422      3.3920    3.4427    0.094    3.2508     3.6346
    15       0.425      3.8560    3.5653    0.260    3.0328     4.0978
    16       0.426      3.4620    3.2451    0.108    3.0237     3.4665
    17       0.434      2.7110    2.7645    0.140    2.4774     3.0517
    18       0.439      2.7430    3.3673    0.092    3.1796     3.5550
    19       0.452      3.7600    3.4879    0.101    3.2819     3.6939
    20       0.455      3.3110    3.4825    0.102    3.2739     3.6912
    21       0.466      2.4040    2.8794    0.113    2.6481     3.1107
    22       0.476      2.9620    2.9747    0.112    2.7459     3.2034
    23       0.476      3.4370    3.5201    0.135    3.2438     3.7965
    24       0.478      2.9060    3.1898    0.092    3.0009     3.3787
    25       0.486      3.1400    3.0937    0.106    2.8774     3.3099
    26       0.488      2.2750    2.1362    0.196    1.7350     2.5373
    27       0.495      2.9540    2.9325    0.116    2.6941     3.1708
    28       0.504      3.3060    2.7484    0.112    2.5182     2.9785
    29       0.535      2.4250    2.2897    0.186    1.9089     2.6706
    30       0.539      2.9710    3.0191    0.140    2.7329     3.3053
    31       0.541      4.0240    3.1584    0.155    2.8405     3.4762
    32       0.582      2.3630    2.5634    0.174    2.2077     2.9191
    33       0.591      2.2580    2.5737    0.180    2.2042     2.9432

                          7
   Obs      ALF        Residual

     1       0.287     -0.2632
     2       0.349      0.3775
     3       0.362      0.4385
     4       0.378      0.4352
     5       0.381      0.3442
     6       0.394      0.0453
     7       0.397     -0.0673
```

(continued on next page)

```
(continued from previous page)
        8          0.4     0.1971
        9        0.405     0.0756
       10        0.409    -0.2798
       11         0.41    -0.3370
       12        0.412    -1.0988
       13        0.417    -0.0930
       14        0.422    -0.0507
       15        0.425     0.2907
       16        0.426     0.2169
       17        0.434    -0.0535
       18        0.439    -0.6243
```

```
                              The SAS System                          2

        Obs        ALF         Residual

        19        0.452     0.2721
        20        0.455    -0.1715
        21        0.466    -0.4754
        22        0.476    -0.0127
        23        0.476    -0.0831
        24        0.478    -0.2838
        25        0.486     0.0463
        26        0.488     0.1388
        27        0.495     0.0215
        28        0.504     0.5576
        29        0.535     0.1353
        30        0.539    -0.0481
        31        0.541     0.8656
        32        0.582    -0.2004
        33        0.591    -0.3157

   Sum of Residuals                      0
   Sum of Squared Residuals         4.3575
   Predicted Resid SS (Press)       5.8459
```

1. The ID statement provides for the identification of individual observations, using the values of the variable specified in that statement. In this case, it is the independent variable ALF. (Although one of the independent variables in the model is most frequently used as the ID variable, any other variable in the data set may be used.)

2. This column, labeled DEP VAR, gives the observed values of the dependent variable, which is CPM. (Compare this with Output 2.1.)

3. This column, labeled Predict Value, results from the P (for predicted) option in the MODEL statement that causes the REG procedure to compute the $\hat{y}$ values corresponding to each observation in the data set.

4., 5., and 6. are the results of the CLM option. This option computes the upper and lower 95% confidence limits for the expected value (conditional mean) for each observation. Computation of these limits requires the standard errors of the predicted values, which are listed in the output under number 4. These are computed according to the formula:

$$\text{STD ERR PREDICT} = ((\mathbf{x}'(\mathbf{X}'\mathbf{X})^{-1}\mathbf{x})*\text{MSE})**0.5$$

where $\mathbf{x}$ is a row vector of the design matrix $\mathbf{X}$ corresponding to a single observation and MSE is the error mean square. This is equal to the square root of the variance of $\hat{y}$ given in Section 1.1.2, "Partitioning the Sums of Squares." The upper and lower 95% confidence limits are then calculated by

$$(\hat{y} \pm t^*(\text{STD ERR PREDICT}))$$

where t is the 0.05 level tabulated t value with degrees of freedom equal to those of the error mean square. For example, for observation 1, for which ALF=0.287 and the actual CPM is 3.306, you can see that the predicted value is 3.569, and the 95% confidence limits are (3.148 to 3.991).

7. This column, labeled Residual, is also produced by the P option in the MODEL statement and contains the set of residual values

$$\text{RESIDUAL} = \text{ACTUAL} - \text{PREDICT} \quad .$$

It is sometimes useful to scan this column of values for relatively large values (see Chapter 3).

One of the useful features of PROC REG (as well as other SAS regression procedures) is that the $\hat{y}$ values can be computed for observations not in the data set from which the regression equation was estimated. Uses for this feature are presented in Section 2.8.

CLI, an additional MODEL statement option, computes the 95% prediction interval for a single observation. The formula for this is similar to that for the confidence interval for the mean, except that the variance of the predicted value is larger than that for the interval of the mean by the value of the residual mean square. The results of the CLI option are not printed here. However, a plot of prediction intervals is presented in Section 2.7, "Creating Data: the OUTPUT Statement."

The interpretation of the CLM and CLI statistics are sometimes confused. Specifically, CLM yields a confidence interval for the subpopulation mean and CLI yields a prediction interval for a single unit to be drawn at random from that subpopulation.* The CLI limits are always wider than the CLM limits because the CLM limits need accommodate only the variability in the predicted value, whereas the CLI limits must accommodate the variability in the predicted value as well as the variability in the future value of y. This is true even though the same predicted value ($\hat{y}$) is used as the point estimate of the subpopulation mean as well as the predictor of the future value.

To draw an analogy, suppose you walk into a roomful of people and are challenged to guess the average weight of all the people in the room and guess the weight of one particular person to be chosen at random. You make a visual estimate of, say, 150 lbs. You would guess the average weight to be 150 lbs., and you would also guess the weight of the mystery person to be 150 lbs. But you would have more confidence in your guess of the average weight for the entire roomful than in your guess of the weight of the mystery person.

In the airline cost data, the 95% confidence interval for the mean of the first airline is from 3.1477 to 3.9906 cents (see Output 2.6). This means that you can state with 95% confidence that these limits include the true mean cost per

---

* You may now see that the STD ERR PREDICT, which is used for CLM, is actually the standard error of the estimated mean, rather than the standard error of a single predicted value. This distinction is recognized in textbooks (Myers 1990, Section 2.9), but no uniform nomenclature or notation has been adopted.

passenger mile of the hypothetical population of airlines having the characteristics of that airline. On the other hand, the CLI option for this airline provides the interval from 2.6578 to 4.4805 cents. This means that there is a 95% probability that a single airline chosen from that population of airlines will have a cost that is within those limits.

The following guidelines are offered to assist in deciding whether to use CLM or CLI:

□ Use CLM if you want the limits to show the region that should contain the population regression curve.

□ Use CLI if you want the limits to show the region that should contain (almost all of) the population of all possible observations.

One final note: the confidence coefficients for CLM and CLI are valid on a single-point basis. Bands that are valid simultaneously for all points require computations not directly available in PROC REG, but which can be computed with the IML procedure.

At the bottom of Output 2.6 there are three statistics that are sometimes useful. These (as identified) are the sum of the computed residuals and sum of squares of the computed residuals and PRESS statistics. Within reasonable roundoff error the sum of residuals should be zero and the sum of squares should equal the error sum of squares in the analysis of variance at the top of the PROC REG output. If different results are obtained, there is reason to suspect that there has been excessive roundoff error (see Section 2.4.5). The PRESS statistics are among the several available for detecting the possibility of outlying or influential observations. If the sum of squares of the PRESS statistics is considerably larger than the residual sum of squares, outliers may exist. Further details are presented in Section 3.2, "Outlier Detection."

2.4.2 SS1 and SS2: Two Types of Sums of Squares

PROC REG can compute two types of sums of squares associated with the estimated coefficients in the model. These are referred to as Type I (sequential) and Type II (partial) sums of squares. These are computed by specifying SS1 and SS2 as MODEL statement options. The following statements produce Output 2.7:

```
proc reg;
    model cpm = alf utl asl spa / ss1 ss2;
run;
```

(The partitioning of the sums of squares and parameter estimates, which appear in Output 2.3, are not affected by these options and are not reproduced.)
The requested sums of squares are printed as additional columns in the Parameter Estimates section and are labeled Type I SS and Type II SS.

```
                                          The SAS System                         1
               Variable   DF     Type I SS    Type II SS

               INTERCEP    1     318.296671    14.108036
               ALF         1       1.526822     4.640865
               UTL         1       2.297567     1.663826
               ASL         1       0.171646     0.524096
               SPA         1       2.575119     2.575119
```

The interpretation of these sums of squares is based on the material in Section 1.1.2. In particular, the following concepts are useful in understanding the different types of sums of squares:

□   partitioning of sums of squares

□   complete and reduced models

□   reduction notation.

The Type I SS are commonly called sequential sums of squares and represent a partitioning of the MODEL SS into component sums of squares due to each variable as they are added sequentially to the model in the order prescribed in the MODEL statement.

The Type I SS for INTERCEP is simply $(\Sigma y)^2/n$, which is commonly called the correction for the mean. The Type I SS for ALF (1.5268) is the MODEL SS for a regression equation containing only ALF and the intercept. This is easily verified as the MODEL SS in Output 2.3. The Type I SS for UTL (2.2976) is the reduction in the ERROR SS due to adding UTL to a model that already contains ALF and the intercept. Since MODEL SS+ERROR SS=TOTAL SS, this is also the increase in the MODEL SS due to the addition of UTL to the model containing ALF.

Equivalent interpretations hold for the Type I SS for ASL and SPA. In general terms, the Type I SS for any particular variable is the reduction in ERROR SS due to adding that variable to a model that already contains all the variables preceding that variable in the MODEL statement.

Note that the sum of the Type I SS is the overall MODEL SS:

$$6.5711 = 1.5268 + 2.2976 + 0.1716 + 2.5751 \quad .$$

This equation shows the sequential partitioning of the MODEL SS into Type I components corresponding to the variables as they are added to the model in the order given. In other words, the Type I sums of squares are order dependent; if the variables in the MODEL statement are given in different order, the Type I sums of squares will change.

The Type II sums of squares are commonly called partial sums of squares. The Type II SS for a variable is the reduction in ERROR SS due to adding that variable to the model that already contains all the other variables in the model list. For a given variable, the Type II SS is equivalent to the Type I SS for that variable if it were the last variable in the model list. This is easily verified by the fact that both types of sums of squares for SPA, which is the last variable in the list, are the same. The Type II sums of squares, therefore, do not depend on the order in which the independent variables are listed in the MODEL statement. Furthermore they do not yield a partitioning of the MODEL SS unless the independent variables are mutually uncorrelated.

Reduction notation (see Section 1.1.2) provides a convenient device to determine the complete and reduced models that are compared if the corresponding one degree of freedom sum of squares is used as the numerator for an F test. In reduction notation the two types of sums of squares are:

PARAMETER	TYPE I (Sequential)	TYPE II (Partial)
ALF	R(ALF | INTERCEPT)	R(ALF | INTERCEPT, UTL,ASL,SPA)
UTL	R(UTL | INTERCEPT,ALF)	R(UTL | INTERCEPT, ALF,ASL,SPA)
ALS	R(ASL | INTERCEPT,ALF,UTL)	R(ASL | INTERCEPT, ALF,UTL,SPA)
SPA	R(SPA | INTERCEPT,ALF,UTL,ASL)	R(SPA | INTERCEPT, ALF,UTL,ASL)

F tests derived by dividing the Type II SS by the error mean square are equivalent to the t tests for the parameters provided in the computer output. In fact, the Type II F statistic is equal to the square of the t statistic.

Tests derived from the Type I SS are convenient to use in model building in those cases where there is a predetermined order for selecting variables. Not only does each Type I SS provide a test for the improvement in the fit of the model when the corresponding term is added to the model, but the additivity of the sums of squares can be used to assess the significance of a model containing, say, the first $k < m$ terms.

Associated with the Type I sums of squares is the MODEL statement option SEQB, which prints the coefficients of the successive models fitted by adding terms in the order given in the MODEL statement. Type I sums of squares and the SEQB option are very useful in fitting polynomial models, which are presented in Section 5.2, "Polynomial Models with One Independent Variable."

PROC REG does not provide the F tests associated with the Type I and Type II sums of squares. This causes no difficulty for the Type II sums of squares since these are the squares of the corresponding t statistics. F ratios corresponding to the Type I sums of squares must therefore be calculated manually.*

---

*   The F tests for Type I sums of squares are available with PROC GLM, which is primarily designed for models of less than full rank used for analysis of variance and covariance by regression methods (Freund, Littell, and Spector 1991). PROC GLM should, however, not normally be used for ordinary multiple regression models because it is not as efficient nor does it contain many of the useful options available in PROC REG.

2.4.3 Standardized Coefficients: the STB Option

The MODEL statement option STB produces the set of standardized regression coefficients. Output 2.8 contains the additional portion of the output from the statements

```
proc reg data = air;
    model cpm = alf utl asl spa / stb;
run;
```

These estimates appear in the same format as the Type I and Type II sums of squares in the Parameter Estimates section of Output 2.5.

Output 2.8
Standardized
Coefficients

```
                                    The SAS System                          1
                           Standardized
          Variable  DF       Estimate

          INTERCEP   1      0.00000000
          ALF        1     -0.82592086
          UTL        1     -0.52768069
          ASL        1      0.37011165
          SPA        1     -0.75983144
```

These coefficients, labeled Standardized Estimate, are the estimates that would be obtained if all variables in the model were standardized to zero mean and unit variance prior to performing the regression computations. Each coefficient indicates the number of standard deviation changes in the dependent variable associated with a standard deviation change in the independent variable, holding constant all other variables. In other words, the magnitudes of the standardized coefficients are not affected by the scales of measurement of the various model variables and thus may be useful in ascertaining the relative importance of the effects of independent variables not affected by the scales of measurement.

2.4.4 Printing Matrices: the XPX and I Options

The XPX and I options are available for printing the matrices used in the regression computations (see Sections 1.1.1, 1.1.2, and 1.3). The XPX option, standing for X prime X, prints the matrix:

$$\begin{bmatrix} X'X & X'Y \\ Y'X & Y'Y \end{bmatrix}$$

In other words, it is the matrix of sums of squares and crossproducts of all the variables in the MODEL statement. The I option, standing for Inverse, prints the matrix:

$$\begin{bmatrix} (\mathbf{X'X})^{-1} & \hat{\beta} \\ (\hat{\beta})' & \text{ERROR SS} \end{bmatrix}$$

The output (not including the usual regression printout) from the following statements appears in Output 2.9:

```
proc reg;
    model cpm = alf utl asl spa / xpx i;
run;
```

Output 2.9
Results of PROC REG with XPX and I Options

```
                            The SAS System                          1
Model: MODEL1


                   Model Crossproducts X'X X'Y Y'Y

        X'X             INTERCEP            ALF               UTL

        INTERCEP              33           14.711           287.67
        ALF              14.711         6.701339          127.6024
        UTL              287.67         127.6024         2574.8875
        ASL              48.479        21.489977         441.54459
        SPA              6.0581         2.6055474         54.159475
        CPM             102.488        45.220067         883.33621


        X'X               ASL              SPA               CPM

        INTERCEP         48.479           6.0581           102.488
        ALF           21.489977         2.6055474        45.220067
        UTL           441.54459         54.159475        883.33621
        ASL           84.737677        10.0323764       146.297362
        SPA          10.0323764        1.36961579        18.3154399
        CPM          146.297362        18.3154399       329.225344


                X'X Inverse, Parameter Estimates, and SSE

                     INTERCEP            ALF               UTL

        INTERCEP    5.2369479797     -6.606496223      -0.264323466
        ALF        -6.606496223      11.205647867       0.1644020761
        UTL        -0.264323466       0.1644020761      0.0272207146
        ASL         0.5549364635     -0.640165877      -0.047184442
        SPA        -4.208572139       6.0925283374      0.1256213977
        CPM         8.5955250497     -7.211373248      -0.212815723


                          ASL              SPA               CPM

        INTERCEP    0.5549364635     -4.208572139       8.5955250497
        ALF        -0.640165877       6.0925283374     -7.211373248
        UTL        -0.047184442       0.1256213977     -0.212815723
        ASL         0.2112878183     -0.918587822       0.3327689316
        SPA        -0.918587822       9.5162522535     -4.950301373
        CPM         0.3327689316     -4.950301373       4.3575188862
```

The rows and columns of the matrices are identified by the names of the variables in the model. The variable INTERCEP corresponds to the dummy variable whose value is unity for all observations and which is used to estimate the intercept coefficient (β_0). Thus in the $X'X$ matrix the first row (or column) consists of the sample size and the sums of the variables. All other elements are (uncorrected) sums of squares and crossproducts of the variables.

The portion of the inverse corresponding to INTERCEP and the independent variables is the inverse of $X'X$. The row (or column) corresponding to the dependent variable contains the estimated coefficients (compare with Parameter Estimates in Output 2.5). The last element, which has both row and column identified by the name of the dependent variable, contains the error (residual) sum of squares. If there are several dependent variables, then the appropriate number of rows and columns corresponding to the dependent variables containing the coefficient estimates and error sums of squares will be printed.

Additional options COVB and CORRB (not illustrated here) print the matrix of variances and covariances and the matrix of correlations of the estimated coefficients, respectively. The ALL option prints all of the statistics corresponding to the various model options we have discussed, plus some descriptive statistics of the model variables.

2.4.5 Regression through the Origin: the NOINT Option

The MODEL statement option NOINT forces the regression response to pass through the origin; that is, the estimated value of the dependent variable is zero when all independent variables have the value zero. An example of this requirement occurs in some growth models where the response (say weight) must be zero at the beginning, that is, when time is zero. In many applications this requirement is not reasonable, especially when this condition does not or cannot actually occur. If this option is used in such situations, the results of the regression analysis are often grossly misleading. Moreover, even when the conditions implied by the NOINT option are reasonable, the results of the analysis have some features that may mislead the unwary practitioner.

The NOINT option is illustrated with the airline data. This example demonstrates the uselessness of this option when it is not justified since, in this example, zero values of the variables in the model cannot occur. Use PROC REG with the following statements:

```
proc reg;
     model cpm = alf utl asl spa / noint p;
run;
```

Note that in addition to the NOINT option, the P option is added to obtain the predicted values. The results appear in Output 2.10.

Output 2.10
Results of PROC
REG with NOINT
and P Options

```
                              The SAS System                              1
Model: MODEL1
NOTE: No intercept in model. R-square is redefined.
Dependent Variable: CPM

                        Analysis of Variance

                           Sum of        Mean
     Source        DF      Squares       Square     F Value     Prob>F

     Model          4    310.75979     77.68995     122.011     0.0001
     Error         29     18.46555      0.63674
     U Total       33    329.22534

          Root MSE      0.79796    R-square      0.9439
          Dep Mean      3.10570    Adj R-sq      0.9362
          C.V.         25.69349

                        Parameter Estimates

                    Parameter     Standard    T for H0:
     Variable  DF    Estimate       Error     Parameter=0   Prob > |T|

     ALF        1    3.632023    1.35217330      2.686        0.0118
     UTL        1    0.221025    0.09400915      2.351        0.0257
     ASL        1   -0.578061    0.31159738     -1.855        0.0738
     SPA        1    1.957326    1.97632390      0.990        0.3302
```

```
                              The SAS System                              2

                       Dep Var     Predict
              Obs        CPM        Value     Residual

               1       3.3060      2.6366      0.6694
               2       3.5270      2.7570      0.7700
               3       3.9590      3.0898      0.8692
               4       4.7370      2.3996      2.3374
               5       3.0960      3.2487     -0.1527
               6       3.6890      2.9286      0.7604
               7       2.3570      2.9600     -0.6030
               8       2.8330      3.1537     -0.3207
               9       3.3130      3.3594     -0.0464
              10       3.0440      3.2583     -0.2143
              11       2.8460      3.4019     -0.5559
              12       2.3410      2.8401     -0.4991
              13       2.7800      2.7355      0.0445
              14       3.3920      3.0495      0.3425
              15       3.8560      2.5304      1.3256
              16       3.4620      3.0421      0.4199
              17       2.7110      2.9350     -0.2240
              18       2.7430      2.8566     -0.1136
              19       3.7600      2.8861      0.8739
              20       3.3110      2.8790      0.4320
              21       2.4040      3.4065     -1.0025
              22       2.9620      3.3846     -0.4226
              23       3.4370      2.7413      0.6957
              24       2.9060      3.0813     -0.1753
              25       3.1400      3.2980     -0.1580
              26       2.2750      3.1124     -0.8374
              27       2.9540      3.3919     -0.4379
              28       3.3060      3.3730     -0.0670
              29       2.4250      3.6856     -1.2606
              30       2.9710      3.1119     -0.1409
              31       4.0240      3.0684      0.9556
              32       2.3630      3.1237     -0.7607
              33       2.2580      3.1204     -0.8624

Sum of Residuals                 1.641323
Sum of Squared Residuals        18.4656
Predicted Resid SS (Press)      25.4386
```

The overall partitioning of the sum of squares and the R-SQUARE statistic certainly suggest a well fitting model. In fact, both the model F and the R-SQUARE statistics are much larger than those for the model with the intercept (see Output 2.5). However, closer examination of the results shows that the error sum of squares for the no intercept model is actually larger than the total sum of squares for the model with intercept. This apparent contradiction arises from the fact that in the no intercept model the total sum of squares is the uncorrected or uncentered sum of squares for the dependent variable, or Σy^2. In contrast, the total sum of squares for the model with the intercept is the corrected or centered sum of squares, $\Sigma(y - \bar{y})^2$. Thus, although the error sum of squares is much larger for the no intercept model, the difference between the total and error sum of squares is much larger for the no intercept model, thus giving a larger value to the R-SQUARE statistic. These differences are noted in the output as U Total for the total sums of squares of the no intercept model and as C Total for the total sums of squares of the intercept model. Furthermore, both total and error degrees of freedom are larger by one in the no intercept model since one less parameter has been estimated. Finally, the statement

```
NOTE: No intercept term in model. R-square is redefined.
```

is intended to alert users to the special interpretation of this statistic and the fact that this value may bear no relationship to the value obtained if the intercept is included.

Looking further you can also see that the coefficient estimates for the no intercept model bear no resemblance to those of the intercept model because you have really fitted two entirely different models. Finally, the statistics that follow the listing of predicted and residual values show that the sum of residuals is not zero. This is in contrast to models with intercepts for which, by definition, the sum of residuals is equal to zero. It is characteristic of no intercept models that the sum of residuals is not zero, although if the true intercept is near zero, the sum of residuals may be quite close to zero.

A simple example is used to illustrate the fact that the use of the NOINT option can result in misleading results even in cases where the true intercept is near zero. Eight data points are generated using the model $y=x$, with a normally distributed error having zero mean and unit variance. Output 2.11 shows the data.

Output 2.11
Data for NOINT Option

```
                          The SAS System                    1

                 OBS    X      Y

                  1     1    -0.35
                  2     2     2.79
                  3     3     1.81
                  4     4     2.00
                  5     5     3.88
                  6     6     6.79
                  7     7     7.67
                  8     8     6.79
```

PROC REG is used for models with and without intercept as follows:

```
proc reg;
    model y = x / P;
    model y = x / noint p;
run;
```

The results of these analyses appear in Outputs 2.12 and 2.13.

Output 2.12
Results of PROC
REG without
NOINT Option

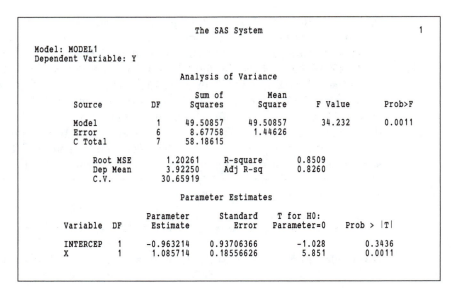

```
                              The SAS System                              1
Model: MODEL1
Dependent Variable: Y

                           Analysis of Variance

                           Sum of        Mean
         Source      DF    Squares      Square     F Value    Prob>F

         Model        1   49.50857    49.50857      34.232    0.0011
         Error        6    8.67758     1.44626
         C Total      7   58.18615

              Root MSE       1.20261    R-square      0.8509
              Dep Mean       3.92250    Adj R-sq      0.8260
              C.V.          30.65919

                          Parameter Estimates

                     Parameter    Standard    T for H0:
         Variable DF  Estimate      Error    Parameter=0   Prob > |T|

         INTERCEP  1  -0.963214   0.93706366     -1.028       0.3436
         X         1   1.085714   0.18556626      5.851       0.0011
```

```
                              The SAS System                              2
                        Dep Var    Predict
               Obs        Y        Value     Residual

                1      -0.3500     0.1225    -0.4725
                2       2.7900     1.2082     1.5818
                3       1.8100     2.2939    -0.4839
                4       2.0000     3.3796    -1.3796
                5       3.8800     4.4654    -0.5854
                6       6.7900     5.5511     1.2389
                7       7.6700     6.6368     1.0332
                8       6.7900     7.7225    -0.9325

Sum of Residuals                      0
Sum of Squared Residuals         8.6776
Predicted Resid SS (Press)      15.5763
```

Output 2.13
Results of PROC
REG with NOINT
Option

```
                              The SAS System                              1
Model: MODEL1
NOTE: No intercept in model. R-square is redefined.
Dependent Variable: Y

                           Analysis of Variance

                           Sum of        Mean
         Source      DF    Squares      Square     F Value    Prob>F

         Model        1  171.06851   171.06851     117.335    0.0001
         Error        7   10.20569     1.45796
         U Total      8  181.27420

              Root MSE       1.20746    R-square      0.9437
              Dep Mean       3.92250    Adj R-sq      0.9357
              C.V.          30.78288

                          Parameter Estimates

                     Parameter    Standard    T for H0:
         Variable DF  Estimate      Error    Parameter=0   Prob > |T|

         X         1   0.915735   0.08453899     10.832       0.0001
```

```
                           The SAS System                                2

                      Dep Var    Predict
                Obs      Y         Value    Residual

                  1    -0.3500    0.9157    -1.2657
                  2     2.7900    1.8315     0.9585
                  3     1.8100    2.7472    -0.9372
                  4     2.0000    3.6629    -1.6629
                  5     3.8800    4.5787    -0.6987
                  6     6.7900    5.4944     1.2956
                  7     7.6700    6.4101     1.2599
                  8     6.7900    7.3259    -0.5359

   Sum of Residuals             -1.58647
   Sum of Squared Residuals     10.2057
   Predicted Resid SS (Press)   13.2594
```

You can see immediately that both the model F and the R-SQUARE values are much larger for the no intercept model whereas the residual mean squares are almost identical. Actually both models have estimated very similar regression lines since the estimated intercept (-0.963) is sufficiently close to zero that a hypothesis test of a zero intercept cannot be rejected ($p=0.3436$). However, the residual mean square of the no intercept model is still somewhat larger and the sum of residuals for the no intercept model is -1.586 even though the intercept is quite close to zero.

The difference between the test statistics for the models is based on which null hypothesis is tested in each case. Remember that the test for the model is based on the difference between the error and total sum of squares. The error sum of squares measures the variability from the estimated regression while the total sum of squares measures the variability from the model specified by the null hypothesis.

In the model with an intercept, the null hypothesis $\beta_1=0$ specifies the model:

$$y = \beta_0 + \varepsilon = \mu + \varepsilon \quad .$$

Now μ is estimated by the sample mean. Therefore, the test for the model compares the variation from the regression to the variation from the sample mean.

In the no intercept model, the null hypothesis $\beta_1=0$ specifies the model $y=\varepsilon$, that is, a *regression* where the mean response is zero for all observations. The test for this model then compares the variation from the regression to the variation from $y=0$. Obviously, unless the mean of the response variable is close to zero, the variation from the mean is smaller than the variation from zero, hence the apparent contradiction.

You can readily make this comparison from the above example. Since the true intercept is indeed zero, the error sums of squares are not very different (8.68 with intercept, 10.21 without intercept) but the total sums of squares are much larger for the no intercept model (181.27 for no intercept, and 58.19 with intercept). Finally, since R-SQUARE is based on the difference between the error and the total sum of squares as defined for the particular model, this statistic is also much larger for the no intercept model. Another way of looking at the no intercept model is afforded by the RESTRICT statement presented in Section 2.5.3, "Restricted Least Squares."

2.5 Further Examination of Model Parameters

In addition to testing the statistical significance of the model and the individual parameters, you can investigate other properties of the model. Specifically, you can

□ test hypotheses on any linear function(s) of the parameters. This is performed by the TEST statement described in Section 2.5.1, "Tests for Subsets and Linear Functions of Parameters."

□ change the model by adding or deleting variables. This can be done by specifying a new model or, interactively, by using ADD and DELETE statements described in Section 2.5.2. Additional model selection methods are presented in Chapter 4.

□ apply restrictions to linear functions of parameter estimates. This is done by using the RESTRICT statement described in Section 2.5.3.

2.5.1 Tests for Subsets and Linear Functions of Parameters

The *t* tests on the parameters in the basic PROC REG output (see Output 2.5) provide the tests of hypotheses that individual regression coefficients are zero. Section 2.4.2 indicates that the TYPE I sums of squares may be used to test whether certain subsets of coefficients are zero. This section shows how the TEST statement can be used to test the hypothesis that one or more linear functions of parameters are equal to specified constants.

One or more TEST statements may accompany a MODEL statement in a PROC REG step. These statements may be entered interactively. The general form of a TEST statement is

label : **TEST** *equation*<, . . ., *equation*>;

The label is any valid SAS name and serves to identify different tests in the output. The equations specify the linear functions to be tested.

The tests can be interpreted in terms of comparing complete with reduced or restricted models in the manner described in previous sections. The complete model for all tests specified by a TEST statement is the model containing all variables on the right-hand side of the MODEL statement. The reduced model is derived from the complete model by imposing the restrictions implied by the equations specified in the TEST statement. For this example the following statements are added to the MODEL statement in Section 2.3:

```
test1 : test spa = 0, alf = 0;
test2 : test utl = 0, alf = 0;
test3 : test utl - alf = 0;
```

The TEST1 statement tests the hypothesis that coefficients for both SPA and ALF are zero. This test compares the full model with one containing only UTL and ASL. The TEST2 statement tests the hypothesis that coefficients for both UTL and ALF are zero. This test compares the full model with the one containing only ASL and SPA. The TEST3 statement tests the hypothesis that the difference between the coefficients for UTL and ALF is zero. This is equivalent to the test that the coefficient for UTL is equal to the coefficient for ALF. (This particular test has no practical interpretation in this example and is used for illustration only.)

A useful feature of these statements is that if the value of the function to be tested is zero, the equality need not be specified. In other words, the TEST1 statement can also be written

```
test1 : spa, alf;
```

The results of these TEST statements appear in Output 2.14.

Output 2.14
Output from TEST
Statements

```
                                The SAS System                              1
Dependent Variable: CPM
Test: TEST1      Numerator:       2.4058  DF:   2   F value:  15.4592
                 Denominator:  0.155626   DF:  28   Prob>F:    0.0001


Dependent Variable: CPM
Test: TEST2      Numerator:       2.5512  DF:   2   F value:  16.3935
                 Denominator:  0.155626   DF:  28   Prob>F:    0.0001


Dependent Variable: CPM
Test: TEST3      Numerator:       4.4919  DF:   1   F value:  28.8634
                 Denominator:  0.155626   DF:  28   Prob>F:    0.0001
```

For each indicated TEST statement, a partial (Type II) sum of squares is computed with degrees of freedom equal to the number of equations in the TEST statement. A mean square is then computed that forms the numerator of an F statistic. The denominator of this statistic is the error mean square for the full model. The values of the two mean squares, the degrees of freedom, the F ratio and its p value are printed in the output.

Note: If there are linear dependencies or inconsistencies among the equations of a TEST statement, PROC REG prints a message that the test failed and no F ratio is computed

It is important to note that each test is performed independently rather than simultaneously with the other tests. Therefore, the results of the various tests are usually not independent of each other. Also, in making multiple hypothesis tests, you run an increased risk of making an experiment-wise type I error.

2.5.2 Changing the Model

Output 2.5 shows that the tests for the coefficient for ASL and UTL resulted in p values that were larger than those for ALF and SPA. You may be interested in examining a model that omits these two variables from the model.

If you are in batch mode, you can simply submit a new job using PROC REG with the desired model. If you are in the interactive mode, you have two choices:

□ Enter a new MODEL statement with any options that may be useful.

□ Use the interactive DELETE and ADD statements.

Before continuing with examples, you need to understand how PROC REG implements multiple models. In the interactive mode as well as in a batch mode execution, PROC REG computes a matrix of sums of squares and crossproducts of all variables involved in all MODEL statements preceding the first RUN statement. For all subsequent models, PROC REG uses elements of this matrix to obtain estimates. Therefore, unless other provisions have been made, any subsequent model may contain any subset of the variables in that matrix but may not contain variables not included in that matrix.

This procedure can be modified by following the PROC REG statement with a VAR (or VARIABLES) statement listing all variables that you may wish to consider for a PROC REG session. The VAR statement causes PROC REG to compute the sums of squares and crossproducts of all variables listed in the VAR statement. Subsequent models can now be analyzed with any subset of these variables without regard to the specification of the initial model.

One by-product of this process is that any observation with a missing value in any one of the variables in the VAR statement or initial set of MODEL statements cannot be used in the computation of the matrix of sums of squares and crossproducts. Therefore, it is possible that some observations will not be used for subset models for which the variables are available. Therefore, if missing values are a problem, you should use separate PROC REG statements for each model.

The interactive ADD and DELETE statements are of the form

    ADD *variables*;

and

    DELETE *variables*;

Assuming that you have used the original four-variable model for the airline cost data, you can delete variables ASL and UTL by entering the following statement:

```
delete asl utl;
```

The SAS log will show the following notations:

```
ASL has been deleted.
UTL has been deleted.
```

No output is produced since you may wish to perform additional interactive modifications. The output is obtained by issuing the following statement:

```
print;
```

This statement produces Output 2.15.

Output 2.15
*Output from
DELETE Statement*

```
                              The SAS System                              1
Model: MODEL1
Dependent Variable: CPM

                         Analysis of Variance

                              Sum of        Mean
        Source         DF    Squares       Square    F Value    Prob>F

        Model           2    4.89725      2.44862     12.179     0.0001
        Error          30    6.03142      0.20105
        C Total        32   10.92867

            Root MSE      0.44838     R-square      0.4481
            Dep Mean      3.10570     Adj R-sq      0.4113
            C.V.         14.43744
```

```
                           Parameter Estimates

                     Parameter      Standard     T for H0:
         Variable  DF   Estimate        Error   Parameter=0   Prob > |T|

         INTERCEP   1   6.555996   0.72271407        9.071       0.0001
         ALF        1  -6.025141   1.36285603       -4.421       0.0001
         SPA        1  -4.163687   1.01691539       -4.094       0.0003
```

This output specifies Model : MODEL1 because PROC REG is still working on the original model. This means that the output will include all MODEL options originally specified for this model. Since some options (especially those presented in Chapter 3) produce rather voluminous output, you may want to specify the following statement:

```
print anova;
```

This statement prints only the basic PROC REG output.

Any ADD or DELETE statement may be followed by additional ADD and DELETE statements, remembering that additions are restricted to those variables for which the sums of squares and crossproducts have been computed. All such statements are cumulative in that they start from the previous statement.

2.5.3 Restricted Least Squares

Restricted least squares are used to place linear restrictions on the estimated regression parameters. For example, a restriction may specify the value of a coefficient to be zero, which is the same as deleting the coefficient. Another restriction may specify that the sum of coefficients is some constant.

PROC REG allows restricted least squares estimation with the use of a RESTRICT statement. The RESTRICT statement follows a MODEL statement and has the general form:

RESTRICT *equation*<, . . ., *equation*>;

where each equation is a linear combination of model parameters set equal to a constant. As for the TEST statement, no constant is needed if the restriction equals zero.

The RESTRICT statement is interactive, but successively implemented RESTRICT statements are not cumulative in that they restrict from the original full model. However, if a RESTRICT statement is followed by a DELETE statement, the deletion is from the restricted model.

The no intercept model is actually a special case of restricted least squares models. That is, you can fit a no intercept model by adding the following statement instead of using the NOINT option in a MODEL statement:

```
restrict intercept = 0;
```

It is of interest to note that, unlike the NOINT option, with this method the total sum of squares is centered, hence the R-SQUARE value has the same connotation as in intercept models. This means that you can get a negative R-SQUARE when, as in the airline cost data, the error sum of squares is larger than the corrected total sum of squares.

The output from the RESTRICT statement with the data set in Output 2.11 is given in Output 2.16. It is instructive to compare the results of the restriction to the NOINT model in Output 2.13, since both are fitting the same model.

Output 2.16
PROC REG with
RESTRICT
Statement

```
                              The SAS System                              1
Model: MODEL1
NOTE: Restrictions have been applied to parameter estimates.
Dependent Variable: Y

                          Analysis of Variance

                            Sum of         Mean
      Source        DF     Squares        Square     F Value    Prob>F

      Model          0    47.98046           .          .          .
      Error          7    10.20569        1.45796
      C Total        7    58.18615

          Root MSE         1.20746     R-square      0.8246
          Dep Mean         3.92250     Adj R-sq      0.8246
          C.V.            30.78288

                          Parameter Estimates

                     Parameter      Standard    T for H0:
      Variable  DF    Estimate         Error    Parameter=0    Prob > |T|

      INTERCEP   1  -2.08167E-16    0.00000000       .             .
      X          1    0.915735      0.08453899     10.832        0.0001
      RESTRICT  -1   -1.586471      1.54962536     -1.024        0.3400
```

You can see that the two methods do give the same error mean square and estimated coefficient and test for the coefficient. The analysis of variance partitioning gives zero degrees of freedom for the MODEL sum of squares, because it compares the error sum of squares of the model containing only the mean (the corrected total sum of squares) to that of the no intercept model, both of which have the same error degrees of freedom. In other words, you are comparing two different models where both have the same number of parameters. Since the MODEL SS gives zero degrees of freedom, there is no legitimate test for the model. However, the RESTRICT statement does provide an R-SQUARE value that is comparable to that provided by the intercept model. Therefore, it may be argued that the RESTRICT statement is really a more reasonable way to fit a no intercept model.

The parameter estimate for the restriction pertains to the Lagrangian parameters that are incorporated in the restricted minimization of the error sum of squares. (See the *SAS/STAT User's Guide, Version 6, Fourth Edition, Volume 2).* The *t* test for the restriction is the same as for the intercept (see Output 2.12) except that a different error mean square is used. (Remember that all tests for any model use the error mean square of the specified model.)

2.6   Examining Observations

After having performed a regression you can determine how the individual observations relate to the regression relationship. Specifically, you can

□   produce plots involving the predicted and residual values or the confidence or prediction limits

□   examine the distribution of residuals

□   compare predicted and residual values for different models

□   see how the estimated regression model is affected by deleting selected observations.

There are two ways to accomplish most of these tasks as follows:

□   by interactively entering statements that produce scatter plots of variables involved in the regression, deleting observations, and adding or deleting variables from the model (as described in Section 2.5, "Further Examination of Model Parameters"). The use of such statements is presented in Section 2.6.1, "Interactive Methods."

□   by creating a data set that, for any model, contains variables such as the predicted and residual values which can be used in any SAS procedure. Instructions for creating and using such data sets are presented in Section 2.7.

Additional methodology for examining individual observations is presented in Chapter 3.

2.6.1   Interactive Methods

While executing PROC REG you can obtain a scatter plot for two variables with the PLOT statement, which is basically the same as the PLOT statement used with PROC PLOT in Section 2.2. The PLOT statement can contain any variables in the data set as well as variables produced by the regression analysis. The variables produced by the regression are specified by a keyword followed by a period, while all other variables are specified as originally named. For example

□   P. (or PREDICTED.) specifies the predicted values.

□   R. (or RESIDUAL.) specifies the residual values.

The most frequently used plots are those involving the residuals. Assuming you are in PROC REG, the following interactive statement produces two plots:

```
plot r.*p. r.*spa = type / hplots=2 vplots=2;
run;
```

The first plot is for the residual values (R.) on the vertical axis and predicted values (P.) on the horizontal axis. The second plot is for the residual values on the vertical axis and the variable SPA on the horizontal axis, using the value of TYPE as the plotting symbol.* Remember, TYPE is a binary variable where the value zero indicates short-haul lines with average stage length less than 1200 miles and unity for long-haul lines. The options HPLOTS=2 and VPLOTS=2 provide for two plots both vertically and horizontally. Since only two plots are specified, the output consists of two side-by-side half-page plots, as seen in Output 2.17.

Output 2.17
Interactive
Residual Plots

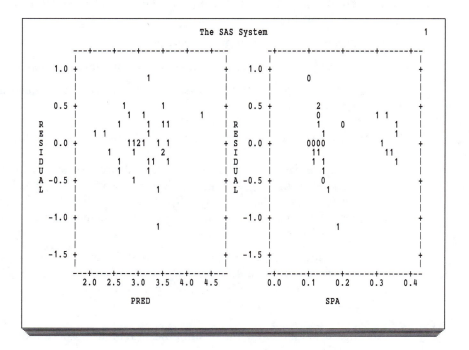

The default plotting symbol in the left-hand plot indicates the number of observations for each point. The plotting symbol for the right-hand plot is the value of the TYPE value, except that if there are multiple data points the sum of TYPE values is used.

The residuals appear adequately random, but using TYPE as the plotting symbol clearly shows two groups of airlines with respect to average plane size (SPA). As expected, the long-haul airlines tend to have larger planes.

Additional plot options include OVERLAY, which operates as in PROC PLOT, some additional SYMBOL options, and a COLLECT option, which is presented below.

The listing of the data in Output 2.1 shows two airlines with CPM values exceeding 4.0. You can redo the above plots with a highlighting of the residuals for these two airlines with the following statements:

```
paint cpm > 4;
plot;
run;
```

---

*   The PLOT statement actually causes PROC REG to refit the latest model, including the effects of any interactive statements preceding the PLOT statement.

The PAINT statement specifies that all observations for which CPM is larger than 4.0 will be highlighted by the default symbol @. The PLOT statement without further specification requests the repeat of the same plots. The results appear in Output 2.18.

Output 2.18
Painting a
Residual Plot

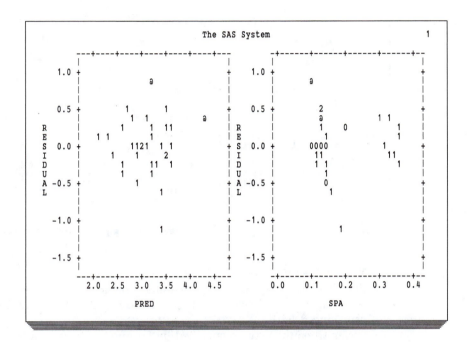

A different symbol for painted observations is specified with the SYMBOL option:

```
paint cpm < 2.5 / symbol = 'S';
plot;
run;
```

This statement paints observations with CPM<2.5 using the symbol S. Additional PAINT statements are cumulative; hence, the above statement would paint the high cost airlines with @ and the low cost airlines with S. A PAINT statement is canceled by the following statement:

```
paint undo;
```

Sometimes it is useful to see what happens to an estimated regression if some observations are deleted. You can estimate the regression model without using the data from airlines with CPM>4.0 as follows:

```
reweight  cpm>4;
print;
plot;
run;
```

The REWEIGHT statement assigns a default weight of zero to the observations for which CPM>4. A zero weight is the same as deleting an observation.

The regression with the reweighted observations is refitted by the PRINT command. Output 2.19 shows the results.

Output 2.19
*Deleting
Observations with
the REWEIGHT
Statement*

```
                              The SAS System                              1

Model: MODEL1
Dependent Variable: CPM

                        Analysis of Variance

                            Sum of        Mean
     Source         DF     Squares       Square     F Value     Prob>F

     Model           4     4.14318      1.03579       8.768     0.0001
     Error          26     3.07137      0.11813
     C Total        30     7.21455

            Root MSE        0.34370     R-square      0.5743
            Dep Mean        3.02345     Adj R-sq      0.5088
            C.V.           11.36780

                        Parameter Estimates

                    Parameter      Standard     T for H0:
     Variable   DF   Estimate        Error     Parameter=0    Prob > |T|

     INTERCEP    1   7.652604     0.92278057       8.293       0.0001
     ALF         1  -6.908211     1.25765796      -5.493       0.0001
     UTL         1  -0.125060     0.06547655      -1.910       0.0672
     ASL         1   0.257663     0.16344098       1.576       0.1270
     SPA         1  -4.423997     1.10141039      -4.017       0.0004
```

You can see that the regression estimates are not changed much by the deletion of these observations. A residual plot for this regression, using the same specifications as the previous plot, can be produced by the PLOT statement, but is not reproduced here.

Other weights* may be specified by an option, for example:

```
reweight cpm > 4 / weight = xx;
```

REWEIGHT statements are cumulative and may be undone by the statement:

```
reweight allobs / reset;
```

You can overlay plots from different regressions with the COLLECT option. For example, you can examine the effect of deleting the SPA variable on the residual plots given in Output 2.17. First, you must return to the original full model. This can be done by simply repeating the original MODEL statement or by various UNDO and RESET options. Then specify the plots as before:

```
plot r.*p. r.*spa=type / collect hplots=2 vplots=2;
run;
```

The COLLECT option causes the plot to be saved so that it can be overlaid by plots to be specified later. Next, delete the variable SPA:

```
delete spa;
```

---

*   For most general applications, weighting that involves all observations is more efficiently done by the WEIGHT statement presented in Section 3.4.1.

At this point you may specify the following statements to examine the resulting model, which is not reproduced here.

```
print; run;
```

Now specify the plots:

```
plot r.*p.='*' r.*spa='.';
run;
```

Note that the plotting symbols have changed so that the plotted points may be compared more readily. The results are shown in Output 2.20.

Output 2.20
Using the
COLLECT Option

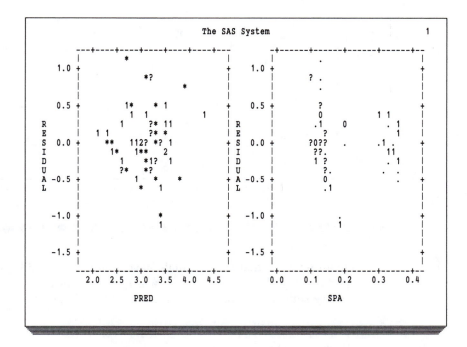

The question mark (?) symbols are data points with multiple symbol specifications. There are only a moderate number of ? symbols, suggesting that the basic pattern of residuals has changed somewhat, but details are difficult to ascertain. This shows that overlaid plots are not always useful because of the lack of definition in a printer plot and the fact that the plots are not rescaled so that some data points on the second plot may be out of range.

You can use the COLLECT option to produce side-by-side plots with no overlays by producing a blank plot for the same position of subsequent collected plots. This is done by specifying ' ' for the plotting symbol.

This is illustrated with residual plots for the full model and the one obtained by deleting SPA. The SAS program, starting with a new MODEL statement, is

```
model cpm = alf utl asl spa;
     plot r.*p. / hplots=2 vplots=2 collect;
delete spa;
     plot r.*p.=' ' r.*p. / nocollect;
run;
```

The first PLOT statement produces the residual plot for the full model (not reproduced here). The DELETE statement deletes SPA. The second PLOT statement refits the model and requests two residual plots. However, since the first has blanks as the plotting symbol, nothing is laid over the first plot. The NOCOLLECT option turns off collecting for future plots. The resulting plots appear in Output 2.21.

Output 2.21
Side-by-Side
Residual Plots

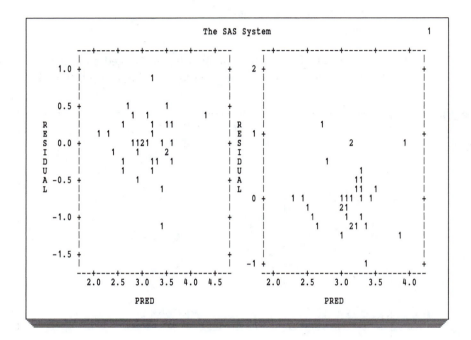

You can now see that the residuals have changed (note different scales), which was expected since the SPA coefficient was quite significant.

Here are some additional notes on the COLLECT option:

□ The first plot is overlaid and the second remains as is if the second PLOT statement specifies only one plot.

□ There is no rescaling of axes for the additional collected plots. This may cause loss of plotted points. For this reason you may wish to start the collection process with plots showing the largest variation of plotted variables.

□ Overlaid plots may be collected.

□ Collection of plots is turned off by using a NOCOLLECT option in the last plot to be collected.

□ Collection of plots may also be done to compare results from REWEIGHT statements.

You can continue with any number of additional interactive statements. However, you must remember that they are cumulative, and after too many such statements you may have forgotten where you are.

2.7 Creating Data: the OUTPUT Statement

An OUTPUT statement following the MODEL statement causes a new SAS data set to be constructed that contains all of the variables in the data set to which PROC REG was applied, plus other variables specified in the OUTPUT statement. The basic form of the OUTPUT statement to create a data set containing, for example, predicted and residual values is

OUTPUT OUT = *dsname* P = *pvarnames* R = *rvarnames*;

where *dsname* is the name chosen for the new data set, *pvarnames* is a list of names chosen for the variables whose values will be the predicted values, and *rvarnames* is the list of names chosen for the variables whose values are the residuals. The names in the *pvarnames* and *rvarnames* lists must correspond to the list of dependent variables in the most recent MODEL statement. A large variety of other output statistics can be included in the OUTPUT data set. Some are used in the example of this section and others are presented in Chapter 3. The complete set of statistics that can be included is given in Chapter 36 of the *SAS/STAT User's Guide, Volume 2.*

The OUTPUT statement produces the statistics only for the estimated model and cannot be altered by any interactive statements. However, the resulting data set can be used for any SAS procedures thus allowing considerable flexibility for summarizing the resulting statistics. Furthermore, the data set may be combined by concatenating or merging results from other models or data sets.

The OUTPUT statement is illustrated using the one-variable regression discussed in Section 2.2 to produce a data set that includes predicted and residual values and the 95% prediction intervals. The SAS statements are

```
proc reg data = air;
    model cpm = alf;
    output out=d p=pcpm r=rcpm u95=up l95=down;
run;
```

The OUTPUT statement includes the following options:

OUT=D   specifies that the name of the new data set is D.

P=PCPM   specifies that the predicted values have the variable name PCPM.

R=RCPM   specifies that the residuals have the variable name RCPM.

U95=UP   specifies that the upper 95% prediction limit has the variable name UP.

L95=DOWN   specifies that the lower 95% prediciton limit has the variable name DOWN.

Additionally, the options U95M and L95M may be employed to provide the upper and lower 95% confidence intervals on the conditional mean (see Section 2.4.1, "The P, CLM, and CLI Options.").

As a result of the OUTPUT statement, the SAS log contains the following information:

```
NOTE: Data set WORK.D has 33 observations and 10 variables.
```

This shows that the procedure has created the new data set: the number of variables comprises the original set of six plus the four additional variables specified in the OUTPUT statement.

The output from PROC REG is the same as in Output 2.3 and is not reproduced here. The data set can now be processed by any SAS procedure, such as the UNIVARIATE procedure, to check the distribution of residuals, or PROC PLOT, which will essentially provide the same plots obtained by the interactive statements presented in the previous section.

The flexibility offered by the OUTPUT statement is illustrated by creating the plot of the actual and predicted values as well as the 95% prediction limits on SAS/GRAPH software, where the more flexible spacing and interpolation options provide a more useful graph.

The required steps (in addition to hardware-specific instructions) are

```
proc sort data=d;
   by alt;
proc gplot data=d;
   plot cpm*alf=1
        pcpm*alf=2
        up*alf=3
        down*alf=4 / overlay;
   symbol1 v=star c=c2;
   symbol2 v=p i=join c=c2;
   symbol3 v=U i=spline c=c2;
   symbol4 v=1 i=spline c=c2;
run;
```

The resulting graph appears in Output 2.22.

Output 2.22
Prediction Plot

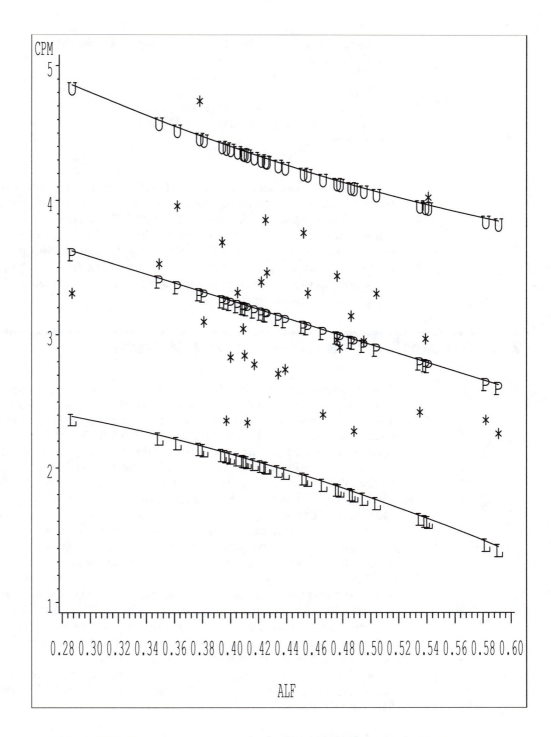

The OUTPUT statement can be used to obtain other statistics, such as confidence intervals for other than the 0.95 confidence level. To do this, first generate a data set containing the predicted values and the standard error of the estimate as follows:

```
output out=b p=yhat stdp=stdmean;
```

Then create a new data set and compute, say, the 0.99 level intervals using the TINV function:

```
data c; set b;
lower = yhat - tinv(0.995,31)*stdmean;
upper = yhat + tinv(0.995,31)*stdmean;
proc print;
run;
```

Other SAS data sets containing the parameter estimates and related statistics as well as data sets containing the correlations or covariances among these estimates are available with the OUTEST and COVOUT options. The **X'X** matrix can also be output to a SAS data set with the OUTSSCP option. Some of these data sets can be used as input to PROC REG as well as other SAS procedures. Instructions for using these options are given in the *SAS/STAT User's Guide* and descriptions of the resulting data sets are given in the Appendix 1, "Special SAS Data Sets," in the same guide.

2.8 Predicting to a Different Set of Data

A regression equation estimated from one set of data can be used to predict values of the dependent variable using the same model for another set of similar data. This type of prediction has been used, for example, to settle charges of pay discrimination against minorities. An equation relating pay to factors such as education, performance, and tenure is estimated using data for nonminority employees, usually white males. This equation predicts what the pay rate should be for all employees in the absence of discrimination or other factors. If this equation predicts substantially higher than actual salaries for minority employees, there is cause to suspect pay discrimination.

This feature may also be used for cross-validation, where a data set is split randomly into two parts and the effectiveness of a statistical procedure used on one of the data sets is determined by finding how well it works on the other.

This type of analysis is illustrated with the airline cost data. The variable TYPE was created to divide the airlines into two groups: the short-haul lines with ASL<1200 miles and the long-haul lines with ASL≥1200 miles. (This is an arbitrary division used here only for illustration.) One way to ascertain if there are differences in the cost structures between these two types is to see how well the cost equation for short-haul lines estimates costs for the long-haul lines.*

Define a new variable SCPM to give the cost per passenger mile of the short-haul lines and missing for the other airlines. This is done by creating a new data set as follows:

```
data short; set air;
if type = 0 then scpm = cpm;
    else scpm = .;
```

---

* Another method for answering this question is given in Section 6.4, "Indicator Variables."

Now use PROC REG:

```
proc reg data=short;
    model scpm = alf utl asl spa ;
    output out=e p=pscpm ;
    run;
```

The SAS log will indicate that although there are 33 observations, only 14 observations are used for calculations. Therefore, the regression estimates from this analysis (see Output 2.23) are based only on the 14 short-haul lines.

Output 2.23
Regression for
Short-Haul Lines

```
                              The SAS System                              1

Model: MODEL1
Dependent Variable: SCPM

                          Analysis of Variance

                           Sum of        Mean
       Source      DF      Squares       Square     F Value     Prob>F

       Model        4      3.90858       0.97714     17.486      0.0003
       Error        9      0.50292       0.05588
       C Total     13      4.41150

            Root MSE       0.23639     R-square      0.8860
            Dep Mean       3.33557     Adj R-sq      0.8353
            C.V.           7.08694

                          Parameter Estimates

                      Parameter      Standard     T for H0:
       Variable  DF    Estimate         Error   Parameter=0    Prob > |T|

       INTERCEP   1    10.700037    1.11685114        9.581        0.0001
       ALF        1    -6.720400    1.65218520       -4.068        0.0028
       UTL        1    -0.413886    0.05584654       -7.411        0.0001
       ASL        1    -0.273706    0.65235057       -0.420        0.6846
       SPA        1    -5.491320    3.45924778       -1.587        0.1469
```

Note that the coefficients are somewhat different from those estimated from the entire data set (Output 2.5). The most striking difference is that the effect of the number of seats per plane (SPA) is not statistically significant ($p=0.1469$). This is probably due to short-haul lines not having a wide assortment of airplane sizes.

Now data set E has predicted values for all 33 observations, but obviously it does not have residuals for the long-haul lines; hence, these must be computed in another DATA step:

```
data f;
    set e;
    rscpm = cpm - pscpm;
```

You can now use PROC PLOT to plot the residuals against the predicted values using the value of TYPE as the plotting symbol and having a reference line at the zero value of the residuals:

```
proc plot data=f;
    plot rscpm*pscpm=type / hpos=30 vpos=25 vref=0;
    run;
```

The resulting plot appears in Output 2.24.

Output 2.24
Regression for
Short-Haul Lines

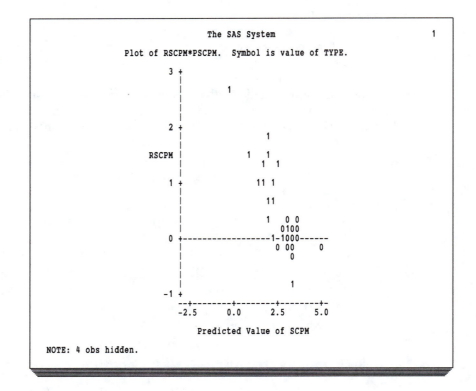

You can see that the cost equation of the short-haul lines does not well predict costs of the long-haul lines. In fact, it appears that this equation underpredicts the costs for the long-haul lines.

2.9 Exact Collinearity: Linear Dependency

Linear dependency occurs when exact linear relationships exist among the independent variables. More precisely, a linear dependency exists when one or more columns of the **X** matrix can be expressed as a linear combination of other columns. This means that the **X′X** matrix is singular and cannot be inverted in the usual sense to obtain parameter estimates.* PROC REG is programmed to detect the existence of exact collinearity and, if it exists, uses a generalized inverse (see Section 1.1.4, "Using the Generalized Inverse") to compute *parameter estimates*. The words *parameter estimates* are stressed to emphasize that care must be exercised to determine exactly what parameters are being estimated. More technically, the generalized inverse approach yields only one of many possible solutions to the normal equations.

---

*   Exact collinearity should not be confused with multicollinearity, which is a term used to describe a high degree of correlation among the independent variables. Multicollinearity can be described as *almost* exact collinearity. In fact, cases of multicollinearity may be diagnosed as exact collinearity due to computer roundoff. Thus these are related topics but do, in fact, represent different conditions requiring different methodology. Multicollinearity and associated methodology are discussed in Chapter 4.

PROC REG computations with an exact linear dependency are illustrated with an alternate model of the airline cost data.

First, create a data set with an additional variable PASS, as follows:

```
data depend; set air;
pass = alf*spa;
```

PASS represents the average number of passengers per flight. Adding this variable does not create a linear dependency since PASS is defined with a multiplicative relationship. Next use a model in which all variables have been converted to logarithms. (The logarithmic model is discussed in some detail in Section 6.2, "Log-Linear (Multiplicative) Models".) This is done by adding the following statements to the DATA step above:

```
array a alf utl asl spa cpm pass;
do over a;
    a = log(a);
end;
```

Because PASS=ALF*SPA, then log(PASS)=log(ALF)+log(SPA), which constitutes an exact collinearity. In this model, then, PASS=ALF+SPA. Now implement PROC REG using all five variables:

```
proc reg data = depend;
    model cpm = alf utl asl spa pass;
run;
```

The results appear in Output 2.25.

Output 2.25
Exact Collinearity

```
                              The SAS System                               1
Model: MODEL1
Dependent Variable: CPM

                            Analysis of Variance

                             Sum of        Mean
        Source       DF      Squares      Square     F Value      Prob>F

        Model         4      0.70234     0.17558      12.364      0.0001
        Error        28      0.39764     0.01420
        C Total      32      1.09997

            Root MSE        0.11917     R-square       0.6385
            Dep Mean        1.11647     Adj R-sq       0.5869
            C.V.           10.67377

NOTE: Model is not full rank. Least-squares solutions for the parameters are
      not unique. Some statistics will be misleading. A reported DF of 0 or B
      means that the estimate is biased.
      The following parameters have been set to 0, since the variables are a
      linear combination of other variables as shown.

      PASS     = +1.0000 * ALF     +1.0000 * SPA
                         Parameter Estimates

                         Parameter      Standard    T for H0:
        Variable  DF      Estimate         Error    Parameter=0    Prob > |T|

        INTERCEP   1      0.638787    0.39010340      1.637        0.1127
        ALF        B     -1.033775    0.18011628     -5.739        0.0001
        UTL        1     -0.467788    0.15840127     -2.953        0.0063
        ASL        1      0.110809    0.08472969      1.308        0.2016
        SPA        B     -0.337168    0.08083128     -4.171        0.0003
        PASS       0      0              .             .            .
```

The existence of collinearity is indicated by the NOTE in the model summary, followed by the equation describing the linear relationship:

PASS = + 1.0000 * ALF + 1.0000 * SPA

The parameter estimates that are printed are equivalent to those that are obtained if PASS were not included in the MODEL statement. In general, the parameter estimates are those that would be obtained if any variable that is a linear function of variables that precede it in the MODEL statement were deleted from the MODEL statement. These deleted variables are indicated with zeroes under the DF and Parameter Estimate headings. Other variables involved in the linear dependencies are indicated with a B, standing for *bias*, under the DF heading. These estimates are in fact unbiased estimates of the parameters of the model that does not include the deleted variable(s), but are biased estimates for other models.

The bias can readily be seen by using a model with the independent variables listed in a different order. For example, in the model

```
model cpm = pass alf utl asl spa;
```

SPA will be designated with 0 and PASS and ALF with B under the DF heading.

Due to roundoff error, determining when exact linear dependency occurs is somewhat arbitrary. In PROC REG the matrix inversion procedure computes successive tolerance values. A tolerance of zero signifies an exact collinearity, but since roundoff errors essentially preclude the computing of exact zero values, a tolerance of 1E-7 is normally used to indicate exact collinearity.

This criterion is adequate for virtually all applications, but can be changed by adding the following option to the PROC REG statement:

```
singular = n;
```

n specifies the minimum tolerance for which the matrix is declared nonsingular.

2.10   Summary

The purpose of this chapter has been to provide instruction on how to use PROC REG to perform a regression analysis. This included

□   estimating the model equation and error variance

□   providing predicted values and their standard errors

□   making inferences on the regression parameters

□   checking the residuals and providing plots to check the fit of the model

□   making modifications of the model

□   checking results when some observations have been deleted

□   finding how well the model may fit an equivalent data set.

Some of the analyses outlined above can be performed in different ways. They also do not exhaust all of the possible analyses that can be performed with PROC REG.

You are now ready to further investigate how well the data fit the model (see Chapter 3) and the suitability of the variables you have chosen for your model (see Chapter 4). Later chapters expand the variety of regression models you can analyze with the SAS System.

Chapter **3** Observations

3.1 Introduction

In the linear model

$$\mathbf{Y} = \mathbf{X}\boldsymbol{\beta} + \boldsymbol{\varepsilon}$$

the elements of the vector $\boldsymbol{\varepsilon}$ are the differences between the observed values of the y's and those expected from the model. These elements comprise the so called *error term* of the model and are specified to be a set of independently and normally distributed random variables with mean zero and variance σ^2. This error term represents natural variation in the data, but can also be interpreted as the cumulative effect of factors not specified in the model. Often this variation results in errors that, for practical purposes, behave as specified in which case the use of linear model methodology may be appropriate. However, this is not always the case and, if the assumptions are violated, the resulting analysis may provide results of questionable validity.

Violations of this assumption can occur in many ways. The most frequent occurrences may be categorized as follows:

☐   The data may contain *outliers*, or unusual observations that do not reasonably fit the model.

☐   A *specification error* occurs when the specified model does not contain all of the necessary parameters. This includes the situations where only linear terms have been specified and the true relationships are curvilinear.

☐   The *distribution* of the errors may be distinctly nonnormal; it may be severely skewed or fat tailed.

☐   The errors may exhibit *heteroscedasticity*, that is, the variances are not the same for all observations.

☐   The errors may be *correlated*, which is a phenomenon usually found in time series data, but is not restricted to such situations.

Violations of the assumptions underlying the random errors are often not so severe as to invalidate the analysis, but this is not guaranteed. Therefore, it is useful to examine the data for possible violations and, if violations are found, to employ remedial measures.

Most methods for detecting violations of assumptions are based on the analysis of the estimated errors which are the *residuals*:

$$\hat{\varepsilon} = y - X\hat{\beta} \quad .$$

However, other statistics may be used. This chapter presents some tools available in PROC REG to detect such violations. Some of these tools involve the estimated residuals, while others are concerned with the behavior of the independent variables. Alternative analysis methodologies that may be employed if assumptions fail are also presented. It must, however, be emphasized, that the coverage is not exhaustive, especially with respect to alternate methodologies (Belsley et al. 1980).

3.2 Outlier Detection

Observations that do not appear to fit the model, often called outliers, can be quite troublesome since they can bias parameter estimates and make the resulting analysis less useful. For this reason it is important to examine the results of a statistical analysis to ascertain if there are observations that have the potential of causing the analysis to provide misleading results. This is especially important in regression analyses where the lack of structure of the independent variables makes detection and identification of outliers more difficult.

It is important to note that observations that may cause misleading results may be unusual with respect to the independent variables, the dependent variable, or both, and that each of these conditions may create different types of results. Furthermore, the identification of unusual observations alone does not provide directions as to what to do with such observations. Any action must be consistent with the purpose of the analysis and conform to good statistical practice.

The following example comes from a study of manpower needs for operating a U.S. Navy Bachelor Officers Quarters (BOQ) (Myers, 1990). The observations are records from 25 establishments. The response variable represents the monthly manhours (MANH) required to operate each establishment, and the independent variables are

OCCUP	average daily occupancy
CHECKIN	monthly average number of check-ins
HOURS	weekly hours of service desk operation
COMMON	square feet of common use area
WINGS	number of building wings
CAP	operational berthing capacity
ROOMS	number of rooms.

The data appear in Output 3.1.

Output 3.1
BOQ Data

```
                           The SAS System                              1

OBS    OCCUP    CHECKIN    HOURS    COMMON    WINGS    CAP    ROOMS     MANH

  1     2.00       4.00      4.0      1.26        1      6        6   180.23
  2     3.00       1.58     40.0      1.25        1      5        5   182.61
  3     5.30       1.67     42.5      7.79        3     25       25   199.92
  4     7.00       2.37    168.0      1.00        1      7        8   284.55
  5    16.50       8.25    168.0      1.12        2     19       19   267.38
  6    16.60      23.78     40.0      1.00        1     13       13   164.38
  7    25.89       3.00     40.0      0.00        3     36       36   999.09
  8    31.92      40.08    168.0      5.52        6     47       47   931.84
  9    39.63      50.86     40.0     27.37       10     77       77   944.21
 10    44.42     159.75    168.0      0.60       18     48       48  1103.24
 11    54.58     207.08    168.0      7.77        6     66       66  1387.82
 12    56.63     373.42    168.0      6.03        4     36       37  1489.50
 13    95.00     368.00    168.0     30.26        9    292      196  1845.89
 14    96.67     206.67    168.0     17.86       14    120      120  1891.70
 15    96.83     677.33    168.0     20.31       10    302      210  1880.84
 16    97.33     255.08    168.0     19.00        6    165      130  2268.06
 17   102.33     288.83    168.0     21.01       14    131      131  3036.63
 18   110.24     410.00    168.0     20.05       12    115      115  2628.32
 19   113.88     981.00    168.0     24.48        6    166      179  3559.92
 20   134.32     145.82    168.0     25.99       12    192      192  2227.76
 21   149.58     233.83    168.0     31.07       14    185      202  3115.29
 22   188.74     937.00    168.0     45.44       26    237      237  4804.24
 23   274.92     695.25    168.0     46.63       58    363      363  5539.98
 24   384.50    1473.66    168.0      7.36       24    540      453  8266.77
 25   811.08     714.33    168.0     22.76       17    242      242  3534.49
```

Perform the regression using the following SAS statements:

```
proc reg data=boq;
    model manh = occup checkin hours common wings cap rooms;
```

The results appear in Output 3.2.

Output 3.2
Regression for BOQ Data

```
                           The SAS System                              1

Model: MODEL1
Dependent Variable: MANH

                        Analysis of Variance

                             Sum of        Mean
         Source       DF    Squares       Square     F Value    Prob>F

         Model         7  87387188.137  12483884.02    60.257    0.0001
         Error        17   3522013.1205   207177.24238
         C Total      24  90909201.258

             Root MSE      455.16727     R-square     0.9613
             Dep Mean     2109.38640     Adj R-sq     0.9453
             C.V.           21.57818

                        Parameter Estimates

                         Parameter      Standard    T for H0:
         Variable   DF    Estimate         Error   Parameter=0   Prob > |T|

         INTERCEP    1    134.967902   237.81429561     0.568      0.5778
         OCCUP       1     -1.283767     0.80469103    -1.595      0.1291
         CHECKIN     1      1.803510     0.51623608     3.494      0.0028
         HOURS       1      0.669150     1.84639922     0.362      0.7215
         COMMON      1    -21.422630    10.17159933    -2.106      0.0504
         WINGS       1      5.619226    14.74609416     0.381      0.7079
         CAP         1    -14.480251     4.22017748    -3.431      0.0032
         ROOMS       1     29.324751     6.36590365     4.607      0.0003
```

The test for the model is certainly significant. However, only three of the coefficients appear to be important, and among these, the effect of CAP has an illogical sign. Such results are typical when multicollinearity exists, which is the topic of Chapter 4, "Multicollinearity: Detection and Remedial Measures." For now, the focus is on finding unusual observations.

3.2.1 Residuals and Studentized Residuals

The traditional tool for detecting outliers (as well as specification error, see Section 3.3, "Specification Errors") consists of examining the residuals.

A difficulty with residuals is that they are not all estimated with the same precision. However, you can compute standard errors of residuals, and when the residuals are divided by these standard errors, you will obtain standardized or *studentized* residuals. These studentized residuals follow Student's *t* distribution. For error degrees of freedom exceeding ten, values from the *t* distribution greater than 2.5 are relatively rare. Thus, studentized residuals exceeding this value provide a convenient vehicle for identifying unusually large residuals.

As indicated in Chapter 2, "Using the REG Procedure," these residuals, as well as other statistics used for detecting violations of assumptions, are provided by PROC REG in several ways. They are

□ printed as part of the PROC REG output as specified by options in the MODEL statement

□ output to a data set for printing, plotting, or other statistical analyses

□ plotted with the interactive plotting capabilities of PROC REG.

For printing these statistics as part of the regression output, you specify the R (for RESIDUAL) option in the MODEL statement:

```
proc reg data=boq;
    model manh = occup checkin hours common wings cap rooms/ r;
```

The additional results produced by this option appear in Output 3.3.

Output 3.3
R Option for BOQ
Data

```
                                    The SAS System                              1

          Dep Var   Predict   Std Err            Std Err   Student
   Obs      MANH      Value    Predict  Residual  Residual  Residual

    1       180.2     210.0    230.877  -29.7547  392.267   -0.076
    2       182.6     213.8    182.567  -31.1856  416.949   -0.075
    3       199.9     380.7    174.801   -180.8   420.264   -0.430
    4       284.5     360.1    183.829  -75.5559  416.394   -0.181
    5       267.4     510.4    181.437   -243.0   417.442   -0.582
    6       164.4     360.5    182.870   -196.1   416.816   -0.470
    7       999.1     685.2    194.651    313.9   411.447    0.763
    8       931.8     891.8    163.824   39.9941  424.663    0.094
    9       944.2     815.5    241.202    128.7   386.004    0.334
   10      1103.2    1279.3    272.756   -176.1   364.392   -0.483
   11      1387.8    1397.8    141.699   -9.9665  432.549   -0.023
   12      1489.5    1305.2    204.778    184.3   406.501    0.453
   13      1845.9    1710.9    336.558    135.0   306.440    0.441
   14      1891.7    1973.4    128.903  -81.7158  436.533   -0.187
   15      1880.8    2750.9    275.477   -870.1   362.339   -2.401
   16      2268.1    1632.1    160.373    635.9   425.979    1.493
   17      3036.6    2210.1    120.765    826.5   438.854    1.883
```

```
18    2628.3    2190.3    134.111      438.0    434.961    1.007
19    3559.9    4225.1    339.885     -665.2    302.746   -2.197
20    2227.8    2698.7    276.208     -471.0    361.782   -1.302
21    3115.3    3134.9    288.719   -19.6054    351.879   -0.056
22    4804.2    4385.8    304.143      418.5    338.636    1.236
23    5540.0    5863.9    403.373     -323.9    210.872   -1.536
24    8266.8    7853.5    426.057      413.3    160.164    2.580
25    3534.5    3694.8    452.533     -160.3     48.896   -3.278

                                          Cook's
      Obs   -2-1-0 1 2                        D

        1   |      |      |              0.000
        2   |      |      |              0.000
        3   |      |      |              0.004
        4   |     *|      |              0.001
        5   |    * |      |              0.008
        6   |     *|      |              0.005
        7   |     |*      |              0.016
        8   |      |      |              0.000
        9   |      |      |              0.005
       10   |      |      |              0.016
       11   |      |      |              0.000
       12   |      |      |              0.007
       13   |      |      |              0.029
       14   |     |      |              0.000
       15   | **** |      |              0.417
       16   |     |**     |              0.039
       17   |     |***    |              0.034
       18   |     |**     |              0.012
       19   | **** |      |              0.761
       20   |   ** |      |              0.123
       21   |      |      |              0.000
       22   |     |**     |              0.154
       23   |  *** |      |              1.079
       24   |     |***** |              5.889
       25   |******|      |            115.041
```

```
                              The SAS System                        2

Sum of Residuals                     0
Sum of Squared Residuals     3522013.1205
Predicted Resid SS (Press) 213738242.87
```

The various statistics are identified by column headings: Dep Var MANH, Predict Value, Residual, and Student Residual. The Std Err Predict column provides the standard errors of the estimated conditional means, which is more precisely explained in Section 2.4.1, "The P, CLM, and CLI Options." The Std Err Residual column provides the standard errors of the residual. You can verify that the studentized residuals are the residuals divided by their standard errors.

The column labeled -2-1-0 1 2 contains a schematic plot of the studentized residuals that shows one asterisk for each 0.5 value of the studentized residuals. Thus, five asterisks correspond to studentized residuals exceeding 2.5 in absolute value. The Cook's D column is the Cook's D statistic to be discussed later.

Observation 25 is of particular interest. Note that the residual of −160.3 is not exessively large compared with the other residuals or the residual standard deviation (ROOT MSE) of 455. But the standard error of the residual, 48.896, is by far the smallest, thus producing the largest studentized residual among all observations. You can also see that observations 15 and 17 have the largest residuals, while observations 24 and 25 have the largest studentized residuals, both of which exceed 2.5.

A better appreciation of these residuals is afforded by examining plots, which may be obtained interactively, or by creating a data set and implementing the PLOT procedure, which is the method used here.

```
proc reg data=boq;
    model manh = occup checkin hours common wings cap rooms;
    output out = resid p = pman r = rman student = student;
proc plot data = resid hpercent=50;
    plot rman*pman student*pman / vpos = 20 vref = 0;
```

The OUTPUT statement produces a data set called RESID, which contains the additional variables PMAN, RMAN, and STUDENT that correspond to the keywords P, R, and STUDENT. These are the predicted, residual and studentized residual values, respectively. The PROC PLOT statements request the plots of residuals and studentized residuals against the predicted values. The option HPERCENT=50 provides for the two plots to be side-by-side for better comparison. The PROC PLOT option VPOS=20 produces a more compact plot of only 20 vertical plot positions and VREF=0 provides for a reference line for *zero* on the vertical axis. The results appear in Output 3.4.

Output 3.4
Residual and
Studentized
Residual Plots

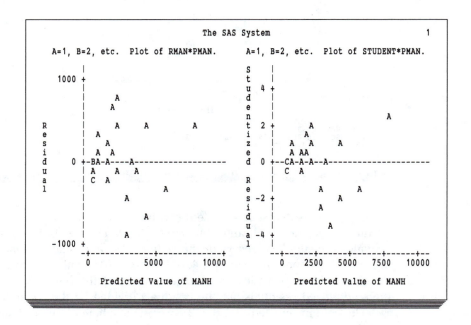

You can see that the pattern of the studentized residuals differs somewhat from that of the actual residuals, and although a number of studentized residuals exceed 2.5 in magnitude, none clearly stands out. The studentized residuals do, however, emphasize that the magnitudes of residuals increase with larger predicted values. This may be an indicator of heterogeneous variances, which are discussed in Section 3.4, "Heterogeneous Variances."

3.2.2 Influence Statistics

Outliers are sometimes not readily detected by an examination of residuals because the least-squares estimation procedure tends to pull the estimated regression response towards observations that have extreme values in either *x* or *y* dimensions. The estimated residuals for such observations may therefore not be especially large, thus hindering the search for outliers. You may be able to overcome this difficulty by asking what would happen to various estimates and statistics if the observation in question were not used in the estimation of the regression equation used to calculate the statistics.

Such statistics are annotated by the subscript (-*i*) to indicate that they are computed by omitting (subtracting) the *i*th observation. For example, s_{-i}^2 is the residual mean square obtained when all but the *i*th observation are used to estimate the regression. Statistics of this type are said to be determining the potential *influence* of a particular observation, hence they are called influence statistics.[*] To print these statistics as part of the PROC REG output, you use the INFLUENCE option as follows:[**]

```
proc reg data=boq;
   model manh = occup checkin hours common wings cap rooms/ influence;
```

The output (not including the default output) produced by this option appears in Output 3.5.

Output 3.5

Output Using the INFLUENCE Option

```
                                  The SAS System                                1

                         Hat Diag      Cov            INTERCEP    OCCUP
 Obs  Residual  Rstudent     H       Ratio    Dffits    Dfbetas   Dfbetas
   1  -29.7547   -0.0736   0.2573   2.1809   -0.0433   -0.0433   -0.0006
   2  -31.1856   -0.0726   0.1609   1.9305   -0.0318   -0.0310   -0.0006
   3   -180.8    -0.4196   0.1475   1.7454   -0.1745   -0.1662    0.0041
   4  -75.5559   -0.1762   0.1631   1.9109   -0.0778    0.0040    0.0026
   5   -243.0    -0.5704   0.1589   1.6437   -0.2479    0.0135    0.0115
   6   -196.1    -0.4594   0.1614   1.7440   -0.2016   -0.1971   -0.0037
   7    313.9     0.7532   0.1829   1.5041    0.3563    0.3234   -0.0274
   8   39.9941    0.0914   0.1295   1.8581    0.0353   -0.0029   -0.0031
   9    128.7     0.3246   0.2808   2.1428    0.2029    0.1271    0.0070
  10   -176.1    -0.4720   0.3591   2.2688   -0.3533   -0.0055   -0.0160
  11   -9.9665   -0.0224   0.0969   1.7980   -0.0073    0.0004    0.0010
  12    184.3     0.4426   0.2024   1.8475    0.2230    0.0069    0.0092
  13    135.0     0.4299   0.5467   3.2687    0.4722   -0.0413    0.0586
  14  -81.7158   -0.1818   0.0802   1.7369   -0.0537    0.0085    0.0068
  15   -870.1    -2.8657   0.3663   0.0932   -2.1787    0.0223   -0.0035
  16    635.9     1.5537   0.1241   0.6025    0.5849   -0.0790    0.0289
  17    826.5     2.0538   0.0704   0.2687    0.5652   -0.0929   -0.0984
  18    438.0     1.0074   0.0868   1.0874    0.3106   -0.0243   -0.0054
  19   -665.2    -2.5192   0.5576   0.2536   -2.8282   -0.0598    0.9457
  20   -471.0    -1.3310   0.3682   1.1097   -1.0162    0.1531    0.2449
  21  -19.6054   -0.0541   0.4024   2.7136   -0.0444    0.0065    0.0124
  22    418.5     1.2566   0.4465   1.3820    1.1286   -0.0431   -0.0822
  23   -323.9    -1.6057   0.7854   2.2901   -3.0715    0.2010    0.2396
  24    413.3     3.2093   0.8762   0.2461    8.5373    0.7391   -1.6514
  25   -160.3    -5.2423   0.9885   0.0473  -48.5179   -0.2455  -44.3791

       CHECKIN    HOURS    COMMON    WINGS      CAP     ROOMS
 Obs   Dfbetas   Dfbetas   Dfbetas   Dfbetas   Dfbetas   Dfbetas

   1   -0.0044    0.0345    0.0036   -0.0020   -0.0007    0.0013
   2   -0.0025    0.0204    0.0046   -0.0020   -0.0008    0.0017
   3    0.0037    0.1231   -0.0128    0.0048   -0.0018    0.0020
```

(continued on next page)

---

[*]   The computations of influence statistics do not require the recomputation of regression omitting each observation. All of these statistics are functions of the results of the original model and the hat matrix (see the discussion of the HAT DIAG statistic later in this section). Computational and other details can be found in Belsley, Kuh, and Welsch (1980).

[**]   You may use the INFLUENCE option in addition to the P and R options, which is not done here.

(continued from previous page)

4	0.0103	-0.0504	0.0261	-0.0006	0.0032	0.0003
5	0.0517	-0.1597	0.0985	-0.0006	0.0165	-0.0119
6	-0.0113	0.1318	0.0374	-0.0025	0.0048	-0.0018
7	-0.0700	-0.2195	-0.1375	-0.0160	-0.0576	0.0820
8	-0.0110	0.0226	-0.0135	0.0020	-0.0033	0.0034
9	-0.0108	-0.1376	0.1242	-0.0116	0.0206	-0.0217
10	-0.0577	-0.1285	0.1666	-0.2715	-0.0783	0.1213
11	-0.0002	-0.0045	0.0022	0.0002	0.0013	-0.0007
12	0.1441	0.0886	-0.0080	0.0454	0.0129	-0.0671
13	-0.0851	0.0377	0.2267	-0.0205	0.3618	-0.2759
14	0.0209	-0.0277	0.0051	-0.0037	0.0106	-0.0113
15	-0.4404	-0.1233	-0.5381	-0.1963	-1.7040	1.4204
16	-0.2033	0.2201	0.1826	-0.2019	0.2104	-0.1149
17	-0.1058	0.2598	0.0756	-0.0191	-0.1389	0.1178
18	0.1403	0.1157	0.0965	0.0305	-0.0209	-0.0446
19	-1.7852	0.0088	-0.5855	1.2009	1.3983	-0.9411
20	0.7725	-0.1946	0.0217	0.6030	0.4888	-0.6953
21	0.0268	-0.0061	-0.0034	0.0275	0.0285	-0.0343
22	0.7506	-0.1382	0.7150	0.1604	-0.0147	-0.2197
23	0.2936	0.3357	0.1652	-2.0577	-0.0658	0.1008
24	0.5958	-1.2140	-5.1382	-0.8793	-0.6539	2.1090
25	1.1685	0.6569	-4.5712	1.1845	-3.9433	7.2839

	The SAS System	2
Sum of Residuals	0	
Sum of Squared Residuals	3522013.1205	
Predicted Resid SS (Press)	213738242.87	

The various statistics are identified in the column labeled with the keywords required in the OUTPUT and PLOT statements except as noted in the descriptions. The first column in the output repeats the actual residuals. The remainder of the statistics are as follows:

□ RSTUDENT is another version of studentized residuals, where the residuals are divided by a standard error which uses s_{-i}^2 rather than s^2 as the estimate of σ^2. It is thus a more sensitive studentized residual than the studentized residual statistic provided by the R option. If there are no outliers, these statistics should obey a t distribution with $(n-m-2)$ degrees of freedom, and therefore the criterion for *large* is the same as for the Student Residual.

□ HAT DIAG (keyword H), represents the diagonal elements of the hat $X(X'X)^{-1}X'$. The individual values, often denoted h_i, indicate the leverage of each observation, which is a standardized measure of how far an observation is from the center of the space of x values. Observations with high leverages, which are indicated by large h_i, have the potential of being influential, especially if they are also outliers in y. The sum of h_i is $(m+1)$, where m is the number of independent variables, hence the mean value of h_i is approximately $(m+1)/n$, where n is the number of observations in the data set. Therefore, observations with values of this statistic exceeding twice this value may be considered as having high leverage.

□ COV RATIO (keyword COVRATIO) indicates the change in the precision of the estimates of the set of partial regression coefficients resulting from the deletion of an observation. This precision is measured by the *generalized variance*, which is computed $(s^2) \, | \, (X'X)^{-1} \, |$. The COVRATIO statistic is the ratio of the generalized variance without the ith observation and the generalized variance using all observations, that is:

$$\text{COVRATIO} = \frac{s_{-i}^2 \, | \, (\mathbf{X'X})_{-i}^{-1} \, |}{s^2 \, | \, (\mathbf{X'X})^{-1} \, |} \quad .$$

In other words, COVRATIO values exceeding unity indicate that the inclusion of the observation results in increased precision, while values less than unity indicate decreased precision.* Belsley, Kuh, and Welsch (1980) suggest that deviations from unity may be considered large if they exceed $3(m+1)/n$.

□ DFFITS measures the difference between predicted value for the ith observation obtained by the equation estimated by all observations and the equation estimated from all observations except the ith, that is $(\hat{y}_{i,-i} - \hat{y}_i)$. The difference is standardized, using the residual variance estimate from all other observations, s_{-i}^2. This statistic is a prime indicator of influence. Belsley, Kuh, and Welsch (1980, p. 28) suggest that DFFITS values exceeding $2[(m+1)/n]^{1/2}$ in absolute value provide a convenient criterion for identifying influential observations.

□ DFBETAS is the standardized difference for each individual coefficient estimate resulting from the omission of the ith observation. It is identified by column headings with the name of the corresponding independent variable. Since there are many DFBETAS values, it is useful to examine only those for observations with large DFFITS values, where large DFBETAS may indicate which independent variable(s) may be the cause of the influence. DFBETAS values are not available in output data sets or for interactive plotting.

A related statistic is Cook's D (keyword COOKD), which is printed by the R option (not included in Output 3.5). Essentially, it is the DFFITS statistic, scaled and squared to make extreme values stand out more clearly. However, the estimated error variance obtained by using all observations is used for standardization.

Finally, the sum and sum of squares of the actually computed residuals and the sum of squares of the PRESS residuals are printed at the bottom of the output. The PRESS sum of squares is the sum of squares of residuals using models obtained by estimating the equation with all other observations, that is $(y_i - \hat{y}_{i,-i})$.** The sum of residuals should be zero and the sum of squares should be the same as the ERROR SS in the regression output; if they are not, severe roundoff has occurred. The sum of squares of the PRESS statistic should be compared to the ERROR SS. When it is appreciably larger than the ERROR SS, as it is here, there is reason to suspect that some influential observations or outliers exist.

The influence statistics now appear to focus more on observations 24 and 25, with 25 being very pronounced with the DFFITS statistic. The DFBETAS indicate that observation 25 is highly influential with respect to the OCCUP coefficient.

---

* Relative magnitudes of the determinant of $\mathbf{X'X}$ are indicators of multicollinearity (Chapter 4). Therefore, a COVRATIO statistic also indicates if the deletion of that observation changes the degree of multicollinearity.

** The sum of squares of PRESS residuals is also printed when the MODEL options P or R are used (see Output 2.12). The individual PRESS residuals may not be printed by a MODEL option but are available in the OUTPUT data set using the keyword PRESS. See also Allen (1970).

A clearer picture is provided by interactive plots. Assuming that PROC REG is active (it is not necessary to have specified the INFLUENCE option), enter the following statements:

```
paint obs. = 25;
plot (student. rstudent. h. dffits.)*p. /
     hplots = 2 vplots = 2;
run;
```

As previously noted, keywords specifying variables created by PROC REG must be followed by a period. In this example, all statistics are to be plotted against the predicted values. The HPLOTS and VPLOTS options specify that all four plots be on one page. The results appear in Output 3.6.

Output 3.6
Interactive Plots
for Influence
Statistics

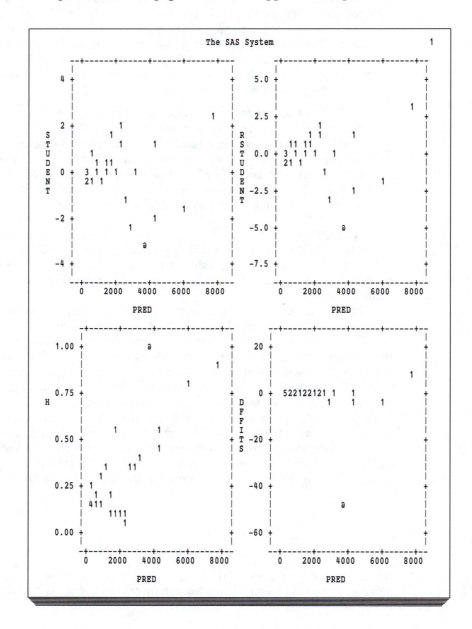

Since observation 25 appears suspicious, you may highlight it with a PAINT statement, which causes the values for this observation to be plotted with a special symbol. This is the first statement in the SAS code above, and since no symbol is specified the symbol is the default @.

You can see that the statistics for observation 25 are all large according to the guidelines outlined above, although none is appreciably larger than the next largest. However, the DFFITS statistic certainly appears to indicate a problem with that observation. Further, returning to Output 3.5, the DFBETAS indicates that the OCCUP variable is the culprit. The DFFITS statistic is also quite large for observation 24, and in this case the cause appears to be in the COMMON variable, although the evidence is not very clearcut.

What to do now is not strictly a statistical problem. *Discarding observations simply because they do not fit is bad statistical practice.* You should first examine the data for obvious discrepancies by various other interactive plots. In addition, you can create an OUTPUT data set and further examine the various statistics with the UNIVARIATE procedure or other descriptive procedures. In this example, looking at observation 25, and focusing on the OCCUP variable, it becomes obvious that this value is impossible: how can average occupancy be 811 with a capacity of only 242? Observation 24 has a very high CHECKIN rate along with a very small COMMON area and high MANH requirements.

Normally, an obvious error such as that in observation 25 would be investigated and probably corrected. Observation 24 is, however, probably correct and should be left alone.

Although it is not necessarily the correct procedure, you can eliminate observation 25 from the data set and redo the regression. This can be done in three ways:

□ by physically eliminating observation 25 from the input file and running PROC REG again

□ by making the dependent variable (MANH) missing in observation 25, which you can do in the DATA step

```
data miss25; set boq;
      if _n_ = 25 then manh = . ;
run;
```

and then running PROC REG again

□ by using the interactive REWEIGHT statement in PROC REG.

The REWEIGHT statement assigns any arbitrary weight* to any specified observation(s). The interactive statement

```
reweight obs. = 25;
print anova;
```

assigns the (default) zero weight to observation 25. A weight of zero is equivalent to deleting the observation.

---

* Principles of weighted regression are presented in Section 3.4.

The REWEIGHT statement causes a re-estimation of the last model, with observation(s) reweighted as instructed, but creates no output. The PRINT ANOVA statement is used to generate the default output for the reweighted regression because the previous MODEL statement included the INFLUENCE option, which is not needed here.

Output 3.7
Omitting
Observation 25
with REWEIGHT
Statement

```
                             The SAS System                                  1

 Model: MODEL1
 Dependent Variable: MANH

                          Analysis of Variance

                                Sum of         Mean
           Source        DF    Squares        Square    F Value    Prob>F

           Model          7  87497672.57  12499667.51   154.318    0.0001
           Error         16  1295986.739  80999.171189
           C Total       23  88793659.309

               Root MSE     284.60353    R-square     0.9854
               Dep Mean    2050.00708    Adj R-sq     0.9790
               C.V.          13.88305

                          Parameter Estimates

                          Parameter      Standard    T for H0:
           Variable  DF    Estimate         Error    Parameter=0   Prob > |T|

           INTERCEP   1   171.473359  148.86168053      1.152      0.2663
           OCCUP      1    21.045622    4.28904939      4.907      0.0002
           CHECKIN    1     1.426323    0.33070989      4.313      0.0005
           HOURS      1    -0.089268    1.16353166     -0.077      0.9398
           COMMON     1     7.650331    8.43835202      0.907      0.3781
           WINGS      1    -5.302310    9.45276086     -0.561      0.5826
           CAP        1    -4.074748    3.30195048     -1.234      0.2350
           ROOMS      1     0.331911    6.81398682      0.049      0.9618
```

The changes in the estimated regression relationship are quite marked. The residual mean square has decreased considerably, the coefficient for OCCUP has become highly significant, while those for CAP and ROOMS are not. Therefore, as indicated by the influence statistics, observation 25 did indeed influence the estimated regression.

Before continuing, it is important to point out that these statistics often do not provide clear evidence of outliers or influential observations. The different statistics are not all designed to detect the same type of data anomalies; hence, they may provide apparently contradictory results. Furthermore, they may fail entirely, especially if there are several outliers. You can verify this by simply duplicating observation 25 and implementing the INFLUENCE option. In other words, these statistics are only tools to aid in outlier detection; they do not replace careful data monitoring.

3.3 Specification Errors

Specification error is defined as the result of an incorrectly specified model and often results in biased estimates of parameters. Specification errors may be detected by examining the residuals from a fitted equation. Because specification errors are usually evidenced by patterns exhibited by residuals, there are essentially no advantages for the use of statistics designed to identify single outliers. A common pattern is for the residuals to suggest a curvilinear relationship, although other patterns such as bunching or cycling are possible.

The following example consists of data collected to determine the effect of certain variables on the efficiency of irrigation. The dependent variable is the percent of water percolation (PERC), and the independent variables are

RATIO   the ratio between irrigation time and advance time

INFT   the exponent of time in the infiltration equation, a calculated value

LOST   the percentage of water lost to deep percolation

ADVT   the exponent of time in the water advance equation, a calculated value.

The data appear in Output 3.8.

Output 3.8
Irrigation Data

```
                            The SAS System                          1

    OBS     PERC    RATIO    INFT     LOST     ADVT

     1     37.75    0.77    0.427    29.10    0.5820
     2     34.83    0.97    0.427    29.10    0.6980
     3     33.75    1.15    0.309    20.90    0.5190
     4     30.26    1.27    0.427    29.10    0.8800
     5     30.60    1.27    0.309    20.90    0.6850
     6     29.05    1.51    0.309    20.90    0.8000
     7     25.76    1.67    0.343    21.27    0.5640
     8     26.26    1.87    0.309    20.90    0.8360
     9     25.75    2.25    0.309    20.90    0.8410
    10     17.16    2.32    0.397    26.53    0.5960
    11     14.73    2.34    0.343    21.27    0.7500
    12     19.04    2.39    0.427    29.10    0.6000
    13     13.16    2.71    0.397    25.45    0.7470
    14     18.03    2.82    0.427    29.10    0.7300
    15     14.46    3.17    0.397    26.53    0.4360
    16     12.96    3.35    0.397    26.53    0.7600
    17     16.80    3.64    0.343    21.27    0.6991
    18     13.72    3.69    0.387    26.53    0.6000
    19     14.56    3.73    0.397    25.45    0.7010
    20     12.71    3.78    0.387    25.45    0.6800
    21      9.06    4.97    0.397    26.53    0.7720
    22      9.52    6.86    0.397    26.53    0.8400
```

Perform the regression analysis with these SAS statements:

```
proc reg data=irrig;
    model perc = ratio inft lost advt;
    output out=irrplot r=rperc p=pperc;
proc plot;
    plot rperc*pperc / vref=0;
run;
```

The results appear in Output 3.9.

Output 3.9
Irrigation Data

```
                           The SAS System                        1

Model: MODEL1
Dependent Variable: PERC

                        Analysis of Variance

                          Sum of         Mean
      Source        DF    Squares       Square     F Value    Prob>F

      Model          4  1300.19826    325.04956     16.234    0.0001
      Error         17   340.38669     20.02275
      C Total       21  1640.58495

            Root MSE       4.47468    R-square      0.7925
            Dep Mean      20.90545    Adj R-sq      0.7437
            C.V.          21.40436

                        Parameter Estimates

                     Parameter      Standard    T for H0:
      Variable  DF    Estimate        Error     Parameter=0    Prob > |T|

      INTERCEP   1    40.558255    11.34544931      3.575       0.0023
      RATIO      1    -4.820525     0.74296236     -6.488       0.0001
      INFT       1  -209.310998   100.93106587     -2.074       0.0536
      LOST       1     2.754826     1.35638415      2.031       0.0582
      ADVT       1     4.285067     8.82267965      0.486       0.6334
```

The regression is certainly statistically significant. The variable RATIO appears to be very important, INFT and LOST contribute marginally, while ADVT appears to have little effect.

The residuals from the regression of the irrigation data are plotted in Output 3.10.

Output 3.10
Residuals for Irrigation Regression

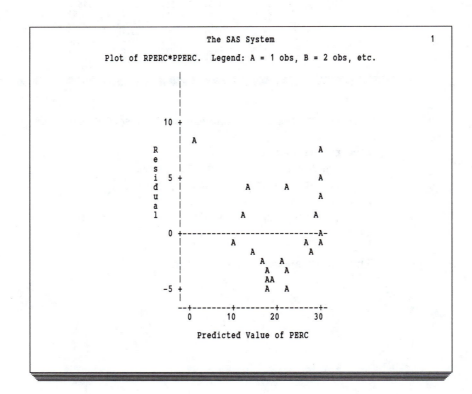

A curved pattern in the residuals is evident. This suggests that a curvilinear component, probably a quadratic term in one or more variables, should be included in the model. Unless there is some prior knowledge to suggest which variable(s) should have the added quadratic you can use the partial residual plots for this purpose.

Partial residuals for any variable in a regression model are the residuals from a regression involving all other variables in the model. In other words, partial residuals show the variability remaining after accounting for or holding constant relationships with the other variables in the model.

Consequently, the partial residuals for x_i, say, are the data for estimating β_i. A plot of these partial residuals will show the partial relationship between x_i and y (Myers 1990, Section 5.6). Now if such a plot shows a curved pattern, there may be a need for curvilinear terms.*

As shown below, plots of partial residuals are available with the PARTIAL option in the MODEL statement. However, a SAS program for computing partial residuals may help to explain the possibly confusing definition of partial residuals and is also useful because it produces a data set containing the actual partial residual values, which are not available with the PARTIAL option. The program shown below provides the partial residuals for the variable RATIO in the irrigation data. Similar programs will be needed for the plots for the other variables.

```
proc reg data=irrig;
    model perc = inft lost advt;
        output out=a r=rperc;
    model ratio = inft lost advt;
        output out=b r=rratio;
data c; merge a b;
    proc plot;
        plot rperc*rratio;
proc reg data=c;
    model rperc = rratio;
run;
```

In this program, the variable RPERC consists of the residuals from the regression of PERC on INFT, LOST, and ADVT, and the variable RRATIO consists of the residuals from the regression of RATIO on INFT, LOST, and ADVT. The results of this program will contain the following (but the results are not shown here):

□ The plot of RRATIO against RPERC is the partial residual plot and will be the same as the leverage plot shown in Output 3.11.

□ The last PROC REG produces the partial regression coefficient for the RATIO variable in the multiple regression as found in Output 3.9.

---

* These plots may also be useful for outlier detection, which is why they are also called leverage plots. For this purpose, the plots are more useful if an ID statement is used with PROC REG, which causes the first character of the ID variable to be used as the plotting symbol. This feature is primarily useful if the ID variable is a character variable.

Output 3.11
Leverage Plot for
RATIO

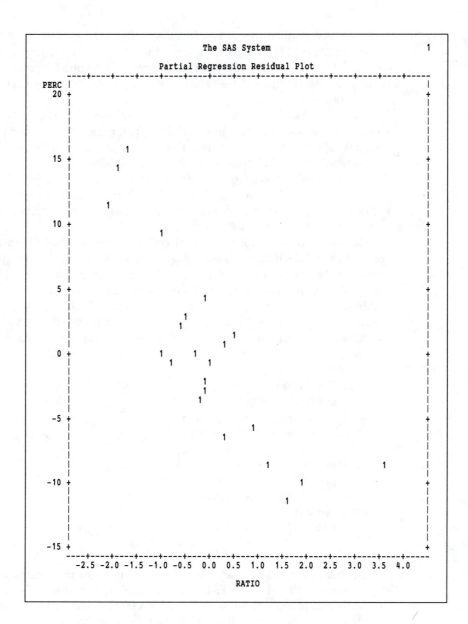

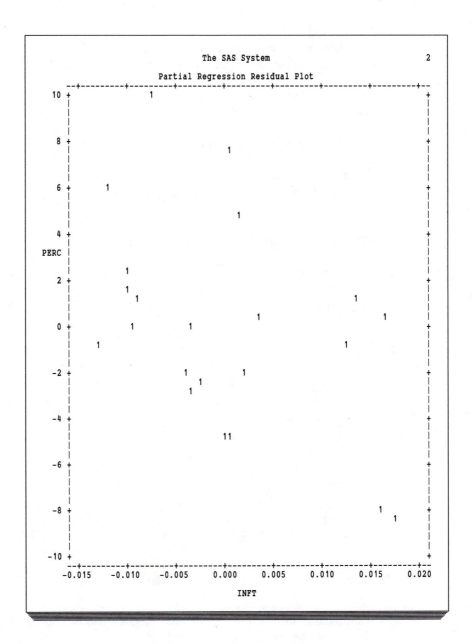

As noted above, you can avoid all this programming and obtain all leverage plots with the MODEL statement option PARTIAL. Output 3.11 shows leverage plots for the variables RATIO and INFT. The others are not shown to save space. The plot involving RATIO shows a strong linear trend as well as a suggestion of a slight upward curved pattern, suggesting that this variable requires the addition of the quadratic term.* The plot involving INFT shows the rather weak negative relationship implied by the p value of 0.536. None of the other leverage plots reveal anything of interest.

---

*   You can see this by drawing a straight line of best fit and seeing an excess of data points below the line at the center and above the line at the two ends.

In order to provide for the addition of the quadratic term suggested by the leverage plot, you must create the quadratic value of RATIO in the DATA step:

```
data quad; set irrig;
ratsq = ratio * ratio;
```

Then perform the regression:

```
proc reg data=quad;
    model perc = ratio ratsq inft lost advt;
run;
```

The results appear in Output 3.12.

Output 3.12
Quadratic
Regression for
Irrigation Data

```
                            The SAS System                              1

Model: MODEL1
Dependent Variable: PERC

                          Analysis of Variance

                              Sum of        Mean
        Source        DF     Squares       Square     F Value     Prob>F

        Model          5   1531.93656    306.38731      45.120     0.0001
        Error         16    108.64838      6.79052
        C Total       21   1640.58495

            Root MSE        2.60586     R-square       0.9338
            Dep Mean       20.90545     Adj R-sq       0.9131
            C.V.           12.46499

                          Parameter Estimates

                      Parameter     Standard     T for H0:
        Variable  DF   Estimate        Error    Parameter=0    Prob > |T|

        INTERCEP   1    53.187314    6.95179512       7.651       0.0001
        RATIO      1   -13.056069    1.47466096      -8.854       0.0001
        RATSQ      1     1.184824    0.20281807       5.842       0.0001
        INFT       1  -108.202970   61.27321116      -1.766       0.0965
        LOST       1     1.308644    0.82778486       1.581       0.1335
        ADVT       1    -0.517066    5.20329863      -0.099       0.9221
```

Comparing these results with those of Output 3.9, you can see that the residual mean square has been halved. In other words, a better fitting equation has been developed. The relationship is one where PERC decreases with RATIO, but the rate of decrease diminishes with increasing values of RATIO. The other variables remain statistically insignificant. Therefore, you may want to consider variable selection (see Chapter 4).

3.4 Heterogeneous Variances

A fundamental assumption underlying linear regression analyses is that all random errors (the ε_i) have the same variance. Outliers may be considered a special case of unequal variances since such observations may be considered to have very large variances.

Violations of the equal variance assumption are usually detected by residual plots that may reveal groupings of observations with large residuals suggesting larger variances. Some of the other outlier detection statistics may also be helpful, especially when the violation occurs in only a small number of observations.

In many applications there is a recognizable pattern for the magnitudes of the variances. The most common of these is an increase in variation for larger values of the response variable. For such cases, the use of a transformation of the dependent variable is in order (Steel and Torrie 1980, Section 9.16). The most popular of these, especially in regression, is the logarithmic transformation discussed in Chapter 6, "Special Applications of Linear Models."

If the use of transformations is not appropriate, it is sometimes useful to alter the estimation procedure by either modifying the least-squares method or implementing a different estimation principle. A discussion of some alternatives, including additional references, is given in Myers (1990, Section 7.7). An illustration of one of these special methods, using iteratively reweighted least squares is shown in Chapter 29, "The NLIN Procedure," in the *SAS/STAT Users Guide, Version 6, Fourth Edition, Volume 2*.

Because the effects of heterogeneous variances are subtle, the effects and remedial methods for this condition are illustrated with a very simple and somewhat pathological example. The data consist of records of sales prices of a set of investment grade diamonds, and are to be used to estimate the relationship of the sales price (PRICE, in $1000) to weight (CARATS) of the diamonds. The data appear in Output 3.13 and the corresponding plot appears in Output 3.14.*

Output 3.13
Diamond Prices

```
                              The SAS System                              1


            CARATS     PRICE        CARATS     PRICE
            0.50       1.918        1.02       27.264
            0.52       2.055        1.02       12.684
            0.52       1.976        1.03       11.372
            0.53       1.976        1.06       13.181
            0.54       2.134        1.23       17.958
            0.60       2.499        1.24       18.095
            0.63       2.324        1.25       19.757
            0.63       2.747        1.29       36.161
            0.68       2.324        1.35       15.297
            0.73       3.719        1.36       17.432
            0.75       5.055        1.41       19.176
            0.77       3.951        1.46       16.596
            0.79       4.131        1.66       16.321
            0.79       4.184        1.90       28.473
            0.91       4.816        1.92       100.411
```

---

* To save space the data are presented in two columns using the whole page access of the PUT statement as shown in the *SAS Language: Reference, Version 6, First Edition.*

Output 3.14
Plot of Diamond
Prices

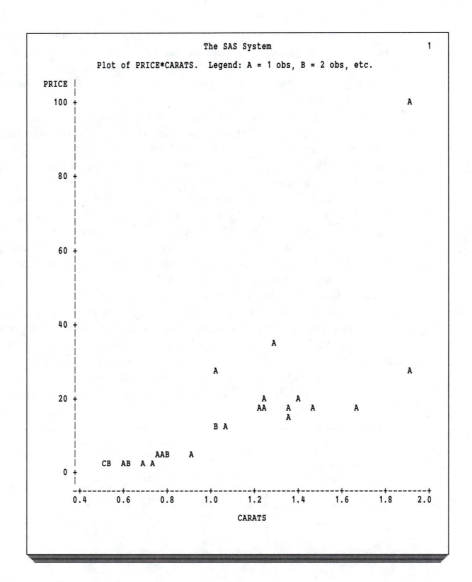

The plot clearly reveals the large variation of prices for larger diamonds. It is difficult to ascertain if the most expensive diamond is an outlier or simply reflects the much higher variability of prices for larger stones. The plot also suggests an upward curving response, hence it is appropriate to specify a quadratic regression. Create the variable CSQ in the DATA step as the square of CARATS, and implement the regression:

```
proc reg data=diamonds;
    model price = carats csq / p cli;
run;
```

The results appear in Output 3.15.

Output 3.15
Diamond Data,
Ordinary Least
Squares

```
                              The SAS System                                1

Model: MODEL1
Dependent Variable: PRICE

                          Analysis of Variance

                          Sum of         Mean
         Source      DF   Squares       Square      F Value      Prob>F

         Model        2  6328.15034   3164.07517     21.590      0.0001
         Error       27  3956.91510    146.55241
         C Total     29 10285.06545

              Root MSE       12.10588     R-square      0.6153
              Dep Mean       13.86623     Adj R-sq      0.5868
              C.V.           87.30477

                          Parameter Estimates

                     Parameter      Standard    T for H0:
         Variable  DF  Estimate       Error    Parameter=0   Prob > |T|

         INTERCEP  1   11.269771   15.30469264     0.736       0.4679
         CARATS    1  -30.614704   29.63090647    -1.033       0.3107
         CSQ       1   28.439561   12.88434421     2.207       0.0360
```

```
                              The SAS System                                2

              Dep Var   Predict   Std Err  Lower95%  Upper95%
      Obs     PRICE     Value     Predict  Predict   Predict   Residual

        1     1.9180    3.0723     4.486   -23.4176  29.5622    -1.1543
        2     2.0550    3.0402     4.227   -23.2694  29.3497    -0.9852
        3     1.9760    3.0402     4.227   -23.2694  29.3497    -1.0642
        4     1.9760    3.0327     4.103   -23.1946  29.2599    -1.0567
        5     2.1340    3.0308     3.985   -23.1191  29.1807    -0.8968
        6     2.4990    3.1392     3.370   -22.6441  28.9225    -0.6402
        7     2.3240    3.2702     3.130   -22.3857  28.9260    -0.9462
        8     2.7470    3.2702     3.130   -22.3857  28.9260    -0.5232
        9     2.3240    3.6022     2.837   -21.9100  29.1144    -1.2782
       10     3.7190    4.0765     2.677   -21.3625  29.5154    -0.3575
       11     5.0550    4.3060     2.646   -21.1195  29.7315     0.7490
       12     3.9510    4.5583     2.633   -20.8613  29.9778    -0.6073
       13     4.1310    4.8333     2.634   -20.5869  30.2535    -0.7023
       14     4.1840    4.8333     2.634   -20.5869  30.2535    -0.6493
       15     4.8160    6.9612     2.840   -18.5520  32.4744    -2.1452
       16    27.2640    9.6313     3.104   -16.0114  35.2740    17.6327
       17    12.6840    9.6313     3.104   -16.0114  35.2740     3.0527
       18    11.3720    9.9082     3.126   -15.7454  35.5617     1.4638
       19    13.1810   10.7729     3.184   -14.9110  36.4568     2.4081
       20    17.9580   16.6399     3.359    -9.1374  42.4172     1.3181
       21    18.0950   17.0362     3.362    -8.7426  42.8150     1.0588
       22    19.7570   17.4382     3.364    -8.3419  43.2183     2.3188
       23    36.1610   19.1031     3.369    -6.6798  44.8859    17.0579
       24    15.2970   21.7710     3.374    -4.0147  47.5568    -6.4740
       25    17.4320   22.2356     3.376    -3.5513  48.0225    -4.8036
       26    19.1760   24.6437     3.399    -1.1556  50.4430    -5.4677
       27    16.5960   27.1941     3.456     1.3629  53.0253   -10.5981
       28    16.3210   38.8174     4.394    12.3932  65.2417   -22.4964
       29    28.4730   55.7686     7.535    26.5113  85.0260   -27.2956
       30   100.4      57.3291     7.891    27.6792  86.9790    43.0819

Sum of Residuals                    0
Sum of Squared Residuals      3956.9151
Predicted Resid SS (Press)    9258.2310
```

As expected, the regression is certainly significant. The estimated equation is

$$\text{PRICE} = 11.27 - 30.614(\text{CARATS}) + 28.440(\text{CARATS})^2 \quad .$$

The coefficient for $(CARATS)^2$ is statistically significant, confirming the upward curve of the relationship of price to carats. The coefficient for (CARATS) has no practical significance (see Chapter 5, "Polynomial Models"). The pattern of residuals and the relative magnitude of the PRESS sum of squares clearly indicate the increasing price variation for the larger diamonds and suggest that these values may be unduly influencing the estimated regression relationship.

Another result of the equal variance assumption can be seen by observing that the widths of the prediction intervals do not vary much between the small and large diamonds. In fact, for the small diamonds, the intervals are so wide that the predictions are completely useless.

3.4.1   Weighted Least Squares

One principle that may be used to reduce influence of highly variable observations is that of *weighted least squares*, which is a direct application of generalized least squares (Myers 1990, Section 7.1). The estimated parameters obtained by this method are those that minimize the weighted residual sum of squares:

$$\Sigma w_i(y_i - \beta_0 - \beta_1 x_1 - \ldots \beta_m x_m)^2$$

where the w_i are a set of nonnegative weights assigned to the individual observations. Observations with small weights contribute less to the sum of squares and thus provide less influence to the estimation parameters, and vice versa for observations with larger weights. Thus, it is logical to assign small weights to observations whose large variances make them more unreliable, and likewise to assign larger weights to observations with smaller variances. It can, in fact, be shown that best linear unbiased estimates are obtained if the weights are inversely proportional to the variances of the individual errors.

The variances of the residuals, however, are not usually known. Multiple observations, or replicates, may be used to estimate this variance (Myers 1990, Section 7.1), or if true replicates are not available, near replicates (Rawlings 1988, Section 11.5.2) may be used. However, these are all estimated variances, and both of the above references warn that the use of weights based on poor estimates of variances may be counterproductive.

Alternately, knowledge about the distribution of residuals may provide a basis for determining weights. It is well known that prices tend to vary by proportions. This implies that standard deviations are proportional to means, hence the variances are proportional to the squares of means. In sample data the means are not known, but estimated means based on an unweighted regression can be used for this purpose.

You can implement this method with the following set of SAS statements:

```
proc reg data=diamonds;
    model price = carats csq;
    output out=a p=pprice u95=upper l95=lower;
data b; set a;
    w = 1/(pprice*pprice);
proc reg data= b; weight w;
    model price = carats csq / p cli;
output out=c p=pwprice u95=wupper l95=wlower;
run;
```

The first PROC REG produces the unweighted analysis that is given in Output 3.15. The OUTPUT statement creates the data set A in which the variable PPRICE is the price as predicted by the unweighted regression. The reciprocal of the square of PPRICE is required for the weighted regression, hence the variable PPRICE in data set A is used to produce the variable W=1/(PPRICE*PPRICE) in data set B. This variable is then used in the WEIGHT statement, which implements the weighted regression specified in the second PROC REG. The output data sets containing variables representing the prediction intervals for both models are requested for later use. The results of the weighted regression appear in Output 3.16.

Output 3.16
Weighted
Regression

```
                            The SAS System                              1
  Model: MODEL1
  Dependent Variable: PRICE

                          Analysis of Variance

                            Sum of         Mean
         Source        DF   Squares       Square     F Value     Prob>F

         Model          2  14.24850      7.12425      33.398     0.0001
         Error         27   5.75948      0.21331
         C Total       29  20.00799

             Root MSE        0.46186     R-square      0.7121
             Dep Mean        3.44598     Adj R-sq      0.6908
             C.V.           13.40285

                          Parameter Estimates

                        Parameter      Standard     T for H0:
         Variable  DF    Estimate         Error    Parameter=0    Prob > |T|

         INTERCEP   1     5.036510     5.14379323       0.979       0.3362
         CARATS     1   -18.743812    13.22756282      -1.417       0.1679
         CSQ        1    23.978563     7.96785521       3.009       0.0056
```

```
                            The SAS System                              2

                    Dep Var   Predict   Std Err  Lower95%  Upper95%
    Obs    Weight    PRICE      Value    Predict   Predict   Predict   Residual

      1    0.1059    1.9180    1.6592    0.658    -1.5504    4.8689    0.2588
      2    0.1082    2.0550    1.7735    0.582    -1.3451    4.8921    0.2815
      3    0.1082    1.9760    1.7735    0.582    -1.3451    4.8921    0.2025
      4    0.1087    1.9760    1.8379    0.549    -1.2488    4.9245    0.1381
      5    0.1089    2.1340    1.9070    0.520    -1.1566    4.9706    0.2270
      6    0.1015    2.4990    2.4225    0.435    -0.6832    5.5282    0.0765
      7    0.0935    2.3240    2.7450    0.448    -0.4874    5.9774   -0.4210
      8    0.0935    2.7470    2.7450    0.448    -0.4874    5.9774    0.00200
      9    0.0771    2.3240    3.3784    0.518    -0.1970    6.9539   -1.0544
     10    0.0602    3.7190    4.1317    0.610     0.0709    8.1925   -0.4127
     11    0.0539    5.0550    4.4666    0.647     0.1755    8.7577    0.5884
     12    0.0481    3.9510    4.8207    0.683     0.2793    9.3620   -0.8697
     13    0.0428    4.1310    5.1939    0.718     0.3827   10.0051   -1.0629
     14    0.0428    4.1840    5.1939    0.718     0.3827   10.0051   -1.0099
     15    0.0206    4.8160    7.8363    0.904     0.9836   14.6889   -3.0203
     16    0.0108   27.2640   10.8651    1.098     1.4641   20.2662   16.3989
     17    0.0108   12.6840   10.8651    1.098     1.4641   20.2662    1.8189
     18    0.0102   11.3720   11.1692    1.120     1.5024   20.8360    0.2028
     19    0.00862  13.1810   12.1104    1.195     1.6113   22.6095    1.0706
     20    0.00361  17.9580   18.2588    1.885     2.0228   34.4948   -0.3008
     21    0.00345  18.0950   18.6636    1.941     2.0351   35.2922   -0.5686
     22    0.00329  19.7570   19.0732    2.000     2.0460   36.1005    0.6838
     23    0.00274  36.1610   20.7597    2.253     2.0756   39.4438   15.4013
     24    0.00211  15.2970   23.4333    2.689     2.0770   44.7895   -8.1363
```

(continued on next page)

```
(continued from previous page)
        25   0.00202    17.4320   23.8957    2.768    2.0722    45.7191    -6.4637
        26   0.00165    19.1760   26.2795    3.190    2.0260    50.5331    -7.1035
        27   0.00135    16.5960   28.7832    3.657    1.9427    55.6238   -12.1872
        28   0.000664   16.3210   39.9971    5.956    1.2349    78.7593   -23.6761
        29   0.000322   28.4730   55.9859    9.598   -0.4130    112.4    -27.5129
        30   0.000304     100.4   57.4430    9.944   -0.5898    115.5     42.9680

Sum of Residuals                          0
Sum of Squared Residuals             5.7595
Predicted Resid SS (Press)           6.8290
NOTE: The above statistics use observation weights or frequencies.
```

A comparison of the results with those of the unweighted least squares regression (see Output 3.15) shows the effect of weighting. Since sums of squares reflect the weights they cannot be compared with results of the unweighted analysis. However, the R-SQUARE statistics are comparable since they are ratios and the effect of the weights cancels. You can see that the R-SQUARE values are somewhat larger for the weighted analysis, which occurs because the effect of the largest residuals has been reduced. Also the estimated equation has a smaller coefficient for $(CARATS)^2$. In other words, the curve has a somewhat smaller upward curvature, which is presumably due to the lesser influence of the very high-priced diamonds. The magnitude of the PRESS sum of squares is now not much larger than that of the residual sum of squares, showing the reduction of influence of the very large diamonds.

Another feature of the weighted analysis is that the prediction intervals are much narrower for the smaller diamonds than for the large diamonds. This can be seen by a plot comparing the prediction intervals for the unweighted and weighted analyses. You can produce these plots by adding the following SAS statements:

```
data all; merge a c;
proc plot data= all hpercent = 50 ;
    plot  upper*carats='U' lower*carats='L'
        / overlay vaxis = -25 to 125 by 25;
    plot  wupper*carats='U' wlower*carats='L'
        / overlay vaxis = -25 to 125 by 25;
```

The resulting plots in Output 3.17 clearly show the differences in the prediction intervals. Although all are possibly too wide to make the estimates very useful, the intervals based on weighted least squares are at least equivalent in relative magnitudes.

Output 3.17
Comparing
Prediction
Intervals

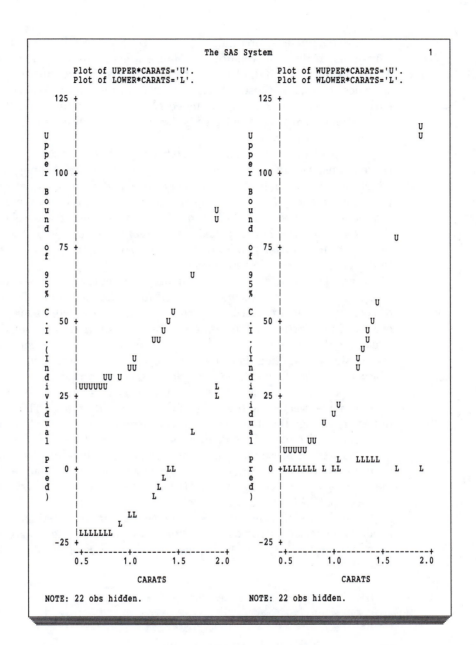

3.5 Correlated Errors

Another aspect of the assumptions underlying the distribution of the random errors is that they be independent. That is, the value of any one residual is independent of the value of any other. Most violations of this assumption occur in time series data, that is, data observed over a sequence of time periods. In such data the observed value at a given point in time, say in period *t*, may be influenced by values observed in previous periods. For example, the weather today is highly influenced by what the weather was yesterday. Non-independent errors may occur in other situations. For example, plants that are too close to each other may compete to the extent that larger plants may be surrounded by smaller, stunted plants.

In linear models, non-independent errors are usually described as being correlated. If these correlations are known, generalized least squares (Rawlings 1988, Sections 9.3 and 11.5) can be used to provide correct estimates and other statistics. However, these correlations are in practice not known. In fact, these correlations cannot even be estimated since there are $(n)(n-1)/2$ such correlations, which greatly exceeds the number of observations (n) on which such estimates must be based.

This problem is alleviated somewhat by imposing a structure on the correlations. The most commonly used structure is the *autoregressive model*, which specifies that the error at time t is related to previous errors by a linear regression model. If the errors at time t are related only to errors at time $(t-1)$, the model is called a first-order autoregressive model, if it is related to errors at time $(t-1)$ and $(t-2)$ it is called a second-order model, and so on. The most commonly used order is one; that is, the errors at time t are directly related only to the errors of the previous period.

It can be shown that if the existence of an autoregressive process is ignored, that is, if ordinary least squares is used for estimation and inference, the estimates of coefficients are unbiased, but estimates of the residual variance and standard errors of the partial coefficients are subject to an unknown, but usually downward bias. It is therefore necessary to consider alternate analysis methodologies. * A rather simple approach is to base the regression on first differences (Neter, Wasserman, and Kutner 1983, Section 13.4). With this procedure, the variables are the period to period differences of all variables. In the SAS System, such variables are created by the DIF function in the data step. This procedure does, however, change the model. Therefore, results are not strictly comparable to those of the original model. This method is not illustrated here.

This section presents an example of one procedure for detecting the existence of a first order autoregressive model, followed by an alternative analysis methodology provided by the AUTOREG procedure, a SAS procedure documented in the *SAS/ETS User's Guide, Version 6, First Edition.*

A consumption function is a model that attempts to estimate consumption of goods and services using other economic variables. Using quarterly data, consumption (CONS) is to be estimated by a regression on the independent variables:

CURR   currency in circulation

DDEP   amount of demand deposits

GNP   the gross national product

WAGES   the hourly wage rate

INCOME   national income

---

*   The analysis of time series data comprises a major specialty within the discipline of statistics. The SAS/ETS library contains some of the most popular methods for analyzing time series data. Usage of the SAS System for these methods is presented in Brocklebank and Dickey (1986).

All variables have been deflated by the consumer price index (January, 1953=100), and all variables except WAGES have been converted to a per capita basis. The data set CONSUME consists of 76 observations from the first quarter of 1951 through the last quarter of 1969. The data appear in Output 3.18.

Output 3.18
Quarterly Data on
Consumption and
Related Variables

```
                            The SAS System                              1

     YR    QTR     CURR     DDEP      GNP     WAGES     CONS
     51     1     181.3    664.5    2296.9    1.713    1256.1
     51     2     181.1    665.0    2332.2    1.739    1247.7
     51     3     181.7    664.0    2353.4    1.736    1254.5
     51     4     180.7    666.3    2340.8    1.746    1256.9
     52     1     183.2    677.2    2365.2    1.779    1265.9
     52     2     182.3    674.3    2333.1    1.764    1276.3
     52     3     182.3    673.3    2350.5    1.796    1287.5
     52     4     184.2    676.4    2422.1    1.828    1306.8
     53     1     186.3    678.2    2467.4    1.868    1321.1
     53     2     185.6    674.6    2461.8    1.865    1317.7
     53     3     184.2    668.0    2424.2    1.874    1309.5
     53     4     183.9    668.1    2386.8    1.891    1307.9
     54     1     182.6    669.0    2377.3    1.891    1320.1
     54     2     180.7    666.6    2360.1    1.898    1322.8
     54     3     179.8    674.7    2384.2    1.904    1338.2
     54     4     178.9    683.1    2438.5    1.942    1355.1
     55     1     178.8    689.3    2511.4    1.953    1367.5
     55     2     178.7    690.9    2553.9    1.974    1379.2
     55     3     177.7    687.9    2582.7    2.009    1382.2
     55     4     177.7    685.9    2613.4    2.032    1408.3
     56     1     177.6    685.6    2614.0    2.053    1422.2
     56     2     174.6    676.0    2605.2    2.059    1414.0
     56     3     173.2    667.9    2601.1    2.075    1416.8
     56     4     171.5    661.7    2621.6    2.100    1419.8
     57     1     170.2    655.4    2636.7    2.095    1428.5
     57     2     167.6    646.0    2614.3    2.082    1416.8
     57     3     166.2    637.9    2621.3    2.087    1429.0
     57     4     164.8    628.3    2570.7    2.099    1427.7
     58     1     161.3    616.5    2485.8    2.070    1410.8
     58     2     160.8    621.0    2490.4    2.083    1423.9
     58     3     160.6    625.6    2553.1    2.103    1439.5
     58     4     160.5    631.7    2614.7    2.153    1447.0
     59     1     161.0    635.4    2658.2    2.173    1464.8
     59     2     160.3    633.0    2701.0    2.177    1469.0
     59     3     159.4    629.8    2659.8    2.147    1478.3
     59     4     157.6    619.7    2675.6    2.190    1482.1
     60     1     157.5    609.9    2732.0    2.207    1494.2
     60     2     155.8    598.6    2712.0    2.192    1505.1
     60     3     154.8    597.5    2692.2    2.197    1498.3
     60     4     153.3    592.0    2660.1    2.204    1500.5
     61     1     152.2    593.4    2651.5    2.204    1508.5
     61     2     151.4    595.8    2698.1    2.231    1513.8
     61     3     151.0    592.9    2719.2    2.218    1514.2
     61     4     152.0    597.1    2779.8    2.268    1532.9
     62     1     152.2    594.6    2807.9    2.267    1536.7
     62     2     152.8    592.0    2838.8    2.270    1544.7
     62     3     152.0    583.0    2841.6    2.253    1546.7
     62     4     152.9    585.5    2877.3    2.297    1569.4
     63     1     154.4    587.5    2884.3    2.298    1577.5
     63     2     155.2    587.5    2896.6    2.308    1580.7
     63     3     156.3    587.3    2922.5    2.306    1591.2
     63     4     157.4    587.7    2952.3    2.333    1588.3
     64     1     159.2    587.8    2998.1    2.331    1619.2
     64     2     160.7    587.7    3030.1    2.343    1631.3
     64     3     161.9    592.0    3060.2    2.362    1659.2
     64     4     162.1    593.9    3067.4    2.371    1663.7
```

```
                              The SAS System                        2
        YR   QTR    CURR      DDEP      GNP     WAGES     CONS
        65    1    163.8     593.6    3137.2    2.376    1677.7
        65    2    163.1     590.1    3155.6    2.371    1698.3
        65    3    165.1     594.0    3209.3    2.387    1720.0
        65    4    166.2     597.5    3261.1    2.396    1742.4
        66    1    167.0     600.2    3303.4    2.393    1758.9
        66    2    168.0     599.8    3317.4    2.400    1771.0
        66    3    167.9     587.7    3326.2    2.401    1775.9
        66    4    168.3     581.5    3357.4    2.415    1773.6
        67    1    169.6     582.9    3358.6    2.426    1800.9
        67    2    169.5     586.0    3359.4    2.431    1803.9
        67    3    169.1     595.4    3386.8    2.434    1808.1
        67    4    169.5     596.1    3450.5    2.462    1807.0
        68    1    170.3     595.2    3486.3    2.477    1841.4
        68    2    171.2     597.1    3533.6    2.481    1845.6
        68    3    172.1     602.0    3557.5    2.488    1863.6
        68    4    172.4     601.2    3570.0    2.514    1857.6
        69    1    173.4     600.4    3572.8    2.492    1862.1
        69    2    173.0     595.3    3570.3    2.484    1861.6
        69    3    171.8     584.1    3583.1    2.506    1862.2
        69    4    171.7     588.5    3553.2    2.506    1862.1
```

Assuming that the data are in sequence, obtain the usual regression as follows:

```
proc reg data=consume;
    model cons = curr ddep gnp wages income / dw;
    output out=a p=pc r=rc;
run;
```

The MODEL statement option DW requests the computation of the Durbin-Watson d statistic for testing for the existence of a first order autoregressive process. The OUTPUT statement requests the creation of a data set containing the predicted and residual values. The results of the procedure appear in Output 3.19.

Output 3.19
Regression for
Estimating
Consumption
Function

```
                              The SAS System                        1
Model: MODEL1
Dependent Variable: CONS

                         Analysis of Variance

                              Sum of        Mean
     Source        DF       Squares       Square     F Value    Prob>F

     Model          5   2702413.9712  540482.79424   3366.924    0.0001
     Error         70     11236.90328    160.52719
     C Total       75   2713650.8745

          Root MSE       12.66993     R-square       0.9959
          Dep Mean     1532.12503     Adj R-sq       0.9956
          C.V.            0.82695

                         Parameter Estimates

                    Parameter      Standard     T for H0:
     Variable  DF    Estimate        Error     Parameter=0    Prob > |T|

     INTERCEP   1   160.387654    95.79100505      1.674        0.0985
     CURR       1     1.482889     0.60086544      2.468        0.0160
     DDEP       1    -0.575372     0.14214897     -4.048        0.0001
     GNP        1     0.115873     0.11466272      1.011        0.3157
     WAGES      1   323.564790    55.09252701      5.873        0.0001
     INCOME     1     0.192557     0.11830923      1.628        0.1081
```

```
                              The SAS System                              2
Durbin-Watson D              0.949
(For Number of Obs.)            76
1st Order Autocorrelation    0.518
```

The model obviously fits the data quite well. The most important coefficients are those for demand deposits and wages. The negative coefficient for demand deposits is puzzling.

The last two items on the output concern autocorrelation. The Durbin-Watson *d* statistic is a test for existence of a first order autoregressive process. According to a table of this statistic (Montgomery and Peck 1982, Table A6; algorithms for computing *p* values are not available), a value of less than 1.60 indicates existence of a positive first order autocorrelation at a significance level of less than 0.01. The second item is the actual sample correlation of adjacent residuals: the value of 0.518 shows a moderate degree of association between adjacent residuals. This first order autocorrelation is also known as the *lag one* autocorrelation as it is the correlation of observations with those that lag behind one period.

A plot of residuals against time may also be useful in detecting autocorrelation. To do this, create a new data set PLOT as follows:

```
data plot; set a;
n = _n_;
run;
```

This DATA step uses the automatic observation counter, _N_, to create the sequential period indicator, N. Because of the spacing limitations of a printer plot, time series plots are more useful if done by SAS/GRAPH software* as follows:

```
symbol1 v=point i=join;
proc gplot data=plot;
    plot rc*n =1;
run;
```

---

* If SAS/GRAPH software is not available, a plot of this type is more useful if each vertical position of the plot represents one period, which you can usually do with the HAXIS option.

Output 3.20
Residual Plot

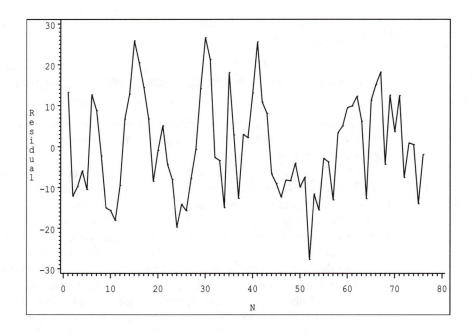

The plot appears to show cycles, that is, a number of sequences of either positive or negative residuals. This is due to the fact that under a first order autoregressive process with a positive autocorrelation, a positive residual is more likely to be followed by another positive residual and likewise for negative residuals. Of course, apparent cycles in the residuals may also be caused by true cyclical effects, such as seasons.*

One popular alternative analysis procedure for data of this type is available in PROC AUTOREG, which is documented in the *SAS/ETS User's Guide*. This procedure uses the residuals from an ordinary least squares analysis to estimate the set of autoregressive parameters for the order of autoregressive model specified by the user. These coefficients are then used to perform the appropriate generalized least squares method, which is implemented by performing a transformation of the variables in the model. (Fuller 1978, Section 2.5.)

Although the primary focus is on the first order autoregressive model, it is still useful to investigate the possibility of higher orders. To do this, you can specify:

```
proc autoreg data=consume;
    model cons = curr ddep gnp wages income / nlag = 4;
run;
```

The statements are in the same form as PROC REG. The only other option needed at this point is the MODEL statement option NLAG=4, which specifies that a fourth-order autoregressive model is to be used. This model is used to allow detection of seasonal cycles. Other MODEL and PROC options are discussed below. Output 3.21 shows the output from PROC AUTOREG.

---

* More general methods for time series analyses are presented in the *SAS System for Forecasting Time Series, 1986 Edition* and in the *SAS/ETS User's Guide*.

Output 3.21
PROC AUTOREG
Output for
Consumption
Function

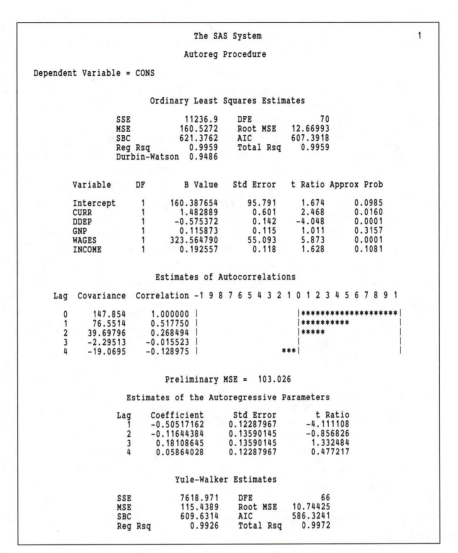

```
                              The SAS System                          1
                            Autoreg Procedure

Dependent Variable = CONS


                    Ordinary Least Squares Estimates

            SSE            11236.9   DFE            70
            MSE          160.5272    Root MSE  12.66993
            SBC          621.3762    AIC       607.3918
            Reg Rsq       0.9959     Total Rsq  0.9959
            Durbin-Watson 0.9486


        Variable    DF    B Value    Std Error    t Ratio  Approx Prob

        Intercept    1   160.387654    95.791      1.674     0.0985
        CURR         1     1.482889     0.601      2.468     0.0160
        DDEP         1    -0.575372     0.142     -4.048     0.0001
        GNP          1     0.115873     0.115      1.011     0.3157
        WAGES        1   323.564790    55.093      5.873     0.0001
        INCOME       1     0.192557     0.118      1.628     0.1081


                    Estimates of Autocorrelations

  Lag  Covariance  Correlation  -1 9 8 7 6 5 4 3 2 1 0 1 2 3 4 5 6 7 8 9 1

   0    147.854     1.000000  |                    |********************|
   1     76.5514    0.517750  |                    |**********          |
   2     39.69796   0.268494  |                    |*****               |
   3     -2.29513  -0.015523  |                    |                    |
   4    -19.0695   -0.128975  |                 ***|                    |


                    Preliminary MSE =  103.026

           Estimates of the Autoregressive Parameters

        Lag    Coefficient      Std Error       t Ratio
         1     -0.50517162     0.12287967     -4.111108
         2     -0.11644384     0.13590145     -0.856826
         3      0.18108645     0.13590145      1.332484
         4      0.05864028     0.12287967      0.477217


                    Yule-Walker Estimates

            SSE           7618.971    DFE            66
            MSE          115.4389     Root MSE  10.74425
            SBC          609.6314     AIC       586.3241
            Reg Rsq        0.9926     Total Rsq  0.9972
```

```
                              The SAS System                          2
                            Autoreg Procedure

        Variable    DF    B Value    Std Error    t Ratio  Approx Prob

        Intercept    1   262.076353   123.93       2.115     0.0382
        CURR         1     0.922011     0.82        1.121     0.2664
        DDEP         1    -0.517861     0.20       -2.534     0.0137
        GNP          1     0.156508     0.14        1.092     0.2789
        WAGES        1   261.044133    70.78        3.688     0.0005
        INCOME       1     0.183093     0.15        1.240     0.2192
```

The upper portion of the output reproduces the coefficients estimated by ordinary least squares, which are the same as appear in Output 3.19. No other statistics for this regression analysis are given. The residuals from this regression are used to compute the autocorrelations for the lags specified by the NLAG option that are printed under the column Estimates of Autocorrelations. The correlation for lag 1 is the same as appears in Output 3.19.

The plot of the autocorrelations provides for a quick check on possible patterns of the various autocorrelations. For example, if there is only a first-order autocorrelation with a correlation of ρ, then it can be shown that the second-order (lag 2) autocorrelation is ρ^2, the third-order correlation is ρ^3, and so forth. For a positive first-order process, then, the plot would show the correlations tending rapidly to zero with increasing lag as they do here.

These correlations are used to estimate the autoregressive parameters, that is, the regression coefficients for the model that relates the residuals of period t to those of the previous periods. These coefficients appear next in the output, together with their standard deviations (standard errors) and t ratios for testing that they are zero. These statistics confirm that there appears to be only a first-order autoregressive process and they suggest that the model should be reestimated using the option NLAG=1. This alternative is not illustrated here.

The autoregressive parameter estimates are used to perform the transformations of the variables required to obtain the generalized least squares estimates. The transformed variables are not printed, but are available in an output data set. The resulting estimates comprise the final portion of the output. A comparison of these estimates and their standard errors with those of the ordinary least squares method shows that they are not very different. Since the upward bias in variance estimates for a first-order autoregressive model is generally accepted to be in the neighborhood of $1/(1-\rho^2)$, these results are not surprising. In other words, if the first-order autocorrelation is 0.5, variance estimates using ordinary least squares should be approximately 33% larger than they actually are.

PROC AUTOREG has a number of PROC and MODEL statement options relating to output of various intermediate results. MODEL statement options are used to restrict the number of autoregressive parameters to be estimated and also to perform, if desired, a backward elimination of autoregressive parameters. The procedure can also be requested to produce an output data set containing predicted and residual values, the parameter estimates, and the transformed variables. These transformed variables may be used as input for repeated implementations of PROC AUTOREG, thus providing an iterative procedure for finding better estimates.

3.6   Summary

This chapter is titled "Observations", because it is concerned with aspects of observations that can cause a regression analysis to be of questionable value. Most of the focus has been on problems with the random error, but it was shown that problems may exist with the independent variables as well.

The problems comprise four major types that may occur singly or in combination:

□   outliers

□   specification error

□   heterogeneous variances

□   non-independent errors.

The most difficult of these is the problem of outliers, a point which is illustrated by the large number of statistics that have been developed to detect outliers. Unfortunately, none of these is uniformly superior because outliers can exist in so many ways. Finally, if you have found an outlier (or several), there is no guide as to what action to take.

The other difficulties are somewhat easier to diagnose and remedy, although even for these a degree of subjectivity is often needed to provide a reasonable analysis.

This chapter has demonstrated how the SAS System can be used to detect violations of assumptions about the error term in the regression model and subsequently to employ some remedial methods. Not only can the violations of assumptions take many forms, but the nature of violations are not always distinct. For example, apparent outliers may be the result of a non-normal distribution of errors. Therefore, it is important not to use these methods blindly by taking a scattershot approach of doing everything. Instead, methods must be chosen carefully, often on the basis of prior information such as, for example, knowledge of distributions that are known to exist with certain types of data, or outliers resulting from sloppiness that occurs with some regularity from some data sources. As usual, the power of even the most sophisticated computer software is no substitute for the application of human intelligence.

Chapter 4 Multicollinearity: Detection and Remedial Measures

4.1 Introduction

The validity of inferences resulting from a regression analysis assumes the use of a model with a specified set of independent variables. But in many cases you do not know specifically what variables should be included in a model. Hence, you may propose an initial model, often containing a large number of independent variables, and use a statistical analysis in hopes of revealing the correct model. This approach has two major problems:

☐ The model and associated hypotheses are generated by the data, thus invalidating significance levels (*p* values). This problem is related to the control of Type I errors in multiple comparisons, and although the problem has been partially solved for that application, it has not been solved for variable selection in regression. Therefore, *p* values provided by computer outputs for models obtained by such methods cannot be taken literally.

☐ The inclusion of a large number of variables in a regression model often results in *multicollinearity*, which is defined as a high degree of correlation among several independent variables.* This occurs when too many variables have been put into the model and a number of different variables measure similar phenomena.

The existence of multicollinearity is not a violation of the assumptions underlying the use of regression analysis. In other words, the existence of multicollinearity does not affect the estimation of the dependent variable. That is, the $\hat{y}$ values are the best linear unbiased estimates of the conditional means of the population. Depending on the purpose of the regression analysis, multicollinearity may, however, inhibit the usefulness of the results as follows:

□   The existence of multicollinearity tends to inflate the variances of predicted values, that is, predictions of the response variable for sets of x values, especially when these values are not in the sample.

□   The existence of multicollinearity tends to inflate the variances of the parameter estimates. Because a partial regression coefficient measures the effect of the corresponding independent variable, holding constant all other variables, the existence of high correlation with other independent variables makes the estimation and interpretation of such a coefficient difficult. In fact, under conditions of multicollinearity, partial coefficients are trying to estimate something that does not occur in the data. Therefore, multicollinearity often results in coefficient estimates that have large variances with consequent lack of statistical significance, or have incorrect signs or magnitude (Myers 1990, Section 3.7). This is an especially troublesome result when it is important to ascertain the structure of the relationship of the response to the various independent variables.

Because the use and interpretation of regression coefficients are very important for many regression analyses, you should ascertain if multicollinearity exists. Then, if multicollinearity is deemed to exist, it is important to ascertain the nature of the multicollinearity, that is, the nature of the linear relationships among the independent variables. The final step is to combat the effects of multicollinearity.

Section 4.2, "Detecting Multicollinearity," presents some methods available in PROC REG for the detection of multicollinearity. You will see that it is not difficult to detect, but once detected, the nature of the multicollinearity may be more difficult to diagnose.

Combatting the effects of multicollinearity is even more difficult, and the methods used depend on the ultimate purpose of the regression analysis. In fact, there is no universally optimum strategy for this task, and, furthermore, results obtained from any strategy are often of questionable validity and usefulness.

The most obvious and therefore most frequently used strategy is to implement a model with fewer independent variables. Since there is often no *a priori* criterion for the selection of variables, an automated, data driven search procedure is most frequently used. Implementation of such variable selection procedures is often called *model building*. However, since these methods use the

---

*   Correlations among independent variables also occur in polynomial models (see Chapter 5, "Polynomial Models") where, for example, there may be a high positive correlation of x and x^2. Remedial measures for this type of multicollinearity are not considered in this chapter.

data to select the model, they are more appropriately called *data dredging*. This approach has two major drawbacks:

□ It is not appropriate if you are trying to ascertain the structure of the regression relationship.

□ The results of the variable selection procedures often do not provide a clear choice of an optimum model.

Procedures for variable selection using the SAS System are presented in Section 4.4, "Variable Selection."

When it is important to study the nature of the regression relationship, it may be useful to redefine the variables in the model. Such redefinitions may be simply based on knowledge of the variables or on a multivariate analysis of the independent variables. Variable redefinition procedures are presented in Section 4.3.1, "Redefining Variables."

Another method that may be useful for studying the structure of the regression relationship is biased estimation. Although least squares is known to provide unbiased estimates of the parameters of a linear model, there are situations in which biased estimates may have smaller variances and thus provide useful estimates. Multicollinearity is a major contributor to large variances of estimates of regression coefficients, hence, a biasing of estimates that reduces the effect of multicollinearity may provide estimates with smaller mean-squared error. A discussion of biased estimators and an example is presented in Section 4.5, "Biased Estimation."

4.2 Detecting Multicollinearity

The example used for detecting and combatting the effects of multicollinearity is the BOQ data used for outlier detection in Chapter 3, "Observations," omitting the impossible observation 25.

Three sets of statistics that may be useful for ascertaining the degree and nature of multicollinearity are available as MODEL statement options in PROC REG. These statistics are

□ the relative degree of significance of the model and its individual parameters

□ the variance inflation factors, often referred to as VIF

□ an analysis of the structure of the **X'X** matrix.

PROC REG provides these statistics when you submit the following statements:

```
proc reg data=boq;
    model manh = occup checkin hours common wings cap rooms /
        vif collinoint;
run;
```

The VIF option requests the calculation of the variance inflation factors that are appended to the listing of parameter estimates, as seen in Output 4.1. The COLLINOINT (or COLLIN) option, shown in Output 4.2, provides for the analysis of the **X'X** structure.

Output 4.1
Regression for
BOQ Data,
Omitting
Observation 25

```
                              The SAS System                               1

Model: MODEL1
Dependent Variable: MANH

                            Analysis of Variance

                          Sum of          Mean
       Source      DF     Squares        Square      F Value      Prob>F

       Model        7   87497672.57   12499667.51    154.318      0.0001
       Error       16   1295986.739   80999.171189
       C Total     23   88793659.309

            Root MSE      284.60353      R-square       0.9854
            Dep Mean     2050.00708      Adj R-sq       0.9790
            C.V.          13.88305

                            Parameter Estimates

                     Parameter      Standard     T for H0:
       Variable  DF   Estimate        Error     Parameter=0    Prob > |T|

       INTERCEP   1   171.473359   148.86168053     1.152        0.2663
       OCCUP      1    21.045622     4.28904939     4.907        0.0002
       CHECKIN    1     1.426323     0.33070989     4.313        0.0005
       HOURS      1    -0.089268     1.16353166    -0.077        0.9398
       COMMON     1     7.650331     8.43835202     0.907        0.3781
       WINGS      1    -5.302310     9.45276086    -0.561        0.5826
       CAP        1    -4.074748     3.30195048    -1.234        0.2350
       ROOMS      1     0.331911     6.81398682     0.049        0.9618

                       Variance
       Variable  DF   Inflation

       INTERCEP   1    0.00000000
       OCCUP      1   43.63221691
       CHECKIN    1    4.54153959
       HOURS      1    1.36076420
       COMMON     1    4.06082971
       WINGS      1    3.79995729
       CAP        1   56.60333046
       ROOMS      1  178.70158599 .
```

A comparison of the relative degrees of statistical significance of the model with those of the partial regression coefficients reveals multicollinearity. The overall model is highly significant with an *F* value of 154.3 and *p* value much smaller than 0.0001, which is the lowest value PROC REG can print. The smallest *p* value for a partial regression coefficient is 0.0002, which is certainly not large but is definitely larger than that for the overall model. This type of result is a natural consequence of multicollinearity: the overall model may fit the data quite well, but because several independent variables are measuring similar phenomena, it is difficult to determine which of the individual variables contribute significantly to the regression relationship.

4.2.1   Variance Inflation Factors

The variance inflation factors are useful in determining which variables may be involved in the multicollinearities. For the *i*th independent variable, the variance inflation factor is defined as $1/(1-R_i^2)$, where R_i^2 is the coefficient of determination for the 'regression' of the *i*th independent variable on all other independent variables. It can be shown that the variance of the estimate of the corresponding regression coefficient is larger by that factor than it would be if there were no multicollinearity. In other words, the VIF statistics show how multicollinearity has increased the instability of the coefficient estimates.

There are no formal criteria for determining the magnitude of variance inflation factors that cause poorly estimated coefficients. Some authorities

(Myers 1990, Chapter 8) state that values exceeding 10 may be cause for concern, but this value is arbitrary. Actually, for models with low coefficients of determination for the regression, estimates of coefficients that exhibit relatively small variance inflation factors may still be unstable, and vice versa. In Output 4.1 the regression R^2 is a rather high 0.9854. Since $1/(1-R^2)=68.5$, any variables associated with VIF values exceeding 68.5 are more closely related to the other independent variables than they are to the dependent variable. Only the coefficient ROOMS has a VIF value larger than 68.5, and it is certainly not statistically significant. However, the variable OCCUP has a VIF value larger than 10 and a very small p value. You may conclude, therefore, that multicollinearity exists that decreases the reliability of the coefficient estimates. The overall regression is so strong however, that some coefficients may still be meaningful. On the other hand, the variable CAP has a rather large VIF and a large p value, so this variable may have been useful if it were not involved in multicollinearity.

4.2.2 Analysis of Structure

The analysis of the structure of relationships among a set of variables is afforded by an analysis of the eigenvalues and eigenvectors of $\mathbf{X'X}$. Such an analysis can be performed in two ways:

□ by using the raw (not centered) variables, including the dummy variable used to estimate the intercept, and scaling the variables such that the $\mathbf{X'X}$ matrix has ones on the diagonal. This method is implemented by the COLLIN option in the MODEL statement.

□ by using scaled and centered variables and excluding the dummy variable. In this case, $\mathbf{X'X}$ is the correlation matrix. This method is implemented by the COLLINOINT option in the MODEL statement.

Because the first method is suggested by use of the dummy variable to estimate the intercept, you may be tempted to think of that variable simply as one of the variables that can be involved in multicollinearity. This is not an appropriate conclusion for many situations. The intercept is an estimate of the response at the origin, that is, where all independent variables are zero. It is chosen for mathematical convenience rather than to provide a useful parameter. In fact, for most applications the intercept represents an extrapolation far beyond the reach of the data. For this reason the inclusion of the intercept in the study of multicollinearity can be useful only if the intercept has some physical interpretation and is within reach of the actual data space.

Centering the variables places the intercept at the means of all the variables. Therefore, if the variables have been centered, the intercept has no effect on the multicollinearity of the other variables (Belsley, Kuh, and Welsch 1980).* Centering is also consistent with the computation of the variance inflation factors which are based on first centering the variables. Since the origin cannot exist in the BOQ example, the COLLINOINT option is used here.

The COLLINOINT option provides the eigenvectors and variance proportions associated with the eigenvalues. A related analysis called principal component

---

*   See especially the comments by Cook et al. following the main discussion.

analysis is presented in Section 4.3.2, "Multivariate Structure: Principal Component Regression."

Output 4.2 shows the portion of the output from the COLLINOINT option.

Output 4.2
COLLINOINT
Option

```
                                      The SAS System                              1
                         Collinearity Diagnostics(intercept adjusted)

                            Condition  Var Prop  Var Prop  Var Prop  Var Prop  Var Prop
    Number   Eigenvalue      Number    OCCUP     CHECKIN   HOURS     COMMON    WINGS

       1      5.04674       1.00000    0.0008    0.0065    0.0097    0.0051    0.0069
       2      0.72303       2.64197    0.0000    0.0095    0.7045    0.0463    0.0496
       3      0.69939       2.68624    0.0016    0.0511    0.2387    0.1325    0.0344
       4      0.31781       3.98494    0.0026    0.0510    0.0264    0.2803    0.4144
       5      0.15871       5.63909    0.0016    0.7776    0.0064    0.0049    0.1162
       6      0.05049       9.99779    0.2717    0.1041    0.0034    0.0586    0.3648
       7      0.00384      36.25398    0.7216    0.0003    0.0109    0.4724    0.0138
```

```
                                      The SAS System                              2

              Var Prop  Var Prop
    Number    CAP       ROOMS

       1      0.0006    0.0002
       2      0.0000    0.0000
       3      0.0017    0.0002
       4      0.0009    0.0000
       5      0.0290    0.0033
       6      0.1025    0.0003
       7      0.8653    0.9960
```

The first column of this output consists of the eigenvalues of the correlation matrix of the set of independent variables. The eigenvalues are arranged from largest to smallest. The severity of multicollinearity is revealed by the relative magnitudes of these eigenvalues. Large variability among the eigenvalues indicates a greater degree of multicollinearity. Two features of these eigenvalues are of interest:

□   Eigenvalues of zero indicate linear dependencies or exact collinearities. Therefore, very small eigenvalues indicate near linear dependencies or high degrees of multicollinearity. There are two eigenvectors that may be considered very small in this set, implying the possibility of two sets of very strong relationships among the variables.

□   The square root of the ratio of the largest to smallest eigenvalue is called the *condition number*, which is the last entry in the column identified by that name. This value provides a single statistic for indicating the severity of multicollinearity. Criteria for a condition number to signify serious multicollinearity are arbitrary, with the value 30 often quoted. Myers (1990, Chapter 7) mentions that the square of the condition number in excess of 1000 indicates serious multicollinearity.* The condition number of 36.25 for this example indicates some multicollinearity.

---

*   The COLLIN option produces larger condition numbers, especially if the origin is outside the region of the data.

The other elements of the Condition Number column are the square roots of the ratio of the largest to each of the other eigenvalues. The number of large values in this column also indicates near linear dependencies among the variables.

The remainder of the output, labeled Var Prop (for variance proportions) may indicate which variables are involved in the near linear dependencies. For a given parameter estimate, these numbers tell you how much of the variance of the parameter estimate is associated with each eigenvalue. For example, looking at the seventh eigenvalue, the value 0.712 in the OCCUP column shows that 72% of the variance of the OCCUP parameter estimate is associated with eigenvalue number 7. Similarly, 27% is associated with eigenvalue number 6, and so on. In other words, relatively large proportion values in any row corresponding to a large condition number (small eigenvalue) may point to variables involved in a near linear dependency.

One approach to the analysis of these variance proportions (Belsley, Kuh, and Welsch 1980) is to identify eigenvalues having condition numbers greater than 30. Then, variables with variance proportions larger than 0.5 for each of these eigenvalues are considered to be involved in the near linear dependency that gives rise to these large condition numbers.

In this example, the condition number is 36.25 (>30) in the row for eigenvalue 7 (0.00384). The variance proportions are clearly large for the variables OCCUP, CAP, and ROOMS, implying a near linear dependency among these variables. These variables also have the largest variance inflation factors. The next largest condition number is 9.997 (<30). Correspondingly, the variance proportions for row 6 do not have any clearly large values. Therefore, it appears that only one set of strongly related variables exists.

4.3 Model Restructuring

In many cases the effects of multicollinearity may be alleviated by redefining the model. For example, in the analysis of economic time series data, variables such as GNP, population, production of steel, and so on, tend to be highly correlated because all are affected by inflation and the total size of the economy. Deflating such variables by a price index and population reduces multicollinearity. Model redefinition is illustrated with the BOQ data in Section 4.3.1.

In situations where a basis for model redefinition is not obvious, it may be useful to implement multivariate techniques to study the structure of multicollinearity and consequently to use the results of such a study to provide a better understanding of the regression relationships. One such multivariate method is principal components, which generates a set of artificial uncorrelated variables that can then be used in a regression model. Implementing a principal component regression using the SAS System is presented in Section 4.3.2, and a biased method based on principal components is presented in Section 4.5.1, "Incomplete Principal Component Regression."

4.3.1 Redefining Variables

The various multicollinearity statistics in the BOQ data demonstrate that many of the variables are related to the size of the establishment. The regression, then, primarily illustrates the relationship that larger establishments require more manpower. It is, however, more interesting to ascertain what other characteristics of Bachelor Officers Quarters require more or less manpower. You may be able to answer this question by redefining the variables in the model to measure per room characteristics; that is, estimate the relationship of the per room manhour requirement to the per room occupancy rate, and so on. Create the following variables in the DATA step:

```
data rel; set boq;
     relocc = occup / rooms;
     relcheck = checkin / rooms;
     relcom = common / rooms;
     relwings = wings / rooms;
     relcap = cap / rooms;
     relman = manh / rooms;
proc print;
     var relocc--relcap rooms hours relman;
run;
```

Output 4.3 shows the resulting variables along with the HOURS variable, which is not redefined, and also the ROOMS variable.

Output 4.3
BOQ Data with
Redefined
Variables

```
                              The SAS System                              1

 OBS   RELOCC   RELCHECK    RELCOM   RELWINGS    RELCAP   ROOMS   HOURS   RELMAN

   1   0.33333    0.6667    0.21000   0.16667    1.00000      6    4.0   30.0383
   2   0.60000    0.3160    0.25000   0.20000    1.00000      5   40.0   36.5220
   3   0.21200    0.0668    0.31160   0.12000    1.00000     25   42.5    7.9968
   4   0.87500    0.2963    0.12500   0.12500    0.87500      8  168.0   35.5687
   5   0.86842    0.4342    0.05895   0.10526    1.00000     19  168.0   14.0726
   6   1.27692    1.8292    0.07692   0.07692    1.00000     13   40.0   12.6446
   7   0.71917    0.0833    0.00000   0.08333    1.00000     36   40.0   27.7525
   8   0.67915    0.8528    0.11745   0.12766    1.00000     47  168.0   19.8264
   9   0.51468    0.6605    0.35545   0.12987    1.00000     77   40.0   12.2625
  10   0.92542    3.3281    0.01250   0.37500    1.00000     48  168.0   22.9842
  11   0.82697    3.1376    0.11773   0.09091    1.00000     66  168.0   21.0276
  12   1.53054   10.0924    0.16297   0.10811    0.97297     37  168.0   40.2568
  13   0.48469    1.8776    0.15439   0.04592    1.48980    196  168.0    9.4178
  14   0.80558    1.7222    0.14883   0.11667    1.00000    120  168.0   15.7642
  15   0.46110    3.2254    0.09671   0.04762    1.43810    210  168.0    8.9564
  16   0.74869    1.9622    0.14615   0.04615    1.26923    130  168.0   17.4466
  17   0.78115    2.2048    0.16038   0.10687    1.00000    131  168.0   23.1804
  18   0.95861    3.5652    0.17435   0.10435    1.00000    115  168.0   22.8550
  19   0.63620    5.4804    0.13676   0.03352    0.92737    179  168.0   19.8878
  20   0.69958    0.7595    0.13536   0.06250    1.00000    192  168.0   11.6029
  21   0.74050    1.1576    0.15381   0.06931    0.91584    202  168.0   15.4222
  22   0.79637    3.9536    0.19173   0.10970    1.00000    237  168.0   20.2711
  23   0.75736    1.9153    0.12846   0.15978    1.00000    363  168.0   15.2617
  24   0.84879    3.2531    0.01625   0.05298    1.19205    453  168.0   18.2489
```

The redefined variables reveal some features of the data that were not originally apparent. For example, the RELCHEK variable shows that establishment 12 has a very high turnover rate while establishments 3 and 7 have low turnover rates. Now perform the regression:

```
proc reg;
     model relman = relocc relcheck relcom relwings relcap hours
                    rooms / vif;
run;
```

The purpose of keeping the ROOMS variable in the model is to ascertain if there are economies of scale, that is, manhour requirements per room decrease for larger establishments. Output 4.4 shows the results of the regression.

Output 4.4
Regression with Redefined Variables

```
                              The SAS System                              1

Model: MODEL1
Dependent Variable: RELMAN

                           Analysis of Variance

                              Sum of        Mean
        Source        DF     Squares      Square    F Value    Prob>F

        Model          7    775.01435   110.71634      1.757    0.1659
        Error         16   1008.44749    63.02797
        C Total       23   1783.46183

              Root MSE      7.93902     R-square      0.4346
              Dep Mean     19.96950     Adj R-sq      0.1872
              C.V.         39.75571

                           Parameter Estimates

                      Parameter      Standard    T for H0:
        Variable  DF   Estimate         Error   Parameter=0   Prob > |T|

        INTERCEP   1   36.881423   21.07922266       1.750       0.0993
        RELOCC     1    1.668914   10.01956781       0.167       0.8698
        RELCHECK   1    1.580586    1.08597638       1.455       0.1649
        RELCOM     1  -12.943365   25.50015448      -0.508       0.6187
        RELWINGS   1   20.207212   26.22189530       0.771       0.4522
        RELCAP     1  -16.028215   13.56251656      -1.182       0.2546
        ROOMS      1   -0.019429    0.01817989      -1.069       0.3010
        HOURS      1   -0.021741    0.03670066      -0.592       0.5619

                       Variance
        Variable  DF   Inflation

        INTERCEP   1   0.00000000
        RELOCC     1   2.75373118
        RELCHECK   1   2.09438390
        RELCOM     1   1.68052258
        RELWINGS   1   1.22609509
        RELCAP     1   1.52130300
        ROOMS      1   1.63476669
        HOURS      1   1.73988902
```

You can see that the multicollinearity has been decreased but the regression is not statistically significant. In other words, there is little evidence that factors other than size affect manpower requirements. It is, however, possible that variable selection may reveal that some of these variables are useful in determining manpower requirements (see Section 4.4.)

4.3.2 Multivariate Structure: Principal Component Regression

Principal component analysis is a multivariate analysis technique that attempts to describe interrelationships among a set of variables. Starting with a set of observed values on a set of *m* variables, this method uses linear transformations to create a new set of variables, called the principal components, which have the following properties:

□ The principal component variables, or simply components, are jointly uncorrelated.

□ The first principal component has the largest variance of any linear function of the original variables (subject to a scale constraint). The second component has the second largest variance, and so on.

Although the principal components exhibit absolutely no multicollinearity, they are not guaranteed to provide useful interpretations.

Principal components may be obtained by computing the eigenvalues and eigenvectors of the correlation or covariance matrix. In most applications, however, the correlation matrix is used so that the components are not affected by the scales of measurement of the original variables.

The eigenvalues are the variances of the components. If the correlation matrix has been used, the variance of each input variable is one. Therefore, the sum of the variances is equal to the number of variables. Because of the scale constraint of the principal component transformation, the sum of variances (eigenvalues) of the components is also equal to the number of variables, but the variances are not equal. A set of eigenvalues of relatively equal magnitudes indicates that there is little multicollinearity, while a wide variation in magnitudes indicates severe multicollinearity. In fact, the number of large (usually greater than unity) eigenvalues may be taken as an indication of the true number of variables (sometimes called factors) needed to describe the behavior of the full set of variables.

These eigenvalues are the same that were produced by the COLLINOINT option where they had the same interpretation. However, instead of computing variance proportions, principal component analysis uses the eigenvectors, which are the coefficients for the linear transformations that relate the components to the original variables. In a sense they are regression coefficients of the equations that relate the component variables to the original (standardized) variables. Therefore, these coefficients may be used to interpret the structure of the components and are also used to create observed values of the component variables. For more complete descriptions of principal components, see Johnson and Wichern (1982) and Morrison (1976).

The set of principal component variables may be used as independent variables in a regression analysis. Such an analysis is called principal component regression. Since the components are uncorrelated, there is no multicollinearity in the regression, and you can easily determine the important coefficients. Then, if the coefficients of the principal components transformations imply meaningful interpretation of the components, the regression may shed light on the underlying regression relationships. Unfortunately, such interpretations are not always obvious.

Principal component regression is illustrated here with the BOQ data. The analysis is composed of two parts:

□   Use PROC PRINCOMP to perform the principal component analysis.

□   Use PROC REG to perform the regression of the dependent variable on the set of component variables.

The SAS statements for the principal component analysis are:

```
proc princomp data = boq out = prin;
    var occup checkin hours common wings cap rooms;
run;
```

The option OUT=PRIN creates a data set called PRIN that contains the variables in the original data set as well as the new principal component variables, which are automatically named PRIN1 through PRIN7. The results of the PRINCOMP procedure using the independent variables from the BOQ data appear in Output 4.5.

Output 4.5
Principal Components

```
                              The SAS System                          1
                        Principal Component Analysis

        24 Observations
         7 Variables


                            Simple Statistics

                      OCCUP          CHECKIN          HOURS          COMMON

      Mean        89.49208333     314.5129167     134.6041667     15.42375000
      StD         91.39426868     382.4113187      59.4962511     14.17183607


                           WINGS            CAP            ROOMS

         Mean     10.87500000     133.0416667     121.4583333
         StD      12.23790441     135.2156021     116.4231335


                          Correlation Matrix

              OCCUP   CHECKIN   HOURS   COMMON   WINGS    CAP     ROOMS

  OCCUP      1.0000   0.8571   0.4785   0.5688   0.7668   0.9270   0.9708
  CHECKIN    0.8571   1.0000   0.4607   0.4640   0.5460   0.8452   0.8545
  HOURS      0.4785   0.4607   1.0000   0.3809   0.3736   0.4634   0.4799
  COMMON     0.5688   0.4640   0.3809   1.0000   0.6827   0.5878   0.6579
  WINGS      0.7668   0.5460   0.3736   0.6827   1.0000   0.6722   0.7581
  CAP        0.9270   0.8452   0.4634   0.5878   0.6722   1.0000   0.9785
  ROOMS      0.9708   0.8545   0.4799   0.6579   0.7581   0.9785   1.0000


                  Eigenvalues of the Correlation Matrix

                 Eigenvalue    Difference    Proportion    Cumulative

     PRIN1        5.04674       4.32371       0.720963      0.72096
     PRIN2        0.72303       0.02364       0.103289      0.82425
     PRIN3        0.69939       0.38158       0.099913      0.92417
     PRIN4        0.31781       0.15910       0.045401      0.96957
     PRIN5        0.15871       0.10822       0.022672      0.99224
     PRIN6        0.05049       0.04665       0.007213      0.99945
     PRIN7        0.00384         .           0.000549      1.00000


                            Eigenvectors

              PRIN1     PRIN2     PRIN3     PRIN4     PRIN5     PRIN6     PRIN7

  OCCUP      0.427129  -.016121  -.223824  -.190675  -.106859  -.773655   0.347686
  CHECKIN    0.385625   0.176465  -.402776   0.271250   0.748651   0.154482  -.002249
  HOURS      0.258063   0.832573   0.476599  -.106772  -.037258   0.015315  -.007541
  COMMON     0.321746  -.368518   0.613557   0.601401   0.056206  -.109608   0.085824
  WINGS      0.362662  -.369182   0.302495  -.707400   0.264716   0.264551   0.014167
  CAP        0.420433   0.003662  -.256780   0.123786  -.510810   0.541268   0.433666
  ROOMS      0.436405  -.057519  -.163207   0.035291  -.304228  -.048847  -.826692
```

The first portion of the output provides the descriptive statistics: the means, standard deviations, and correlation coefficients. You can easily see the very high correlations among OCCUP, CAP, and ROOMS, but other correlations are also quite large.

The second portion provides information on the eigenvalues of the correlation matrix. The eigenvalues are identified by column headings. Since there are seven variables, there are also seven eigenvalues that are arranged from high to low and identified as PRIN1 - PRIN7. As noted, these eigenvalues are the same as those obtained by the COLLINOINT option in the MODEL statement in PROC REG (see Output 4.2).

The principal components have been computed from the standardized variables, that is, from the correlation matrix. Therefore, the sum of the variances of the original seven variables, as well as the sum of variances of the seven new principal component variables, is seven. This is a measure of the total variation inherent in the entire set of data. As previously noted, the variances of the principal components are given by the individual eigenvalues. The first principal component shows a very large variance (5.04), the second and third have modest variances (0.72 and 0.70), and the remainder have very small variances (less than 0.5). Remember, an eigenvalue of zero implies exact linear dependency.

The second Difference column gives the differences between adjacent eigenvalues. This statistic shows the rate of decrease in variances of the principal components.

The proportion of total variation accounted for by each of the components is obtained by dividing each of the eigenvalues by the total variation. These quantities are given in the Proportion column. You can see that the first component accounts for 72% of the total variation, a result that is typical when a single factor, in this case the size of the establishment, is a common factor in the variability among the original variables.

The cumulative proportions printed in the Cumulative column indicate for each component the proportion of the total variation of the original set of variables explained by all components up to and including that one. For example, 92% of the total variation in the seven variables is explained by only three components. This is another indication that the original set of variables contains redundant information.

The columns of the final portion of the output give the eigenvectors for each of the principal components. These coefficients, which relate the components to the original variables, are scaled so that their sum of squares is unity. This allows for finding which, if any, of the original variables dominate a component.

The coefficients of the first principal component show a positive relationship with all variables, with somewhat larger contributions from OCCUP, CAP, and ROOMS. As expected, this component measures the size of the establishment. The second component is dominated by HOURS. This shows that among these establishments there is a variability in operating hours that is independent of size. The third component is dominated by COMMONS and is also somewhat a function of HOURS and, negatively, of CHECKIN. This component indicates some variation among the establishments that reflects large common areas and longer hours of operation but a relatively low number of check ins. Interpretation of components having small eigenvalues, such as components four through seven, is not usually useful, although such components may reveal data anomalies (see Output 4.7).

Next, you can perform a regression of MANH on the principal components. Remember that the implementation of the OUT=PRIN option in the PROC PRINCOMP step created a data set called PRIN that contains all the original variables as well as the seven principal components, PRIN1 - PRIN7. Now perform the regression:

```
proc reg data = prin;
    model manh = prin1 - prin7 / ss2;
run;
```

The results appear in Output 4.6.

Output 4.6
Principal
Component
Regression

```
                            The SAS System                          1

Model: MODEL1
Dependent Variable: MANH

                         Analysis of Variance

                            Sum of        Mean
        Source        DF    Squares      Square     F Value    Prob>F

        Model          7  87497672.57  12499667.51   154.318    0.0001
        Error         16   1295986.739 80999.171189
        C Total       23  88793659.309

             Root MSE       284.60353    R-square     0.9854
             Dep Mean      2050.00708    Adj R-sq     0.9790
             C.V.            13.88305

                         Parameter Estimates

                       Parameter      Standard    T for H0:
        Variable  DF    Estimate         Error    Parameter=0   Prob > |T|

        INTERCEP   1   2050.007083   58.09445297     35.287      0.0001
        PRIN1      1    827.095158   26.41623645     31.310      0.0001
        PRIN2      1     40.582716   69.79100876      0.581      0.5690
        PRIN3      1   -470.672616   70.96047336     -6.633      0.0001
        PRIN4      1   -173.967127  105.26717235     -1.653      0.1179
        PRIN5      1    461.607512  148.96354543      3.099      0.0069
        PRIN6      1  -1733.066763  264.10410257     -6.562      0.0001
        PRIN7      1    405.074579  957.69358445      0.423      0.6779


        Variable  DF    Type II SS

        INTERCEP   1    100860697
        PRIN1      1     79405328
        PRIN2      1        27388
        PRIN3      1      3563571
        PRIN4      1       221222
        PRIN5      1       777797
        PRIN6      1      3487875
        PRIN7      1        14491
```

The statistics for the overall regression (SS Model and SS Error) are, by definition, the same as for the regression with the seven original variables (see Output 4.1). However, the statistics for the variables in the model tell a different story. Since the components are uncorrelated, the VIFs (not printed) are all unity. You can also verify that the Type II sums of squares add to the model sum of squares. According to the t statistics for the parameter estimates, there appear to be four components of importance for estimating manhour requirements.* The most important component is PRIN1, followed in importance by PRIN3 and PRIN6, and to a lesser degree PRIN5.

PRIN1 is clearly the component associated with size of establishment. In fact, this component accounts for over 90% of the variation explained by the model (TYPE II SS/MODEL SS). The second component apparently does nothing, that is, the hours of operation apparently have no effect on manpower requirements. Component three was associated with common areas, hours, and (negatively) with check ins. The negative coefficient indicates lower manhour requirements for establishments having larger common areas and longer desk hours and lower turnover.

Because principal components with very small variances are usually not useful, strong relationships of such components with the dependent variable are

---

* You should not use the p values literally, but the magnitudes of the p values can be used to indicate relative importance of the coefficients.

an apparent contradiction and may very well indicate data anomalies. You can investigate this by plotting the component variables against the dependent variable. In this example, components three and six have small variances and appear important and are therefore logical candidates for such plots. If you are using PROC REG in the interactive mode, enter the following statements:

```
plot prin3*manh prin6*manh  / hplots = 2 vplots = 2;
run;
```

Otherwise, use PROC PLOT as follows:

```
proc plot  data = prin vpercent =50 hpercent = 50 ;
      plot prin3*manh  prin6*manh ;
run;
```

The HPLOT and VPLOT as well as the HPERCENT and VPERCENT options produce side-by-side plots one-half page long. The results, using PROC REG interactively, appear in Output 4.7.

Output 4.7
Plots of Components Three and Six

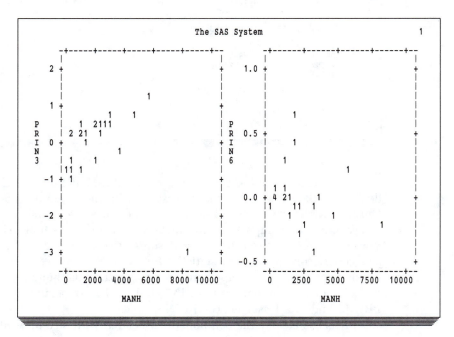

You can see that the relationships of both PRIN3 and PRIN6 with MANH are dominated by one observation, which can be identified as number 24. Remember that observation 24 was unusual in having very high turnover and small common areas, which have relatively large coefficients for component three. Omitting this observation would most certainly change the results. The relationship of PRIN6 to MANH is also affected by observation 24, but the reason for this is not clear. Of course, this is no justification for omitting observation 24.

Principal components that have large eigenvalues can also be used to re-create values of the original variables reflecting only the variation explained by these components. This is a biased estimation procedure and is illustrated in Section 4.5.1.

In summary, principal component regression has helped somewhat to interpret the structure of the regression, although the interpretation is not clearcut, which is common with this type of analysis. Slightly more interpretable results are obtained by using rotated principal components, which are available in the FACTOR procedure. Presentation of such methods is beyond the scope of this book.

4.4 Variable Selection

When a number of variables in a regression analysis do not appear to contribute significantly to the predictive power of the model, it is natural to try to find a suitable subset of important or useful variables. The use of regression methodology assumes that you have specified the appropriate model, but in many cases theory or intuitive reasoning does not supply such a model. In such situations, it is customary to use an automated procedure that uses information on the estimated coefficients to select a suitable subset of variables for a final model.

An optimum subset model is one that, for a given number of variables, produces the minimum error sum of squares, or, equivalently, the maximum R^2. In a sense, the only way to ensure finding optimum subsets is to examine all possible subsets. This procedure, for m independent variables, requires computing for $m!/[p!(m-p)!]$ regression equations for subsets of size p from an m-variable model, or requires computing 2^m equations for finding optimum subsets for all subset sizes. Fortunately, optimal search procedures, highly efficient algorithms, and high speed computing capabilities make such a procedure feasible for models with a moderate number of variables, because they reduce the number of subsets that actually need to be examined. Such a procedure is implemented by an option in PROC REG, and it is normally recommended for models containing fewer than 25 variables when using personal computers, while a somewhat larger number is possible when using mainframe computers. This method is presented in Section 4.4.1, "The R-SQUARE Selection Method."

Because these selection methods often produce a bewildering array of results, statistics have been developed to assist in choosing suitable subset models. The use of such statistics is presented in Section 4.4.2, "Choosing Useful Models." Popular alternatives to the guaranteed optimum subset selection are the step-type procedures that add or delete variables one at a time until, by some criterion, a reasonable stopping point is reached. These procedures do not guarantee finding optimum subsets, but they work quite well in many cases and are especially useful for models with many variables. A number of step-type procedures may be implemented as options in PROC REG and are presented in Section 4.4.3, "Other Variable Selection Procedures."

Before continuing, it necessary to point out that variable selection is not always appropriate, although it is easy to do. In fact, it may produce misleading results. Additional comments on this issue are presented in Section 4.6, "Summary."

4.4.1   The R-SQUARE Selection Method

Guaranteed optimum subsets are obtained by using the MODEL statement option SELECTION=RSQUARE in PROC REG. You can use this method for the BOQ data as follows:

```
proc reg;
    model manh = occup checkin hours common wings cap rooms /
        selection = rsquare  best = 4 cp;
run;
```

Two additional options are specified here (others are presented later) as follows:

BEST=4   specifies that only the best four (smallest error mean square) models for each subset size be printed. This option not only prevents excessive output but also saves computing time.

CP   specifies the printing of the Mallows C(P) statistic (denoted by C(P) in the output) for each subset. This is the most popular of several statistics used to aid selection of a final model (see Section 4.4.2).

The results appear in Output 4.8.

Output 4.8
Regression for
BOQ Data Using
R-SQUARE
Selection

```
                              The SAS System                              1

        N = 24     Regression Models for Dependent Variable: MANH


     Number in    R-square      C(p)   Variables in Model
      Model

         1       0.96190521   21.76062   OCCUP
         1       0.88882403  101.87435   ROOMS
         1       0.81494443  182.86332   CHECKIN
         1       0.79202567  207.98754   CAP
     -------------------------------------------------------------
         2       0.97645669    7.80887   OCCUP CHECKIN
         2       0.96454174   20.87038   OCCUP CAP
         2       0.96341233   22.10847   OCCUP ROOMS
         2       0.96285345   22.72113   OCCUP WINGS
     -------------------------------------------------------------
         3       0.98385346    1.70031   OCCUP CHECKIN CAP
         3       0.98026880    5.62991   OCCUP CHECKIN ROOMS
         3       0.97670694    9.53454   OCCUP CHECKIN COMMON
         3       0.97656403    9.69119   OCCUP CHECKIN WINGS
     -------------------------------------------------------------
         4       0.98511227    2.32036   OCCUP CHECKIN COMMON CAP
         4       0.98454740    2.93959   OCCUP CHECKIN CAP ROOMS
         4       0.98390717    3.64143   OCCUP CHECKIN COMMON ROOMS
         4       0.98386582    3.68676   OCCUP CHECKIN WINGS CAP
     -------------------------------------------------------------
         5       0.98539624    4.00907   OCCUP CHECKIN COMMON WINGS CAP
         5       0.98511633    4.31591   OCCUP CHECKIN HOURS COMMON CAP
         5       0.98511303    4.31953   OCCUP CHECKIN COMMON CAP ROOMS
         5       0.98464867    4.82858   OCCUP CHECKIN WINGS CAP ROOMS
     -------------------------------------------------------------
         6       0.98540235    6.00237   OCCUP CHECKIN HOURS COMMON WINGS CAP
         6       0.98539914    6.00589   OCCUP CHECKIN COMMON WINGS CAP ROOMS
         6       0.98511749    6.31464   OCCUP CHECKIN HOURS COMMON CAP ROOMS
         6       0.98465472    6.82195   OCCUP CHECKIN HOURS WINGS CAP ROOMS
     -------------------------------------------------------------
         7       0.98540451    8.00000   OCCUP CHECKIN HOURS COMMON WINGS CAP ROOMS
     -------------------------------------------------------------
```

The output from the SELECTION=RSQUARE option provides, for each subset size, the variables included in the four best models, listed in order of decreasing R-SQUARE, along with the R-SQUARE and C(P) statistics. You can see that R-SQUARE remains virtually unchanged down to subsets of size three, indicating that the three-variable model including OCCUP, CHECKIN, and CAP may be most useful. Additional considerations in this selection are presented in Section 4.4.2.

Some additional options that are useful for problems with many variables include:

INCLUDE=*n* specifies that the first *n* independent variables in the MODEL statement are to be included in all subset models.

START=*n* specifies that only subsets of *n* or more variables are to be considered. This number includes the variables specified by the INCLUDE option.

STOP=*n* specifies that subsets of no more than *n* variables are to be considered. This number also includes the variables specified by the INCLUDE option.

B specifies that the regression coefficients are printed for each subset model. This option should be used sparingly as it may produce a large amount of unnecessary output. A more efficient way of getting coefficient estimates is to use information from Output 4.8 to choose interesting models and obtain the coefficient estimates by repeated MODEL statements or, interactively, with ADD and DELETE statements.

4.4.2 Choosing Useful Models

An examination of the R-SQUARE values in Output 4.8 does not reveal any obvious choices for selecting a most useful subset model. A number of other statistics have been developed to aid in making these choices and are available as additional options with the RSQUARE option. Among these, the most frequently used is the C(P) statistic, proposed by Mallows (1973). This statistic is a measure of total squared error for a subset model containing *p* independent variables. The total squared error is a measure of the error variance plus the bias introduced by not including important variables in a model. It may, therefore, indicate when variable selection is deleting too many variables. The C(P) statistic is computed as follows:

$$C(P) = (SSE(p)/MSE) - (N - 2p) + 1$$

where

MSE	is the error mean square for the full model (or some other estimate of pure error)
SSE(p)	is the error sum of squares for the subset model containing p independent variables (NOT including the intercept)*
N	is total sample size.

For any given number of selected variables, larger C(P) values indicate equations with larger error mean squares. For any subset model C(P)>(p+1), there is evidence of bias due to an incompletely specified model. On the other hand, if there are values of C(P)<(p+1), the full model is said to be overspecified, that is, it contains too many variables.

Mallows recommends that C(P) be plotted against p, and further recommends selecting that subset size where the minimum C(P) first approaches (p+1), starting from the full model. The magnitudes of differences in the C(P) statistic between the optimum and near optimum models for each subset size are also of interest.

You can obtain such a plot by using the OUTEST option with the RSQUARE selection. Because this is a PROC REG statement option, it cannot be done interactively and you must invoke PROC REG as follows:

```
proc reg outest = est;
    model manh = occup checkin hours common wings cap rooms /
        selection = rsquare CP best = 2;
run;
```

Only the best two models are requested, since adding more models will produce too much output, especially the OUTEST option, which produces the actual coefficients for each model. You can examine the resulting data set using PROC PRINT. Output 4.9 shows the results.

---

*   In the original presentation of the C(P) statistic (Mallows 1973), the intercept coefficient is also considered as a candidate for selection, so that in that presentation the number of variables in the model is one more than what is defined here and results in the +1 elements in the equations. As implied in the discussion of the COLLIN option, allowing the deletion of the intercept is not normally useful.

Output 4.9
Output Data Set
from R-SQUARE
Selection

```
                              The SAS System                                1

    OBS _MODEL_ _TYPE_ _DEPVAR_   _RMSE_ INTERCEP  OCCUP  CHECKIN  HOURS   COMMON

      1 MODEL1  PARMS   MANH     392.114  163.064 21.0850  .        .        .
      2 MODEL1  PARMS   MANH     669.862  117.492  .        .        .        .
      3 MODEL1  PARMS   MANH     315.511  170.791 16.7706 1.20306   .        .
      4 MODEL1  PARMS   MANH     387.204  183.560 23.8142  .        .        .
      5 MODEL1  PARMS   MANH     267.741  207.865 20.6716 1.43624   .        .
      6 MODEL1  PARMS   MANH     295.973  219.157 21.8218 1.31672   .        .
      7 MODEL1  PARMS   MANH     263.772  165.195 20.4184 1.47797   .      6.13854
      8 MODEL1  PARMS   MANH     268.729  186.088 18.4129 1.46375   .        .
      9 MODEL1  PARMS   MANH     268.403  162.255 21.2042 1.42403   .      7.85875
     10 MODEL1  PARMS   MANH     270.963  173.044 20.4290 1.48045 -0.077225 6.19315
     11 MODEL1  PARMS   MANH     276.126  171.875 21.2203 1.42686 -0.094768 7.93259
     12 MODEL1  PARMS   MANH     276.157  162.435 21.0039 1.42360   .      7.53828
     13 MODEL1  PARMS   MANH     284.604  171.473 21.0456 1.42632 -0.089268 7.65033

    OBS   WINGS     CAP      ROOMS   MANH  _IN_ _P_ _EDF_   _RSQ_    _CP_

      1    .         .         .       -1    1   2   22   0.96191   21.761
      2    .         .       15.9109    -1    1   2   22   0.88882  101.874
      3    .         .         .       -1    2   3   21   0.97646    7.809
      4    .      -1.98990     .       -1    2   3   21   0.96454   20.870
      5    .      -3.45397     .       -1    3   4   20   0.98385    1.700
      6    .         .      -4.4143     -1    3   4   20   0.98027    5.630
      7    .      -3.77319     .       -1    4   5   19   0.98511    2.320
      8    .      -5.31452   3.8103     -1    4   5   19   0.98455    2.940
      9 -5.21267 -3.92549     .       -1    5   6   18   0.98540    4.009
     10    .      -3.77339     .       -1    5   6   18   0.98512    4.316
     11 -5.23336 -3.92634     .       -1    6   7   17   0.98540    6.002
     12 -5.29354 -4.09664   0.3826     -1    6   7   17   0.98540    6.006
     13 -5.30231 -4.07475   0.3319     -1    7   8   16   0.98540    8.000
```

As you can see, this data set contains much information, including the coefficients as variables whose names are those of the independent variables. For model selection, you want to plot the C(P) statistic, which is identified as the variable _CP_, against the number of independent variables selected, which is identified as the variable _IN_. Following Mallow's suggestion, compare the C(P) values to $(p+1)$, which is the variable _P_ in this data set. You can plot both of these values as follows:

```
proc plot;
    plot _cp_*_in_ = 'C' _p_*_in_ = '*' / overlay
          vaxis = 0 to 25 by 1 haxis = 0 to 7 by 1
          hpos=40 vpos=30;
RUN;
```

In this plot, the C(P) values are represented with the C symbol while the values of $(p+1)$ are represented by the * symbol. The VAXIS option is used to plot only the most relevant part, since including in the plot the essentially irrelevant C(P) value of 101.874 for the second best one-variable model squeezes the plot and makes it difficult to interpret. The resulting plot appears in Output 4.10.

Output 4.10

C(P) Plot

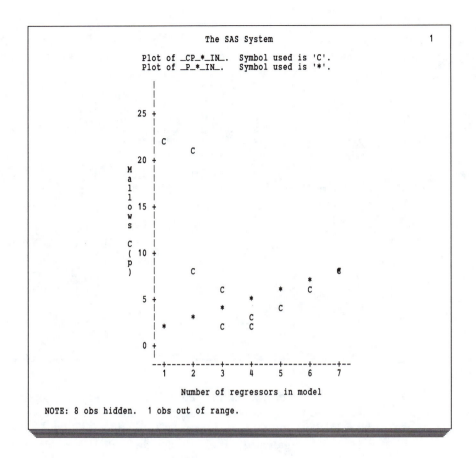

```
                         The SAS System                        1

              Plot of _CP_*_IN_.   Symbol used is 'C'.
              Plot of _P_*_IN_.    Symbol used is '*'.
         |
         |
     25  +
         |
         |
         |  C
         |          C
     20  +
   M     |
   a     |
   l     |
   l     |
   o 15  +
   w     |
   s     |
         |
   C     |
   ( 10  +
   P     |
   )     |          C                              *       C
         |                C                *       C
      5  +                *       *
         |        *               C
         |                C       C
      0  +
         |
        --+-----+-----+-----+-----+-----+-----+--
          1     2     3     4     5     6     7
                Number of regressors in model

NOTE: 8 obs hidden.   1 obs out of range.
```

The pattern of C(P) values is quite typical for situations where multicollinearity is serious. Starting with $\_P\_=7$, they initially become smaller than $(p+1)$, as fewer variables are included, but eventually start to increase. In this plot, there is a definite corner at $\_IN\_=3$, where the C(P) values increase rapidly with smaller subset sizes. Hence, a model with three variables appears to be a good choice.

A second criterion is the difference in C(P) between the optimum and second optimum subset for each subset size. In the above models with four or more variables, these differences are very small, which implies that the multicollinearity allows interchange of variables without affecting the fit of the model. However, the difference is larger with three variables, implying that the degree of multicollinearity has decreased. You can now estimate the best three-variable model using the information from Output 4.8 as follows:

```
proc reg data = boq;
    model manh = occup checkin cap / vif;
run;
```

Results of the regression appear in Output 4.11.

Output 4.11
Regression for
BOQ Data, Best
Three Variable
Model

```
                              The SAS System                               1
Model: MODEL1
Dependent Variable: MANH

                            Analysis of Variance

                                Sum of        Mean
        Source        DF       Squares       Square     F Value    Prob>F

        Model          3 87359949.237 29119983.079     406.219    0.0001
        Error         20 1433710.0716  71685.50358
        C Total       23 88793659.309

            Root MSE      267.74149     R-square      0.9839
            Dep Mean     2050.00708     Adj R-sq      0.9814
            C.V.           13.06052

                          Parameter Estimates

                         Parameter     Standard    T for H0:
        Variable  DF      Estimate        Error   Parameter=0   Prob > |T|

        INTERCEP   1    207.864860   78.28539211        2.655       0.0152
        OCCUP      1     20.671626    1.75123474       11.804       0.0001
        CHECKIN    1      1.436243    0.29365829        4.891       0.0001
        CAP        1     -3.453968    1.14109505       -3.027       0.0067

                          Variance
        Variable  DF     Inflation

        INTERCEP   1    0.00000000
        OCCUP      1    8.21907889
        CHECKIN    1    4.04615481
        CAP        1    7.63824793
```

You can see that the multicollinearity has greatly decreased.

Note: Since this model has been specified by the data, the *p* values cannot be used literally but may be useful for determining the relative importance of the variables.

It does appear that more turnover (CHECKIN) requires additional manpower. The negative coefficient for CAP may reflect lower manhours for a larger proportion of vacant rooms.

A number of other statistics are available to assist in choosing subset models. Some are relatively obvious, such as the residual mean square or standard deviations, while others are related to R-SQUARE, with some providing adjustments for degrees of freedom or scaling preferences. They are all essentially equivalent, although some may have different theoretical justification. A number of these are available as options with the selection methods described in this section. Keywords and literature references for these options are provided in "Model-Selection Methods," in Chapter 36, "The REG Procedure" in *SAS/STAT User's Guide, Version 6, Fourth Edition, Volume 2.*

For those who find the results of the SELECTION=RSQUARE method somewhat bewildering, PROC REG provides for two less bewildering but also less informative methods for selecting optimum subsets. These selection methods are SELECTION=ADJRSQ and SELECTION=CP. For each of these, PROC REG prints a total of *n* sets of subset models judged optimum according to the respective criterion (ADJ R-SQ or C(P)), where *n* is specified by the BEST=*n* option.

Now, for a given subset size, there is a monotonic relationship among all three selection criteria, but this is not true when they are compared across different subset sizes. Thus, for example, using the SELECTION=CP BEST=4 option you get the four models with the smallest C(P) values regardless of subset size. From Output 4.8, you can verify that this is the optimum three-variable model followed by the three best four-variable models. Thus, you will have a compact output for a few optimum models according to this criterion, but you will not, for example, have the comprehensive summary of selection results provided by the plot in Output 4.10.

In the same manner, SELECTION=ADJRSQ provides *n* models with the largest adjusted R-SQUARE values (see Section 2.3, "A Model with Several Independent Variables").

4.4.3 Other Variable Selection Procedures

Several step-type selection procedures are available as alternatives to the RSQUARE selection method. Starting with some given model, these procedures can

□   add a variable to the model

□   delete a variable from the model

□   exchange a variable in the model for one that is not in the model.

Five different step-type selection methods are available as MODEL options in the PROC REG step. Each is implemented with a SELECTION=KEYWORD, where the keyword is given in parentheses in the descriptions below. Additional options for these methods are detailed after the descriptions. Only one selection option is available with any MODEL statement, but several MODEL statements may be used with different selection options. The selection methods are as follows:

Forward Selection
(FORWARD or F)
>   begins by finding the variable that produces the optimum one-variable model. In the second step, the procedure finds the variable that, when added to the already chosen variable, results in the largest reduction in the residual sum of squares (largest increase in R^2). The third step finds the variable that, when added to the two already chosen, gives the minimum residual sum of squares (maximum R^2). The process continues until no variable considered for addition to the model provides a reduction in sum of squares considered statistically significant at a level specified by the user (see SLE specification later in this section). An important feature of this method is that once a variable has been selected, it stays in the model.

Backward Elimination
(BACKWARD or B)
>   begins by computing the regression with all independent variables specified in the MODEL statement. The statistics for the partial coefficients are examined to find the variable that contributes least to the fit of the model, that is, the coefficient with the largest *p* value (smallest partial *F* value). That variable is deleted from the model and the resulting equation is examined for the variable now contributing the least, which is then deleted, and so on. The procedure stops when all coefficients remaining in the model are statistically significant at a level specified by the user (see SLS specification later in this section). With this method, once a variable has been deleted, it is deleted permanently.

Stepwise Selection
(STEPWISE)

begins like forward selection, but after a variable has been added to the model, the resulting equation is examined to see if any coefficient has a sufficiently large p value (see SLS specification later in this section) to suggest that a variable should be dropped. This procedure continues until no additions or deletions are indicated according to significance levels (SLE and SLS) chosen by the user.

Maximum R-SQUARE Improvement
(MAXR)

begins by selecting one- and two-variable models as in forward selection. At that point, the procedure examines all possible pairwise interchanges with the variables not in the model. If any interchanges increase R^2, then that interchange resulting in the largest increase in R^2 is implemented. This process is repeated until no pairwise interchange improves the model. At this point, a third variable is selected as in forward selection. Then the interchanging process is repeated, and so on. This method usually requires more computer time than the other three, but it also tends to have a better chance of finding more nearly optimum models. In addition, the maximum R-SQUARE improvement method often produces a larger number of equations, a feature that may be of some value in the final evaluation process.

Minimum R-SQUARE Improvement
(MINR)

is similar to maximum R-SQUARE improvement, except that interchanges are implemented for those with minimum improvement. Since interchanges are not implemented when R^2 is decreased, the final results are quite similar to those of the maximum R-SQUARE improvement method, except that a larger number of equations may be examined.

A number of options are available to provide greater control over the selection procedures. One option available for all procedures is the INCLUDE=n, which specifies that the first n independent variables in the MODEL statement are to be kept in the model at all times.

For the FORWARD, BACKWARD, and STEPWISE methods, you may specify desired significance levels for stopping the addition or elimination of variables as follows:

SLE = .*xxx*   specifies the significance level for stopping the addition of variables in the forward selection mode. If not specified, the default is 0.50 for FORWARD and 0.15 for STEPWISE.

SLS = .*xxx*   specifies the significance level for stopping the backward elimination mode. If not specified, the default is 0.10 for BACKWARD and 0.15 for STEPWISE.

The smallest permissible value for SLS is 0.0001, which almost always ensures that the final equation obtained by backward elimination contains only one variable, while the maximum SLE of 0.99 usually includes all variables when forward selection has stopped. It is again important to note that, since variable selection is an exploratory rather than confirmatory analysis, the SLE and SLS values do not have the usual connotation as probabilities of erroneously rejecting the null hypothesis of the nonexistence of the coefficients in any selected model.

MAXR and MINR selection do not use significance levels, but you may specify the starting and stopping of these procedure with these options:

START=*s*   specifies that the interchanging procedure starts with first *s* variables in the MODEL statement.

STOP=*s*   specifies that the procedure stops when the best *s* variable model has been found.

For MAXR and MINR, the INCLUDE option works as it does with R-SQUARE. That is, if the INCLUDE option is used in addition to the START or STOP option, the INCLUDE option overrides the START or STOP specification. For example, if you use START=3 and INCLUDE=2, the selection starts with the first three variables, but the first two may not be candidates for deletion.

Because the outputs from the step-type selection procedures are quite lengthy, they are illustrated here only with the SELECTION=FORWARD option using the redefined variables of the BOQ data. Since the overall seven-variable model has a rather high *p* value, the default SLE of 0.15 most likely selects only a few variables. Consider these SAS statements:

```
proc reg;
     model relman = relocc relcheck relcom relwings relcap
           hours rooms / selection = f ;
```

The results appear in Output 4.12.

Output 4.12
Forward Selection for Redefined Variables

```
                              The SAS System                              1

                Forward Selection Procedure for Dependent Variable RELMAN

   Step 1    Variable RELCAP Entered    R-square = 0.18493577   C(p) = 3.06334795

                     DF       Sum of Squares      Mean Square        F     Prob>F

   Regression         1         329.82588205      329.82588205     4.99     0.0360
   Error             22        1453.63595251       66.07436148
   Total             23        1783.46183456

                  Parameter       Standard        Type II
   Variable         Estimate         Error     Sum of Squares       F     Prob>F

   INTERCEP      46.25587237      11.88177407    1001.39206715     15.16    0.0008
   RELCAP       -25.15406243      11.25854468     329.82588205      4.99    0.0360

   Bounds on condition number:            1,            1
   -----------------------------------------------------------------------------
   Step 2    Variable RELCHECK Entered  R-square = 0.29084171   C(p) = 2.06659553

                     DF       Sum of Squares      Mean Square        F     Prob>F

   Regression         2         518.70509660      259.35254830     4.31     0.0271
   Error             21        1264.75673796       60.22651133
   Total             23        1783.46183456

                  Parameter       Standard        Type II
   Variable         Estimate         Error     Sum of Squares       F     Prob>F

   INTERCEP      44.18015114      11.40419713     903.88394046     15.01    0.0009
   RELCHECK      1.30004064       0.73410587     188.87921455      3.14    0.0911
   RELCAP       -25.90675595      10.75719110     349.31401191      5.80    0.0253

   Bounds on condition number:      1.001564,      4.006254
   -----------------------------------------------------------------------------
```

```
Step 3   Variable ROOMS Entered    R-square = 0.38677327   C(p) = 1.35208210

                  DF      Sum of Squares      Mean Square       F    Prob>F

Regression        3       689.79536214      229.93178738     4.20   0.0185
Error            20      1093.66647242       54.68332362
Total            23      1783.46183456

                 Parameter        Standard         Type II
Variable         Estimate           Error     Sum of Squares       F    Prob>F

INTERCEP        39.37032978     11.20177003     675.49121163    12.35   0.0022
RELCHECK         1.53969966      0.71250840     255.35652108     4.67   0.0430
RELCAP         -18.83124664     11.00307190     160.17146358     2.93   0.1025
ROOMS           -0.02562072      0.01448459     171.09026555     3.13   0.0922

Bounds on condition number:     1.19609,     10.16797
-------------------------------------------------------------------------------

No other variable met the 0.1000 significance level for entry into the model.
```

```
                          The SAS System                                  2

         Summary of Forward Selection Procedure for Dependent Variable RELMAN

            Variable   Number  Partial    Model
     Step   Entered      In     R**2      R**2      C(p)        F    Prob>F

       1    RELCAP        1     0.1849    0.1849    3.0633    4.9917   0.0360
       2    RELCHECK      2     0.1059    0.2908    2.0666    3.1361   0.0911
       3    ROOMS         3     0.0959    0.3868    1.3521    3.1287   0.0922
```

For each step, the output describes the action taken. In this case, Step 1 selects RELCAP, and an abbreviated output summarizes the resulting model. In the same fashion, the Step 2 adds RELCHECK and Step 3 adds ROOMS. The note at the end of Step 3 indicates that no other variables are added for the stated SLE. The Bounds on condition numbers are provided to detect possible roundoff error. Values in the millions may indicate the presence of a roundoff error (Berk 1977). At the end of the selection is a summary of the selection process.

Remember that the *p* values cannot be taken literally, but you can use them as a measure of relative importance. In the three-variable model, RELCHECK appears to have some importance and the other variables have *p* values sufficiently small to indicate that they should not be ignored. Also, the signs of the coefficients do make sense, in that manpower requirements increase with greater turnover but decrease with overall size (economy of scale) and fewer unused rooms.

This example provides an illustration of the fact that the step-type procedures do not necessarily produce optimum selections.* You can verify this fact by implementing the SELECTION=RSQUARE and CP options, which produces the results in Output 4.13.

---

* In the model using the original variables, all step-type procedures produce the optimum subsets.

Output 4.13
R-SQUARE
Selection with
Redefined
Variables

```
                              The SAS System                               1

         N = 24      Regression Models for Dependent Variable: RELMAN


             R-square      C(p)  Variables in Model
        In

         1   0.1849358   3.0633  RELCAP
         1   0.1558407   3.8866  RELOCC
         1   0.1460384   4.1640  ROOMS
         1   0.1122826   5.1192  RELWINGS
        ------------------------------------------------------------------
         2   0.2969640   1.8934  RELCHECK ROOMS
         2   0.2908417   2.0666  RELCHECK RELCAP
         2   0.2832976   2.2801  RELOCC ROOMS
         2   0.2658832   2.7728  RELOCC RELCAP
        ------------------------------------------------------------------
         3   0.3867733   1.3521  RELCHECK RELCAP ROOMS
         3   0.3477129   2.4573  RELCHECK RELWINGS ROOMS
         3   0.3417358   2.6265  RELCHECK RELWINGS RELCAP
         3   0.3306014   2.9415  RELOCC RELCAP ROOMS
        ------------------------------------------------------------------
         4   0.4115443   2.6512  RELCHECK RELWINGS RELCAP ROOMS
         4   0.4002139   2.9718  RELCHECK RELCOM RELCAP ROOMS
         4   0.3914877   3.2187  RELOCC RELCHECK RELCAP ROOMS
         4   0.3914551   3.2196  RELCHECK RELCAP ROOMS HOURS
        ------------------------------------------------------------------
         5   0.4216847   4.3642  RELCHECK RELCOM RELWINGS RELCAP ROOMS
         5   0.4171831   4.4916  RELOCC RELCHECK RELWINGS RELCAP ROOMS
         5   0.4161815   4.5199  RELCHECK RELWINGS RELCAP ROOMS HOURS
         5   0.4133487   4.6001  RELCHECK RELCOM RELCAP ROOMS HOURS
        ------------------------------------------------------------------
         6   0.4335757   6.0277  RELCHECK RELCOM RELWINGS RELCAP ROOMS HOURS
         6   0.4254512   6.2576  RELOCC RELCHECK RELWINGS RELCAP ROOMS HOURS
         6   0.4221540   6.3509  RELOCC RELCHECK RELCOM RELWINGS RELCAP ROOMS
         6   0.4135690   6.5939  RELOCC RELCHECK RELCOM RELCAP ROOMS HOURS
        ------------------------------------------------------------------
         7   0.4345562   8.0000  RELOCC RELCHECK RELCOM RELWINGS RELCAP ROOMS
                                 HOURS
        ------------------------------------------------------------------
```

This output shows that the optimum two-variable model includes RELCHECK and ROOMS with a C(P) value of 1.8934 while the FORWARD method picked RELCHECK and RELCAP with a C(P) value of 2.0666. Admittedly, the difference is not large, but the FORWARD choice is not optimal. Actually, the BACKWARD method does pick the optimum two-variable model but also picks the definitely nonoptimal one-variable model with ROOMS.

4.4.4   A Strategy for Models with Many Variables

Because SELECTION=RSQUARE allows you to investigate all models, it not only provides the optimum models for all subset sizes, but it also provides information on other subsets that, although not strictly optimal, may be very useful. However, the RSQUARE method simply cannot be used for problems with a large number of variables. In such cases, step-type procedures provide an alternative. An especially attractive alternative is to use both the FORWARD and BACKWARD methods with the SLE and SLS parameters set to provide the entire range (usually SLE=.99 and SLS=.0001). The closeness of agreement of the two methods provides some clues to true optimality: if they are identical it is quite likely that optimality has been achieved.

In addition, these methods may indicate approximately how many variables are needed. Then, for example, if only a few are needed, you may be able to implement the RSQUARE method for that limited number of variables.

4.5 Biased Estimation

Least-squares estimators provide unbiased estimates of parameters. That is, on the average, the estimate targets the true value of the parameter. For some situations, it may be possible to provide a biased estimator that has a smaller variance than does the unbiased estimator. The precision of a biased estimate, called the *mean squared error*, is the square of the bias plus the variance. In some cases, the mean squared error of a biased estimate may be smaller than the variance of the unbiased estimate.

Biased estimation methods appear to be more useful for predicting the response for one sample using models estimated from another sample. One reason for this is that the results of variable selection are often unstable; hence, using the results of a variable selection based on one sample may not provide a good model for another sample from the same population. Biased estimation may also be useful for subsequent variable selection since such a procedure may delete variables because of weak relationships to the response rather than multicollinearity.

Currently, the SAS System has no procedures for performing biased estimation procedures. However, they can be programmed using the IML procedure. Section 4.5.1 presents an example of PROC IML code for a biased estimation method called incomplete principal component regression. A second method called ridge regression is described in Section 4.5.2 "Ridge Regression," but no code is provided.

4.5.1 Incomplete Principal Component Regression

As noted in Section 4.3.2, principal components provide a linear transformation of a set of variables to a new set of uncorrelated variables. Variables in the transformed set having very small variances may be considered as indicators of multicollinearity. The idea behind incomplete principal component regression is to delete from the principal component regression one or more of the transformed variables having small variances and then convert the resulting regression to the original variables.

PROC IML is used here to illustrate incomplete principal component regression with the BOQ data, omitting the outlier observation.

As noted in Section 4.3.2, principal components are normally computed from the correlation matrix, that is, all variables are centered and scaled. You can do this within PROC IML, or create the standardized variable with the STANDARD procedure. Because the latter results in a more easily understood PROC IML code, it is used here. Display 4.1 shows the SAS log where PROC STANDARD is used to create a data set STANDARD containing the standardized variables.

Display 4.1
Standardizing the Variables

```
1    data boq;
2    input id $ occup checkin hours common wings cap rooms manh;
3    *** delete 25***;
4    if _n_ = 25 then delete;
5    cards;

NOTE: The data set WORK.BOQ has 24 observations and 9 variables.
NOTE: The DATA statement used 0.04 CPU seconds and 1522K.

31   ;
32   *** incomplete pc regression ***;
33   *****   standardize to mean zero and standard deviation of unity
34       so that X'X/(n-1)  is the correlation matrix. *****;
35   proc standard data=boq out = stand m=0 s=1;
36   var occup -- rooms manh;
37   run;
```

The next step is to use PROC IML. PRINT statements are used to show the more important results.

The READ statements fetch the standardized variables into matrices **X** and **Y**. The remainder of the steps compute the sample size, number of variables and degrees of freedom, and the matrices of the sums of squares and crossproducts. The principal components are provided by the EIGEN function, which computes the eigenvalues (A) and the coefficients of the transformation (V), as seen in Output 4.14. You can see that the results are identical to those produced by PROC PRINCOMP in Output 4.5. The following code produces Output 4.14.

```
proc iml;
use stand;
read all var {occup checkin hours common wings cap rooms} into x;
read all var {manh} into y;
***** n= sample size df=n-1, p=no vars *****;
n = nrow(x);
df = n-1;
p = ncol (x);
***** compute correlation matrices *****;
corr = x`*x/(n-1);
****** do principal components, a= eigenvalues, v = eigenvectors *****;
call eigen (a,v,corr);
print a v;
```

Output 4.14
Principal Components Provided by EIGEN Function

```
                                                                              1
        A         V
5.0467391 0.4271291 -0.016121 -0.223824 -0.190675 -0.106859 -0.773655 0.3476864
0.7230258 0.3856252 0.1764647 -0.402776 0.2712504 0.7486509 0.1544818 -0.002249
0.6993905 0.2580631 0.8325725 0.4765989 -0.106772 -0.037258 0.0153148 -0.007541
0.3178095 0.3217455 -0.368518 0.6135569 0.6014008 0.0562062 -0.109608 0.0858244
0.1587058 0.362662 -0.369182 0.302495 -0.7074 0.2647161 0.2645511 0.0141673
0.0504897 0.4204329 0.0036616 -0.25678 0.1237858 -0.51081 0.5412682 0.4336658
0.0038397 0.4364053 -0.057519 -0.163207 0.035291 -0.304228 -0.048847 -0.826692
```

You can now compute the complete principal component regression as in Section 4.3.2. To do this, obtain the matrix of component variables and then compute the least-squares regression as illustrated in Output 4.15. The coefficients have different magnitudes from those in Output 4.6 because, for the current procedure, the dependent variable has been standardized. The following code produces Output 4.15.

```
****** compute components and principal component regression *****;
z = x*v;
bpc = inv(z`*z)*z`*y;
print bpc;
```

Output 4.15
Computing the Principal Components

```
                                                                              1
                              BPC
                          0.420948
                          0.0206545
                         -0.239548
                         -0.08854
                          0.234934
                         -0.88204
                          0.2061617
```

The incomplete principal component regression is obtained by deleting the last element of the set of principal component regression coefficients and the last row and column of the set of eigenvectors. This is done with PROC IML by creating submatrices that specify what rows and columns are to be retained. The incomplete principal component regression is obtained by a transformation (Rawlings 1988, p. 347). The results, denoted by B6, are based on the standardized variables and are therefore not directly comparable to the original regression coefficients (see Output 4.1).

These coefficients can be transformed to the original units by using the original data. The code for this transformation and resulting coefficients, denoted by INT and B6S for the intercept and set of coefficients, is shown below. In addition, standard errors and *t* ratios are computed to compare with those of the original regression, although the distribution of the *t* ratios is not strictly comparable to the Student *t* distribution. The names of the coefficients have been added manually for easier comparison. The following code produces Output 4.16:

```
***** delete last component, retaining six *****;
bpc6 = bpc [{1 2 3 4 5 6}];
v6 = v [,{1 2 3 4 5 6}];
***** incomplete principal component regression;
b6 = v6*bpc6;
print b6;
***** standard errors of coefficients***;
***** for variance use MSE from full component regression ***;
mse = (y`*y - bpc`*z`*y)/ (df - p);
zz = z`*z;
zz6 = zz[{1 2 3 4 5 6},{1 2 3 4 5 6}];
stdb6 = sqrt(mse # vecdiag(v6*inv(zz6)*v6`));
print stdb6;
***** rescale to get nonstandardized coefficients *****;
use boq;
read all var {occup checkin hours common wings cap rooms} into x1;
read all var {manh} into y1;
* sumx is row vector *;
sumx = x1[+,];
sumy = y1[+];
sscp = x1`*x1 - sumx`*sumx/n;
ssy  = y1`*y1 - sumy`*sumy/n;
stdx= sqrt(vecdiag (sscp));
stdy= sqrt(ssy);
***** compute coefficients, standard errors and t ratios*****;
b6s = stdy#(b6/stdx);
stdb6s = stdy#(stdb6/stdx);
t6s = b6s/stdb6s;
* intercept*;
int = sumy/n - b6s`*(sumx/n)`;
print int b6s stdb6s t6s;
```

Output 4.16
Computing
Incomplete
Principal
Component
Regression

```
              INT       B6S    STDB6S       T6S
         168.14502 19.504618 2.2632466 8.6179817
                    1.4287048 0.3306619 4.3207417
                   -0.037927 1.1571827 -0.032775
                    5.1972053 6.1293028 0.8479276
                   -5.771248  9.387519 -0.614779
                   -5.373911 1.2118459 -4.434483
                    3.2082454 0.4309398 7.4447639
```

The most striking differences are for the coefficients associated with CAP and ROOMS, which have become much more important. This is, in fact, reasonable, since these variables were involved in the multicollinearities among all the variables associated with the size of the establishments. In fact, the negative coefficient for CAP may now be taken to imply increased manpower cost for excess capacity.

You can also compute the relationship between the incomplete principal component and original regression coefficients (Rawlings 1988, p. 348). The results appear in Output 4.17, which is produced by the following code:

```
***** matrix of coefficients relating OLS to PC coefficients
      see Rawlings, p. 351 ****;
rel = v6*v6`;
print rel;
```

Output 4.17
Computing
Incomplete
Principal
Component
Regression

```
         REL
 0.8791142 0.0007819 0.0026219  -0.02984 -0.004926  -0.15078 0.2874296
 0.0007819 0.9999949 -0.000017  0.000193 0.0000319 0.0009752 -0.001859
 0.0026219 -0.000017 0.9999431 0.0006472 0.0001068 0.0032702 -0.006234
  -0.02984  0.000193 0.0006472 0.9926342 -0.001216 -0.037219 0.0709504
 -0.004926 0.0000319 0.0001068 -0.001216 0.9997993 -0.006144  0.011712
  -0.15078 0.0009752 0.0032702 -0.037219 -0.006144 0.8119339 0.3585081
 0.2874296 -0.001859 -0.006234 0.0709504  0.011712 0.3585081 0.3165804
```

Each row in this matrix consists of the coefficients relating the component regression coefficient to the set of least-squares coefficients. You can see that for coefficients two through five, the relationship is essentially one to one, that is, the coefficients have changed very little. The most interesting relationship involves the last coefficient (ROOMS), which is almost an average of the old coefficients for OCCUP, CAP, and ROOMS.

Deleting additional components is done by changing the specifications when deleting components denoted bpc6, v6, and zz6 in the code preceding Output 4.16. However, deleting the sixth component in this example may not be reasonable since in the full component regression this component appears to be important.

4.5.2 Ridge Regression

The least-squares estimates of a standardized regression are obtained by

$$\hat{\beta} = \mathbf{R}_{xx}^{-1}\mathbf{R}_{xy},$$

where $\mathbf{R}_{xx}$ is the correlation matrix of the independent variables, and $\mathbf{R}_{xy}$ is the one-column matrix of correlations of the independent variables with the dependent variable.

The cause of multicollinearity is the existence of large correlations among the independent variables. If you now add a small constant, call it k, to the diagonal elements of $\mathbf{R}_{xx}$, the effective correlations have all been reduced by the factor $[1/(1+k)]$. The resulting correlation matrix is

$$\mathbf{R}_{xx,k} = \mathbf{R}_{xx}(\mathbf{I} + \mathbf{D}_k)$$

where $\mathbf{D}_k$ is a diagonal matrix with diagonal values of k and can be used to estimate a set of biased regression coefficients:

$$\hat{\beta}_k = [\mathbf{R}_{xx}(\mathbf{I} + \mathbf{D}_k)]^{-1}\mathbf{R}_{xy} \quad.$$

This equation is called a ridge regression estimate.

The larger the value of k, the smaller the effective correlations are among the independent variables, but the larger the bias of the estimates is. The problem in ridge regression is to find some optimum compromise value for k.

The most popular method is to compute ridge regression estimates for a set of values of k starting with $k=0$ (the unbiased estimate). In many applications, a plot of the coefficients against k shows that as the value of k increases from zero, the coefficients involved in multicollinearities change rapidly. However, as k increases further, these coefficients change more slowly until all coefficients tend to get smaller at a rather uniform rate. The selection of k is done by examining such a plot and picking that value of k where the rapid changes cease, that is, where the coefficients settle down. This is a very subjective procedure, and although other more objective procedures have been proposed, none has gained universal acceptance.

As previously indicated, no procedure for performing ridge regression is currently available in the SAS System. It can, however, be programmed with PROC IML, which is not presented here. Actually, ridge regression results are often quite similar to those obtained by incomplete principal components regression.

4.6 Summary

This chapter has presented several methods for detecting multicollinearity and three types of remedial methods for combatting the effects of multicollinearity. It can be argued that the three types have different purposes:

□ Model redefinition, including complete principal components regression, is used to investigate the structure of the relationships.

□ Variable selection is used to find the smallest (most economical) set of variables needed for estimating the dependent variable.

□ Biased estimation is used to find coefficients that have more definite interpretations.

These different objectives are, of course, not mutually exclusive, and most regression analyses involve all of these to some degree. It is, however, useful to keep these in mind when planning a strategy for analysis.

However, because it is the easiest to use, variable selection is the most frequently used method. This is unfortunate, not only because it may be the incorrect strategy, but also because there are some side effects from using variable selection.

The least-squares properties of providing unbiased estimates of the regression coefficients and error variance assume that the true model has been specified. However, models resulting from variable selection may not be the true model; hence, the resulting estimates may not have these favorable properties. In fact, if the selection process deletes variables that are in the true model, it is clear that all estimates are biased. On the other hand, if variables not in the true model have not been deleted, the purpose of variable selection has not been accomplished.

The other negative aspect of variable selection has already been noted, that is, p values obtained with selected models may not be taken literally. There is, in fact, no theory that specifies what the true p values can be, except that they are probably quite a bit larger than those printed by the output.

If variable selection is used, it is important to stress that, if possible, the use of prior information to choose a set of suitable variables is preferable to automated variable selection. In other words, the brute force of the computer is no substitute for knowledge about the data and existing relationships. For example, the relative cost of measuring the different independent variables should have a bearing on which variables to keep in a model that you use to predict values of the dependent variable. Another case in point is the polynomial model where a natural ordering of parameters exists, which suggests a predetermined order of variable selection. See Chapter 5, "Polynomial Models."

An interesting demonstration of how poorly automatic variable selection works is to randomly split a data set into two parts and perform these methods on each part. The differences in the results are often quite striking and informative. For this reason, results of all analyses, and especially those resulting from variable selections, should be interpreted with caution.

Chapter 5 Polynomial Models

5.1 Introduction

In the regression models presented in earlier chapters, all relationships among variables have been described by straight lines. In this chapter, linear regression methods are used to estimate parameters of models that cannot be described by straight lines. The most popular type of model used for this purpose is the *polynomial* model, in which the dependent variable is related to functions of the powers of one or more independent variables.

5.2 Polynomial Models with One Independent Variable

A one-variable polynomial model is defined as follows:

$$y = \beta_0 + \beta_1 x + \beta_2 x^2 + \ldots + \beta_m x^m + \varepsilon$$

where y represents the dependent variable and x the independent variable. The highest exponent, or power, of x used in the model is known as the *degree* of the model, and it is customary for a model of degree m to include all terms with lower powers of the independent variable.

A regression analysis for a polynomial model is performed by using the values of all the required powers of the independent variable as the set of independent variables in a multiple linear regression model. Since the resulting model is linear in the parameters, all statistics and estimates produced by the implementation of that model have the same connotation as in any linear regression analysis, although the practical implications of some of the results may differ.

Polynomial models are primarily used as a means to fit a relatively smooth curve to a set of data. In this situation, the polynomial model itself is of little practical use, and therefore the degree of polynomial required to fit a set of data is not usually known a priori. Therefore, it is customary to build an appropriate polynomial model by sequentially fitting equations with higher order terms until a satisfactory degree of fit has been accomplished. In other words, you start by fitting a simple linear regression of y on x. Then you specify a model with linear and quadratic terms, to ascertain if adding the quadratic term improves the fit by significantly reducing the residual mean square. You can then continue by adding and testing the contribution of a cubic term, then a fourth power term, and so on, until no additional terms are needed.

A polynomial regression model is illustrated here using data collected to determine how growth patterns of fish are related to temperature. A curve describing how an organism grows with time is called a *growth curve*. It usually shows rapid initial growth which gradually becomes slower and may eventually cease. Mathematical biologists have developed many sophisticated models to fit growth curves (see Section 7.3 "Fitting a Growth Curve with the NLIN Procedure"). However, a polynomial model often provides a convenient and easy approximation to such curves.

Fingerlings of a particular species of fish were put into four tanks, that were kept at temperatures of 25, 27, 29, and 31 degrees Celsius, respectively. After 14 days, and weekly thereafter, one fish was randomly selected from each tank and its length was measured. The data from this experiment are given in Output 5.1.*

Output 5.1
Data Set FISH

```
                          The SAS System                          1


        TEMP      25       27       29       31

        AGE


         14      620      625      590      590
         21      910      820      910      910
         28     1315     1215     1305     1205
         35     1635     1515     1730     1605
         42     2120     2110     2140     1915
         49     2300     2320     2725     2035
         56     2600     2805     2890     2140
         63     2925     2940     3685     2520
         70     3110     3255     3920     2710
         77     3315     3620     4325     2870
         84     3535     4015     4410     3020
         91     3710     4235     4485     3025
         98     3935     4315     4515     3030
        105     4145     4435     4480     3025
        112     4465     4495     4520     3040
        119     4510     4475     4545     3177
        126     4530     4535     4525     3180
        133     4545     4520     4560     3180
        140     4570     4600     4565     3257
        147     4605     4600     4626     3166
        154     4600     4600     4566     3214
```

The data set FISH consists of 84 observations containing the variables AGE, TEMP, and LENGTH. The data for the fish kept at 29 degrees are used to approximate the growth curve with a fourth-degree polynomial in AGE for the dependent variable LENGTH. (The entire data set is used later).

The polynomial regression is estimated using PROC REG, with LENGTH as the dependent variable, and AGE, AGE^2, AGE^3, and AGE^4 as independent variables.

---

* To save space, a PUT statement has been used to present the data with each column representing the weights for each temperature.

Before continuing, it is important to point out that the estimation of polynomial regression model might be subject to severe roundoff errors. To counter this problem, you can use the ORTHOREG procedure, which employs special methods to reduce roundoff errors. This procedure was used for this example and produced identical results to those from PROC REG. However, PROC ORTHOREG does not offer any of the various diagnostic and special output options available with PROC REG.

In order to use PROC REG for a polynomial regression, it is first necessary to generate the values of the powers of AGE to use as independent variables. This is done in the following DATA step, which in this case also selects the data for TEMP=29.* This data set is then used for PROC REG as follows:

```
data temp29; set fish;
    if temp = 29;
    asq = age*age;
    acub = age*age*age;
    aqt = asq*asq;
proc reg data=temp29;
    model length = age asq acub aqt / ss1 seqb;
run;
```

The results of these statements appear in Output 5.2.

Output 5.2
Polynomial Regression Using PROC REG

```
                              The SAS System                                1

Model: MODEL1
Dependent Variable: LENGTH

                          Analysis of Variance

                              Sum of        Mean
     Source          DF     Squares        Square      F Value     Prob>F
                                                                     1
     Model            4  38250790.379  9562697.5948     724.314     0.0001
     Error           16   211238.57331  13202.41083
     C Total         20  38462028.952

          Root MSE      114.90174     R-square      0.9945
          Dep Mean     3524.61905     Adj R-sq      0.9931
          C.V.            3.25998

                          Parameter Estimates

                     Parameter      Standard     T for H0:
     Variable   DF    Estimate        Error     Parameter=0    Prob > |T|
                          2
     INTERCEP    1   280.188216   287.02298969      0.976        0.3435
     AGE         1    -2.802825    20.35327746     -0.138        0.8922
     ASQ         1     1.956435     0.45368989      4.312        0.0005
     ACUB        1    -0.021584     0.00394465     -5.472        0.0001
     AQT         1   0.000066279    0.00001167      5.679        0.0001

                                              (continued on next page)
```

---

* Alternately these statements may be used in the DATA step in which the data are initially read.

(continued from previous page)

Variable	DF	Type I SS **3**
INTERCEP	1	260881728
AGE	1	30305600
ASQ	1	7484973
ACUB	1	34496
AQT	1	425721

Sequential Parameter Estimates **4**

INTERCEP	AGE	ASQ	ACUB	AQT
3524.6190476	0	0	0	0
1143.9593074	28.341187384	0	0	0
-816.6419686	90.96908972	-0.372785133	0	0
-1037.459406	103.27930553	-0.545667933	0.0006860429	0
280.18821563	-2.802824794	1.9564354263	-0.021583744	0.0000662791

The bold numbers in Output 5.2 have been added to key the descriptions that follow:

1. The test for the entire model is statistically significant since the *p* value for the test for MODEL is less than 0.0001. The large value for the coefficient of determination (R-SQUARE) is 0.9945 and shows that the model accounts for a large portion of the variation in fish lengths. The residual standard deviation (Root MSE) is 114.9 and indicates how well the fourth-degree polynomial curve fits the data.

2. The Type I sums of squares, often also called *sequential* sums of squares, are used to determine what order of polynomial model is really needed. The Type I sums of squares give the contribution to the MODEL SS for each independent variable as it is added to the model in the order listed in the MODEL statement (see Section 2.4.2 "SS1 and SS2: Two Types of Sums of Squares"). Dividing these Type I sums of squares by the residual mean square provides *F* statistics that are used to test if these additional contributions to the regression sum of squares justify addition of the corresponding terms to the model.*

   In this example, the Type I sum of squares for the linear regression on AGE is 30,305,600; dividing by the residual mean square of 13,202 gives an *F* ratio of 2295.46, which clearly establishes that a linear regression fits better than no regression.** The additional contribution of the quadratic term, designated ASQ, is 7,484,973, and the *F* ratio is 566.94. Therefore, the addition of this term can be justified. The *F* ratio for adding the cubic term is 2.61. This is not statistically significant, so the inclusion of this term cannot be justified. Nevertheless, you can continue to check for additional terms. The

---

* PROC GLM allows the implementation of a polynomial model without having to generate the powers of the independent variable in the DATA step and also gives the *F* ratios for the Type I sums of squares. However, PROC GLM uses more computer resources than PROC REG and also does not have many desirable diagnostic and ouput options for regression. Therefore, it is not the best procedure to use, even if it is a bit more convenient for this purpose.

** The Type I sum of squares for INTERCEP is the correction for the mean. This can be used to test the hypothesis that the mean is zero, which is seldom of interest.

F ratio for adding the fourth-degree term is 32.25, which is significant, providing evidence that this term should be included. You could, of course, continue if you had specified a higher order polynomial in the MODEL statement. However, polynomials beyond the fourth degree are not often used.

3. In this example, it is appropriate to recommend the fourth-degree polynomial. The estimated equation, obtained from the portion of the output labelled Parameter Estimate, is

$$\widehat{\text{LENGTH}} = 280.19 - 2.8028(\text{AGE}) + 1.9564(\text{AGE})^2$$
$$- 0.02158(\text{AGE})^3 + 0.00006628(\text{AGE})^4 \quad .$$

As noted, the polynomial model is only used to approximate a curve. Therefore, the individual polynomial terms have no practical interpretation and the remainder of the statistics for the coefficients are of little interest.[*]

4. If the tests based on the Type I sums of squares had indicated that a lower order polynomial would suffice, the coefficients for such lower order polynomial regression models are found under the heading Sequential Parameter Estimates. These were produced by PROC REG using the MODEL statement option SEQB. In this portion of the output, the first line is the zero-order polynomial, that is, the mean of the dependent variable (3524.62). The second line contains the coefficients of the first-order, or linear, regression:

$$1143.96 + 28.3412(\text{AGE}) \quad .$$

The third line contains the coefficients of the quadratic model, and so on. The last line contains the coefficients of the full, or in this case, the fourth-order polynomial and is the same as the list of coefficients under Parameter Estimate in number 3 above.

5.3 Polynomial Plots

In testing for the appropriate degree of polynomial required to fit the growth curve, you can see that while the fourth-degree term was required, it was also evident that the major improvement in fit occurred with the addition of the quadratic term. A plot illustrating how the fit of a polynomial regression improves with the addition of higher order terms may provide information to help decide if the improvement due to adding additional terms is indeed worthwhile.

---

[*] Remember that a partial regression coefficient is the change in the response due to a unit change in the independent variable, holding constant the other variables. Since it is impossible to change, say, x^2 holding x constant, the coefficients measure relationships that really do not exist.

In order to construct such a plot, you need the estimated values associated with the linear, quadratic, cubic, and fourth-order regression model estimates. This is accomplished with the following statements:

```
proc reg data = temp29;
    model length = age;
    output out=l p=pl r=rl;
    model length = age asq;
    output out=q p=pq r=rq;
    model length = age asq acub;
    output out=c p=pc r=rc;
    model length = age asq acub aqt;
    output out=qt p=pqt r=rqt;
data all; merge l q c qt;
    run;
```

The four MODEL statements are for the linear, quadratic, cubic, and fourth-order polynomial models. The four OUTPUT statements create data sets with the predicted and residual values for these models. The predicted values are PL, PQ, PC, and PQT, respectively. The residual values, RL, RQ, RC, and RQT are used later. The MERGE statement places all of these into one data set named ALL.

The desired plot is produced by the following statement:

```
proc plot data=all;
    plot length*age='*' pl*age='L' pq*age='Q' pc*age='C'
        pqt*age='4' / overlay;
run;
```

Unfortunately, the resulting printer plot does not possess sufficient resolution to illustrate the improvement in fit for the cubic and fourth-order polynomial terms, and it is not reproduced here. Instead, the equivalent plot produced by the GPLOT procedure in SAS/GRAPH software is shown in Output 5.3, using the cubic spline interpolation for the fitted curves.

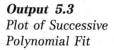

Output 5.3
*Plot of Successive
Polynomial Fit*

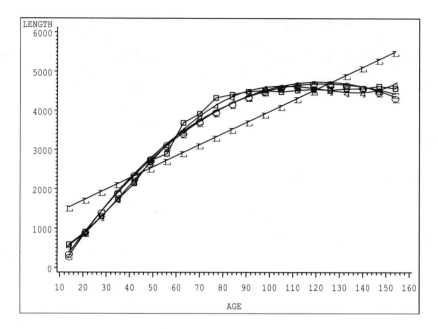

The statements needed to produce this plot, not including those that are hardware specific, are:

```
proc gplot data = all;
   symbol1 v=square i=join;
   symbol2 v=l i=spline ;
   symbol3 v=q i=spline ;
   symbol4 v=c i=spline ;
   symbol5 v=4 i=spline ;
plot
     length*age=1
     pl*age=2
     pq*age=3
     pc*age=4
     pqt*age=5 / overlay;
run;
```

This plot clearly shows the limited improvement due to the cubic and fourth-degree terms. In fact, the fourth-order polynomial curve shows a peculiar hook at the upper end that is not typical of growth curves. Of course, the quadratic curve shows negative growth in this region, so it is also unsatisfactory. In other words, the polynomial model may be unsatisfactory for this data set. Alternate models for use with this data set are presented in Section 7.2.

Another method for checking the appropriateness of a model is to plot the residual values. The plot of residual values from the quadratic polynomial (for which the predicted and residual values are in data set Q) is obtained by the following statements:

```
proc plot data=q;
     plot rq*age / vref=0;
run;
```

The resulting plot, which appears in Output 5.4, shows a systematic pattern that is typical of residual plots when the specified degree of polynomial is inadequate. In this case the W-shaped pattern is due to the fourth-degree term, which was statistically significant.

Output 5.4
Plot of Residuals from Quadratic Model

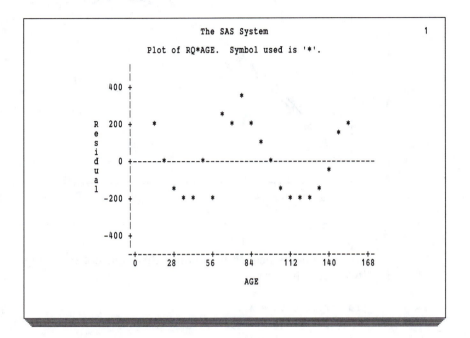

5.4 Polynomial Models with Several Variables

Polynomial models for several variables contain terms involving powers of the various variables as well as crossproducts among these variables. The crossproduct terms measure interactions among the effects of the variables. For example, consider the two variable model:

$$y = \beta_0 + \beta_1 x_1 + \beta_2 x_2 + \beta_{12} x_1 x_2 \quad .$$

The coefficient β_{12} indicates how the linear effect of x_1 is affected by x_2, or vice versa. This is apparent in the following rearrangement of terms:

$$y = \beta_0 + (\beta_1 + \beta_{12} x_2) x_1 + \beta_2 x_2 \quad .$$

The coefficient β_{12} specifies how the linear effect of x_1 changes with x_2. This change is linear in x_2. This effect is referred to as the linear-by-linear interaction. The interaction effect is symmetric since it also shows how the linear coefficient in x_2 is affected by x_1. Crossproducts involving higher order terms have equivalent connotations, although their interpretation might become more difficult.

Regressions using such models can be performed by generating the desired powers and crossproducts variables in the DATA step and implementing a multiple regression analysis using PROC REG.

One consequence of the greater complexity of models with polynomials in several variables is that the sequential sums of square (Type I) are no longer useful in selecting the appropriate degree of model. Likewise, the partial sums of squares (Type II) are of little use since, as was the case for one variable models, it is not customary to omit lower order terms. A similar restriction also applies to crossproduct terms. For example, if a crossproduct of two linear terms has been included, you should include the individual linear terms. In such models, the following questions are of primary interest:

□ Does the entire model help to explain the behavior of the response variable?

□ Are all factors or variables needed?

□ Is there a need for quadratic and higher order terms?

□ Is there a need for crossproduct terms?

□ Is the model adequate?

Obviously, the statistics supplied by a single run of a regression model cannot answer all of these questions.

Since polynomial models with several variables can easily become extremely cumbersome and consequently difficult to interpret, it is common practice to restrict the degree of polynomial terms to be used for such models. The most frequently used model of this type is called the *quadratic response surface model*, in which the maximum total exponent of any term is two. In other words, this model includes all linear and quadratic terms in the individual variables and all pairwise crossproducts of linear terms.

The RSREG procedure (for response surface regression) is the SAS procedure for building and evaluating such a quadratic response surface model. The implementation of this procedure for estimating the response surface regression is illustrated by estimating the quadratic response surface regression relating the LENGTH of fish to AGE and TEMP using the data in Output 5.1.

The procedure is implemented with the following statements:

```
proc rsreg data=fish;
    model length = age temp;
run;
```

Note that the MODEL statement requires only the listing of the dependent and independent variables or factors, because PROC RSREG creates the necessary squares and products variables. For this example, the regression model estimated by the procedure is:

$$\widehat{\text{LENGTH}} = \beta_0 + \beta_1(\text{AGE}) + \beta_2(\text{AGE})^2 + \beta_3(\text{TEMP}) + \beta_4(\text{TEMP})^2 + \beta_5(\text{AGE})(\text{TEMP}) \quad .$$

Options are available in this procedure to create an ouput data set containing predicted, residual, and other statistics associated with individual observations. These options are presented in Section 5.5, "Response Surface Plots." Another option (not illustrated) is the COVARIATES option, which allows the inclusion of variables that are not part of the response surface model. This option is useful for adjusting estimates for experimental conditions. The results of implementing PROC RSREG on the fish data appear in Output 5.5.

Output 5.5
Quadratic
Response Surface
Regression Using
PROC RSREG

```
                              The SAS System                              1

                Coding Coefficients for the Independent Variables

                    Factor    Subtracted off    Divided by

                    AGE          84.000000       70.000000
                    TEMP         28.000000        3.000000
```

```
                              The SAS System                              2
                      Response Surface for Variable LENGTH

                    Response Mean          3153.345238
                    Root MSE                262.038473
                    R-Square                  0.9611
                    Coef. of Variation        8.3099
```

	Regression	Degrees of Freedom	Type I Sum of Squares	R-Square	F-Ratio	Prob > F
2	Linear	2	107867300	0.7835	785.5	0.0000
2	Quadratic	2	21762116	0.1581	158.5	0.0000
3	Crossproduct	1	2682926	0.0195	39.073	0.0000
1	Total Regress	5	132312342	0.9611	385.4	0.0000

	Residual	Degrees of Freedom	Sum of Squares	Mean Square
5	Total Error	78	5355805	68664

Parameter	Degrees of Freedom	Parameter Estimate	Standard Error	T for H0: Parameter=0	Prob > |T|
INTERCEPT	1	-56025	5625.614035	-9.959	0.0000
AGE	1	123.822451	8.988307	13.776	0.0000
TEMP	1	3934.862900	401.275363	9.806	0.0000
AGE*AGE	1	-0.266708	0.017852	-14.940	0.0000
TEMP*AGE	1	-1.885584	0.301652	-6.251	0.0000
TEMP*TEMP	1	-69.205357	7.147685	-9.682	0.0000

Parameter	Parameter Estimate from Coded Data
INTERCEPT	3978.557760
AGE	1835.337662
TEMP	-297.078571
AGE*AGE	-1306.870189
TEMP*AGE	-395.972727
TEMP*TEMP	-622.848214

```
                              The SAS System                              3
```

Factor	Degrees of Freedom	Sum of Squares	Mean Square	F-Ratio	Prob > F
AGE **4**	3	121756815	40585605	591.1	0.0000
TEMP **4**	3	13238453	4412818	64.267	0.0000

```
                        The SAS System                          4

                Canonical Analysis of Response Surface
                       (based on coded data)
                                  6
                              Critical Value
                 Factor        Coded        Uncoded

                 AGE          0.775671     138.296998
                 TEMP        -0.485049      26.544854


         Predicted value at stationary point   4762.416003


                                      Eigenvectors
              Eigenvalues          AGE           TEMP

              -569.675554       -0.259376       0.965776
             -1360.042850        0.965776       0.259376


                 Stationary point is a maximum.
```

Because the interpretation of results from the search for the optimum response (see number 6 below) may be affected by the scales of measurement of the factor variables, they are coded to have maximum and minimum values of $+1$ and -1 for the computations required for this procedure. However, all of the statistics in the output are, except where noted, converted to the original scales.

The bold numbers in Output 5.5 have been added to key the descriptions that follow:

1. The F ratio of 385.39 indicates a statistically significant model, which is supported by an R-SQUARE of 0.96.

2. The need for linear and quadratic terms is established in this portion of the output. The Linear line tests the effectiveness of the model including only the strictly linear terms. The Quadratic line tests the additional contribution of the quadratic terms, $(AGE)^2$ and $(TEMP)^2$. Some linear and quadratic terms are needed, although these statistics do not specify which of these are needed.

3. The test for the crossproduct terms (in this case there is only one) is provided in this line. This term should also be included in the model.

4. The contribution of the variables, or factors, is evaluated in this portion. Here, the AGE line tests the hypothesis that the factor AGE can be omitted from the model. That is, it tests the hypothesis that all terms involving the AGE variable may be omitted without decreasing the fit of the model. The resulting F ratio tests the increase in the residual mean square if all terms involving AGE, namely AGE, $(AGE)^2$, and (AGE)(TEMP) are deleted from the model. Obviously, the factor AGE should not be omitted from the model. Similarly, the TEMP line determines if the factor TEMP can be omitted. Although this factor contributes less than AGE, it also appears to help describe the growth of the fish.

5. The error sum of squares and mean square are given here. A lack-of-fit test for the adequacy of the model is provided in this part of the output if replicated observations exist. Since such observations are not available in this example, only the error mean square is printed. An example of the lack-of-fit test is provided in Section 5.6, "A Three-Factor Response Surface Experiment."

6. Because response surface analysis is sometimes performed to obtain information on optimum estimated response, PROC RSREG also supplies information to assist in determining if the estimated response surface exhibits such an optimum. First, the partial derivatives of the estimated response surface equation are calculated and a stationary point is found. The values of the factors for the stationary point are given in the Critical Values column, and the estimated response at this point is denoted as Predicted Value at Stationary Point. For this example, the stationary points are AGE=138.3 and TEMP=26.5, where the estimated response is 4762.4. The program does not check to see if these values are in the range of data. The critical values are also given for the coded variables. Because the stationary point may be a maximum, minimum, or saddle point, a canonical anlysis is performed to ascertain which of these it is. In this case, the point is a maximum. The eigenvalues and eigenvectors required for the analysis might yield additional information on the shape of the response surface (Myers 1976). See also the RIDGE statement in Section 5.6.

Additional statistics on the output include some overall descriptive measures, the residual sum of squares, and the mean square. Also given are the statistics for coding the factor variables. The various statistics for the individual coefficients, including the coefficients for the coded variables, are given in the columns named Parameter Estimate and Parameter Estimate from Coded Data. However, as before, the statistics for the lower order terms are not particularly useful.

5.5 Response Surface Plots

As in the case of a one-variable polynomial regression, graphic representations can be used to show the nature of the estimated curve. For multidimensional polynomial regressions, such plots are called response surface plots. A popular plot of this type is a contour plot, in which contours of equal response are plotted for a grid of values of the independent variables. Such a plot may be obtained using the PLOT procedure. Also available are three-dimensional representations, which may be performed using the G3D procedure in SAS/GRAPH software.

As an example of a response surface plot, a plot is made for the estimated quadratic response surface for the fish lengths produced in the previous section. In addition, a residual plot might be useful for investigating specification error or detecting possible outliers.

All SAS System plotting procedures construct plots that illustrate relationships among values of variables in a data set. Therefore, in order to produce a response surface plot, it is first necessary to produce a data set of values representing the estimated response for a grid of values of the independent variables to be used in the plot. This is not difficult since, in the SAS System, all regression procedures can produce the estimation of predicted values for data points that are not in the data set used to estimate the regression model.

The first step is to generate the grid of values of the independent variables. The number of grid points required depends on the size of the page used for the output. In this example, the page size allows 80 columns and 50 rows. Allowing for legends and titles, about 30 rows (representing TEMP) and 60 columns (representing AGE) are used for this plot. Plots involving more than two independent variables are presented in Section 5.6.

The following statements produce a grid of values in the F1 data set:

```
data f1;
     do temp = 25 to 31 by .2;
         do age = 10 to 160 by 2.5;
             id = 1;
output; end; end;
run;
```

The data set F1 has 31*61=1891 observations, containing the variables TEMP and AGE, and a variable ID, whose value is unity (the need for this variable is shown later in this section). The next step is to concatenate data set F1 with the original data set:

```
data f2;
     set fish f1;
run;
```

Note that the data set FISH does not have the variable ID, and F1 does not have the variable LENGTH, so these variables are denoted as missing when not available in data set F2. If you now run PROC RSREG on data set F2, the estimation is based on the 72 observations for which the dependent variable is not missing. However predicted values, when requested, are computed for all observations.

The instructions for producing a data set with estimated values and other statistics as well as the format of the resulting output are different for PROC RSREG than for PROC REG or PROC GLM. The following statements are required:

```
proc rsreg data=f2 out=p1;
     model length = age temp /predict residual;
     id id;
run;
```

The PROC RSREG statement must include the option OUT=P1, which specifies that the output data set containing the predicted values is data set P1. The MODEL statement options PREDICT and RESIDUAL request that the output data set contains the predicted and residual values. Other statistics, such as the actual values, confidence intervals, and Cook's D statistic, may be obtained by adding other keywords. For more information, see Chapter 37, "The RSREG Procedure," in the *SAS/STAT User's Guide, Version 6, Fourth Edition, Volume 2*.

The output data set produced by PROC RSREG has a different format than a data set produced by PROC REG. To illustrate this format, the first 20 observations from the data set produced from the instructions given above are reproduced in Output 5.6.

Output 5.6
Partial Listing of
Output Data Set

```
                              The SAS System                        1

         OBS     AGE    TEMP    _TYPE_      LENGTH

          1      14      25     PREDICT      114.61
          2      14      25     RESIDUAL     505.39
          3      21      25     PREDICT      586.04
          4      21      25     RESIDUAL     323.96
          5      28      25     PREDICT     1031.34
          6      28      25     RESIDUAL     283.66
          7      35      25     PREDICT     1450.50
          8      35      25     RESIDUAL     184.50
          9      42      25     PREDICT     1843.53
         10      42      25     RESIDUAL     276.47
         11      49      25     PREDICT     2210.42
         12      49      25     RESIDUAL      89.58
         13      56      25     PREDICT     2551.16
         14      56      25     RESIDUAL      48.84
         15      63      25     PREDICT     2865.78
         16      63      25     RESIDUAL      59.22
         17      70      25     PREDICT     3154.25
         18      70      25     RESIDUAL     -44.25
         19      77      25     PREDICT     3416.59
         20      77      25     RESIDUAL    -101.59
```

The data set P1 has one observation for each statistic requested in the MODEL statement and contains the following variables:

□ the independent variables or factors (AGE and TEMP).

□ a variable called _TYPE_, which identifies the output statistic. In this example, PREDICT and RESIDUAL were requested. Hence, two observations are created for each observation in the input data set. One observation, identified by _TYPE_=PREDICT, has the predicted values and the second observation, identified by _TYPE_=RESIDUAL, contains the residual values. The predicted and residual values are identified by the name of the response variable(s).

□ variables used in a BY or ID statement or COVAR option, which are not used here.

The format for the data set P1 is not directly suitable for each of the desired plots. This is because the data set for the residual plot must contain the predicted and residual values for the originally observed data, while the data set for the contour plot requires only the values of the factor variables and predicted values for the grid data set. The required data sets are created as follows:

```
data plot
     pred (rename=(length=pred))
     resid (rename=(length=resid));
set p1;
     if id = 1 and _type_= 'PREDICT' then output plot;
     else if id = . then do;
          if _type_= 'PREDICT' then output pred;
          if _type_= 'RESIDUAL' then output resid;
     end;
data resid2;
     merge pred resid;
run;
```

The data for the response surface plot, named PLOT, correspond to the original set F1 in which ID=1. Only the factor and predicted values are needed.

The residual plot requires the original data set in which ID=. (missing). For this purpose, the DATA step creates the other two data sets: the data set renamed PRED contains the predicted values, and the data set renamed RESID contains the residual values. Finally, a second DATA step produces data set RESID2 by merging PRED and RESID.* The residual plot is obtained as follows:

```
proc plot data = resid2;
    plot resid*pred / vref = 0;
run;
```

The plot appears in Output 5.7. Although some patterns are apparent in these residuals, they are not sufficiently consistent to identify specification errors.

Output 5.7
Residual Plot

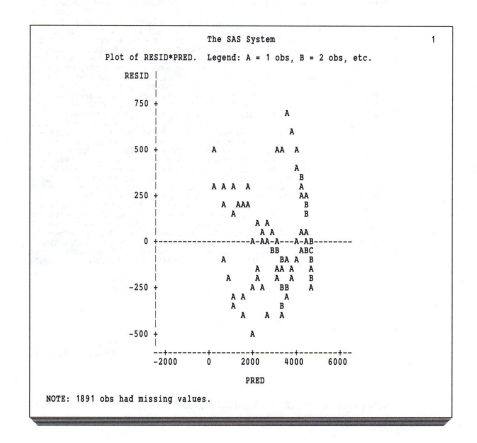

Use the following statements to produce the desired contour plot:

```
proc plot data=plot;
    plot temp*age=length / contour = 8;
run;
```

---

* It is actually somewhat easier to produce these data sets with PROC REG, which has a format for the OUTPUT data set that is easier to use, but then you must remember to create the polynomial variables in both the input and grid data sets.

The PLOT statement specifies TEMP as the row variable and AGE as the column variable. The contours represent the estimated response (LENGTH), with values represented by the symbols specified in the legend at the bottom of the plot. The option CONTOUR=8 specifies a contour plot with eight levels. The resulting plot appears as Output 5.8. The plot shows the growth of fish with age, although the growth becomes negative with increasing age. The plot also shows that fish grow faster at temperatures of 26 to 28 degrees Celsius.

Output 5.8
*Contour Plot of TEMP*AGE*

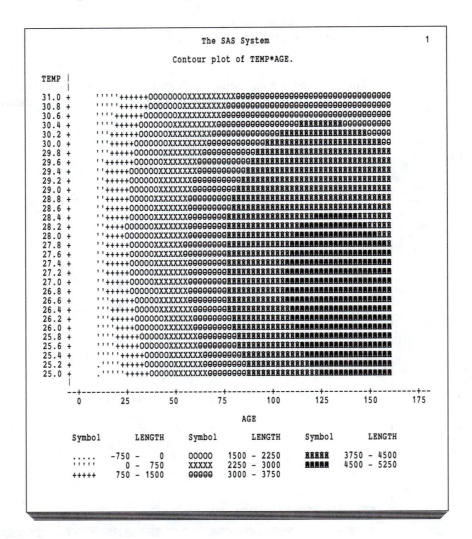

5.6   A Three-Factor Response Surface Experiment

The data for this example come from an experiment concerning a device for automatically shelling peanuts. Dickens and Mason (1962) maintain that

> ... peanuts flow through stationary sheller bars and rest on the grid which has perforations just large enough to pass shelled kernels. The grid is reciprocated and the resulting forces on the peanuts between the moving grid and the stationary bars break open the hulls. ... the problem became one of determining the combination of bar grid spacing, length of stroke and frequency of stroke which would produce the most satisfactory performance. The performance criteria are ... kernel damage, shelling time and unshelled peanuts.

The paper cited above describes three separate experiments; the second one is used for this illustration. The experimental design is a three-factor composite design consisting of 15 points, with 5 additional observations at the center point (Myers 1976). The data consist of responses resulting from the shelling of 1000 grams of peanuts. The factors of the experiment are the following:

LENGTH   length of stroke (inches)

FREQ   frequency of stroke (strokes per minute)

SPACE   bar grid spacing (inches).

The response variables are the following:

TIME   time needed to shell 1000 grams of peanuts (minutes)

UNSHL   unshelled peanuts (grams)

DAMG   damaged peanuts (percent).

Output 5.9 shows the peanut sheller data.

Output 5.9
Peanut Sheller
Data for Response
Surface Analysis

```
                              The SAS System                              1

       OBS    LENGTH    FREQ    SPACE    TIME    UNSHL    DAMG

         1     1.00     175     0.86    16.00     284     3.55
         2     1.25     130     0.63     9.25     149     8.23
         3     1.25     130     1.09    18.00     240     3.15
         4     1.25     220     0.63     4.75     155     5.26
         5     1.25     220     1.09    15.50     197     4.23
         6     1.75     100     0.86    13.00     154     3.54
         7     1.75     175     0.48     3.50     100     8.16
         8     1.75     175     0.86     7.00     176     3.27
         9     1.75     175     0.86     6.25     177     4.38
        10     1.75     175     0.86     6.50     212     3.26
        11     1.75     175     0.86     6.50     200     3.57
        12     1.75     175     0.86     6.50     160     4.65
        13     1.75     175     0.86     6.50     176     4.02
        14     1.75     175     1.23    12.00     195     3.80
        15     1.75     250     0.86     5.00     126     4.05
        16     2.25     130     0.63     4.00      84     9.02
        17     2.25     130     1.09     7.00     145     3.00
        18     2.25     220     0.63     2.25      97     7.41
        19     2.25     220     1.09     5.75     168     3.78
        20     2.50     175     0.86     3.50     168     3.72
```

Because this experiment has six replications at the center point (observations 8 through 13, where LENGTH=1.75, FREQ=175, and SPACE=0.86), you can obtain an estimate of pure error and consequently perform a test for lack of fit. For this example, only the variable UNSHL is analyzed. You might want to perform analyses for the other responses and ponder the problem of multiple responses. The following SAS statements are used:

```
proc sort data=peanuts;
    by length freq space;
proc rsreg data=peanuts;
    model unshl = length freq space / lackfit;
    ridge min;
run;
```

PROC SORT is used to ensure that all observations from the same set of treatment or factor combinations are together (see Output 5.9). When the data are sorted in this manner, the LACKFIT option in the PROC RSREG step computes pure error sum of squares from all observations occurring within identical factor level combinations. In this example, the statistic comes from the six replications identified above.

This sum of squares is subtracted from the residual sum of squares (from the model) to obtain the lack-of-fit sum of squares. This quantity indicates the additional variation that can be explained by adding to the model all additional parameters allowed by the construct of the treatment design. Thus, the ratio of the resulting lack of fit and pure error mean squares provides a test for the possible existence of such additional model terms. In other words, it is a test for the adequacy of the model.

The RIDGE statement is explained below in the section on the canonical analysis. The results of the RSREG procedure appear in Output 5.10.

Output 5.10
PROC RSREG with
LACKFIT Option

```
                         The SAS System                              1

            Coding Coefficients for the Independent Variables

                  Factor      Subtracted off    Divided by

                  LENGTH         1.750000        0.750000
                  FREQ         175.000000       75.000000
                  SPACE          0.855000        0.375000
```

```
                         The SAS System                              2

                  Response Surface for Variable UNSHL

                  Response Mean        168.150000
                  Root MSE             19.222839
                  R-Square              0.9144
                  Coef. of Variation   11.4320


                     Degrees
                        of      Type I Sum
     Regression      Freedom    of Squares    R-Square   F-Ratio   Prob > F

     Linear             3          27642       0.6401    24.936     0.0001
     Quadratic          3          10989       0.2545     9.913     0.0024
     Crossproduct       3        856.375000    0.0198     0.773     0.5354
     Total Regress      9          39487       0.9144    11.874     0.0003
```

1

Residual	Degrees of Freedom	Sum of Squares	Mean Square	F-Ratio	Prob > F
Lack of Fit	5	1903.675307	380.735061	1.063	0.4742
Pure Error	5	1791.500000	358.300000		
Total Error	10	3695.175307	369.517531		

2

Parameter	Degrees of Freedom	Parameter Estimate	Standard Error	T for H0: Parameter=0	Prob > |T|
INTERCEPT	1	-130.386632	210.102546	-0.621	0.5488
LENGTH	1	-319.784414	111.964075	-2.856	0.0171
FREQ	1	3.006709	1.180000	2.548	0.0290
SPACE	1	789.775578	232.083714	3.403	0.0067
LENGTH*LENGTH	1	52.110564	23.973433	2.174	0.0548
FREQ*LENGTH	1	0.405556	0.302058	1.343	0.2091
FREQ*FREQ	1	-0.009684	0.002524	-3.836	0.0033
SPACE*LENGTH	1	-1.086957	59.098259	-0.0184	0.9857
SPACE*FREQ	1	-0.471014	0.656647	-0.717	0.4896
SPACE*SPACE	1	-331.287196	100.067743	-3.311	0.0079

Parameter	Parameter Estimate from Coded Data
INTERCEPT	184.350375
LENGTH	-50.515924
FREQ	-5.684025
SPACE	52.104286
LENGTH*LENGTH	29.312192
FREQ*LENGTH	22.812500
FREQ*FREQ	-54.474119

The SAS System   3

Parameter	Parameter Estimate from Coded Data
SPACE*LENGTH	-0.305707
SPACE*FREQ	-13.247283
SPACE*SPACE	-46.587262

3

Factor	Degrees of Freedom	Sum of Squares	Mean Square	F-Ratio	Prob > F
LENGTH	4	16591	4147.864308	11.225	0.0010
FREQ	4	6462.244483	1615.561121	4.372	0.0266
SPACE	4	17546	4386.601785	11.871	0.0008

4

Canonical Analysis of Response Surface
(based on coded data)

Factor	Critical Value Coded	Uncoded
LENGTH	0.842171	2.381628
FREQ	0.057503	179.312738
SPACE	0.548273	1.060602

Predicted value at stationary point   177.199118

Eigenvalues	LENGTH	Eigenvectors FREQ	SPACE
30.850993	0.990957	0.133509	-0.013376
-43.243358	0.072745	-0.450813	0.889649
-59.356824	-0.112747	0.882578	0.456448

(continued on next page)

(continued from previous page)

```
                    Stationary point is a saddle point.


              Estimated Ridge of Minimum Response for Variable UNSHL


     Coded    Estimated    Standard              Uncoded Factor Values
    Radius    Response      Error       LENGTH        FREQ        SPACE

      0.0    184.350375   7.789077    1.750000    175.000000    0.855000
      0.1    176.949575   7.766784    1.796364    175.374746    0.825583
      0.2    169.149158   7.714192    1.831772    175.248503    0.792137
      0.3    160.752551   7.676618    1.858325    174.550896    0.756422
      0.4    151.620193   7.730364    1.878628    173.258186    0.719767
      0.5    141.657266   7.977460    1.894789    171.369838    0.682995
      0.6    130.797678   8.525890    1.908265    168.898882    0.646596
      0.7    118.992786   9.459711    1.920022    165.870412    0.610878
      0.8    106.204776  10.818957    1.930682    162.321155    0.576038
      0.9     92.403026  12.603536    1.940650    158.297515    0.542198
      1.0     77.562102  14.791640    1.950185    153.852091    0.509420
```

The bold numbers in Output 5.10 have been added to key the descriptions that follow. Numbers 2 through 4 are similar to those in the example in Section 5.4, "Polynomial Models with Several Variables."

1. The residual sum of squares from the nine-term model in the lack-of-fit portion of the output is 3695.1753, with 10 degrees of freedom. The pure error is the sum of squares among the 6 replicated values and has 5 degrees of freedom. The difference, 1903.6753, with 5 degrees of freedom, is the additional sum of squares that could be obtained by adding 5 terms to the model. The F statistic derived from the ratio of the lack of fit to pure error mean square has a p value of 0.4742. You may conclude that additional terms are not needed.

2. The crossproduct terms are not significant, indicating that there are no interactions. In other words, the responses to any one factor have similar shapes across levels of the other factors.

3. The factor FREQ has the smallest effect, in fact, it is not significant at the 0.01 level.

4. The canonical analysis shows that the response surface has a saddle point. This means it has no point at which the response is either maximum or minimum.

Since you are looking for a minimum amount of unshelled peanuts, the existence of a saddle point may be disappointing. Of course it is possible that the saddle point is not well defined and that a broad range of points may provide a guide for finding optimum operating conditions.

The RIDGE statement provides help in determining where optimum operating conditions may occur. This statement produces the ridge of optimum responses. In this example, optimum response means lower values of UNSHL. The following statement provides sets of values of the factor levels producing the fastest decrease in the estimated response starting at the stationary point:

```
ridge min;
```

The results are in the last section of Output 5.10 and show that increasing LENGTH but decreasing FREQ and SPACE lowers the estimated percent of unshelled peanuts. This analysis does not, of course, show what happens to the other response variables.

It is not possible to produce a three-factor response surface plot, but you can produce a plot that represents the response curve for two factors for several levels of the third factor. Since there are three different factor combinations for such plots, you must choose which combination is most useful. Often this decision is not easy to make and several possibilities might have to be explored. In this example, the factor FREQ has the smallest effect, so it appears logical to plot the response to LENGTH and SPACE for selected values of FREQ.

The response surface plot is produced here for LENGTH and SPACE for FREQ values of 175, 200, and 225. The residual plot is also obtained.

As before, you must first generate the data representing the grid of points needed for the response surface plot. Use the following statements:

```
data p1;
    id=1;
        do freq = 175 to 225 by 25;
            do length = 1 to 2.5 by .05;
                do space = .6 to 1.2 by .02;
                    output;
                end;
            end;
        end;
run;
```

The data set P1 consists of a 31-by-31 grid of values of LENGTH and SPACE for three values of FREQ. The data set P1 is concatenated with the original data set and PROC RSREG is used as follows:

```
data p2;
    set peanuts p1;
proc rsreg data=p2 out=p1;
    model unshl = length freq space / predict residual;
    id id;
run;
```

Next, you create the data sets for the plots using the procedure that generated the data for Outputs 5.7 and 5.8.

```
data plot (rename = (unshl = predict))
    p4 (rename = (unshl = predict))
    p5 (rename = (unshl = residual));
set p1;
    if id = 1 and _type_ = 'PREDICT' then output plot;
    if id = . and _type_ = 'PREDICT' then output p4;
    if id = . and _type_ = 'RESIDUAL' then output p5;
run;
data p6;
    merge p4 p5;
run;
```

The data set PLOT contains the predicted values for the grid needed for the response surface plots. The data sets P4 and P5 contain the predicted and residual values for the actual data points, since the variable ID was undefined in that set of data. Finally, sets P4 and P5 are merged to produce the data set P6 required for the residual plot.

The residual plot is constructed with the following statements:

```
proc plot data = p6;
    plot residual*predict / vref = 0;
```

Output 5.11 shows the plot that is produced by the preceding statements.

Output 5.11
Residual Plot

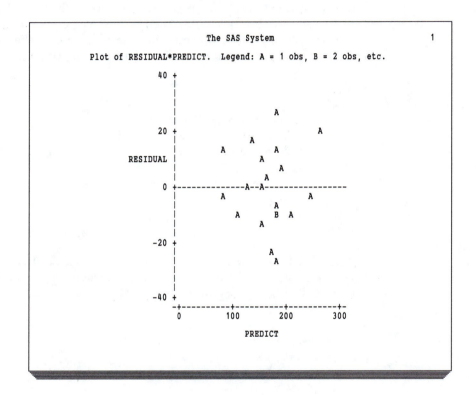

No obvious outliers or specification appear in this plot, confirming the results of the lack-of-fit analysis.

Response surface plots may be produced either by PROC PLOT or PROC G3D in SAS/GRAPH software. For PROC PLOT, the following statements are needed:

```
proc plot data=plot;
    plot length*space = predict / contour = 6;
by freq;
run;
```

For PROC G3D, these statements are needed:

```
proc g3d data=plot;
    plot length*space = predict;
    by freq;
run;
```

Output 5.12 shows the output from PROC G3D.

Output 5.12
Results of PROC G3D

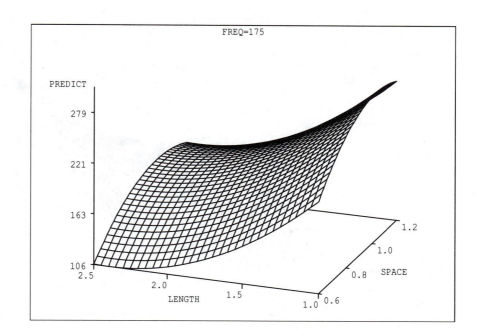

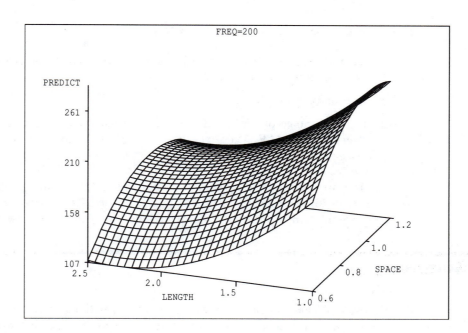

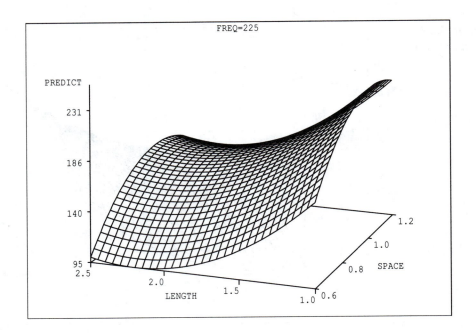

From these plots you can see that

□ the increase in FREQ uniformly increases the percent of unshelled of peanuts by a relatively small amount.

□ the saddle point is not of interest.

□ the percentage of unshelled peanuts decreases with increasing LENGTH and decreasing SPACE. These results confirm the results from the RIDGE statement.

The optimum operating conditions for unshelled peanuts should concentrate in regions of higher FREQ and LENGTH and lower SPACE. However, this recommendation is subject to the behavior of the other response variables.

5.7 Summary

Polynomial models provide reasonable approximations to response models that cannot be described by straight lines. In the SAS System, they can be analyzed with PROC REG and PROC RSREG, although PROC GLM can also be useful since it allows the use of polynomial terms in the model and is the procedure of choice if there are to be indicator variables for more than two groups (for example, blocks or replications).

An important limitation of polynomial models is that they only provide approximations to a curve, and the model coefficients usually have no practical interpretation. Therefore, if you want a regression where the coefficients have practical interpretation, you might need to look for other types of models. Some of these are explored in Chapter 6, "Special Applications of Linear Models," and Chapter 7, "Nonlinear Models."

Chapter 6 Special Applications of Linear Models

6.1 Introduction

In Chapter 5, "Polynomial Models," you are introduced to the use of polynomial models to analyze relationships that cannot be described by straight lines. Although these polynomial models are very useful, they cannot provide adequate descriptions for all types of relationships. For example, in the data on fish growth, the polynomial model provided a statistically significant fit, but the plot of the resulting curve, even for the fourth-order polynomial, showed some features that did not fit the desired characteristics for such a curve. A number of other regression methods are available for such cases.

Methods presented in this chapter may be analyzed with the SAS System by adaptations and options of the standard linear regression procedures available in the REG procedure. In Chapter 7, "Nonlinear Models," you are introduced to the estimation of models that cannot be analyzed in this manner.

Models presented in this chapter include

☐ log-linear models, where logarithms in a linear regression model provide for estimating a multiplicative model

☐ spline functions, which allow different functions, usually polynomial models, to be fitted for different regions of the data

☐ indicator variables, which provide for the estimation of the effect of binary categorical variables.

6.2 Log-Linear (Multiplicative) Models

A linear regression model using the logarithms of the variables is equivalent to estimating a multiplicative model.* The log linear model:

$$\log(y) = \beta_0 + \beta_1(\log(x_1)) + \beta_2(\log(x_2)) + \beta_m(\log(x_m)) + \varepsilon$$

---

* Either base 10 or base e may be used with identical results except for a change in the definition of the intercept. Base e is used in all examples.

is equivalent to the model:

$$y = (e^{\beta 0})(x_1^{\beta 1})\,(x_2^{\beta 2}) \ldots (x_m^{\beta m})\,(e^\varepsilon) \quad .$$

In this multiplicative model the coefficients or *elasticities* measure the percent change in the dependent variable associated with a one percent change in the corresponding independent variable, holding constant all other variables. The intercept is a scaling factor. The error component in this model is also multiplicative and exhibits variation which is proportional to the magnitude of the dependent variable (Myers 1990, Section 7.1).

The log-linear model is illustrated with an example in which the weight of lumber is to be estimated from external measurements of the trees. The data set PINES contains information on a sample of individual pine trees. The dependent variable WEIGHT represents the weight of lumber from a tree. The four independent variables are

HEIGHT	the height of the tree
DBH	the diameter of the tree at breast height (about four feet)
AGE	the age of the tree
GRAV	a measure of the specific gravity of the tree.

Obviously, the first two variables are relatively easy to measure; hence, a model for predicting tree weights using these variables could provide a low-cost estimate of timber yield. The other two variables are included to see if their addition to the model provides for better prediction. Output 6.1 shows the data for estimating tree weights.

Output 6.1
Data for
Estimating Tree
Weights

```
                            The SAS System                              1

         OBS     DBH    HEIGHT    AGE     GRAV     WEIGHT

          1      5.7      34      10     0.409      174
          2      8.1      68      17     0.501      745
          3      8.3      70      17     0.445      814
          4      7.0      54      17     0.442      408
          5      6.2      37      12     0.353      226
          6     11.4      79      27     0.429     1675
          7     11.6      70      26     0.497     1491
          8      4.5      37      12     0.380      121
          9      3.5      32      15     0.420       58
         10      6.2      45      15     0.449      278
         11      5.7      48      20     0.471      220
         12      6.0      57      20     0.447      342
         13      5.6      40      20     0.439      209
         14      4.0      44      27     0.394       84
         15      6.7      52      21     0.422      313
         16      4.0      38      27     0.496       60
         17     12.1      74      27     0.476     1692
         18      4.5      37      12     0.382       74
         19      8.6      60      23     0.502      515
         20      9.3      63      18     0.458      766
         21      6.5      57      18     0.474      345
         22      5.6      46      12     0.413      210
         23      4.3      41      12     0.382      100
         24      4.5      42      12     0.457      122
         25      7.7      64      19     0.478      539
         26      8.8      70      22     0.496      815
         27      5.0      53      23     0.485      194
         28      5.4      61      23     0.488      280
         29      6.0      56      23     0.435      296
         30      7.4      52      14     0.474      462
         31      5.6      48      19     0.441      200
         32      5.5      50      19     0.506      229
         33      4.3      50      19     0.410      125
```

```
        34    4.2    31    10    0.412     84
        35    3.7    27    10    0.418     70
        36    6.1    39    10    0.470    224
        37    3.9    35    19    0.426     99
        38    5.2    48    13    0.436    200
        39    5.6    47    13    0.472    214
        40    7.8    69    13    0.470    712
        41    6.1    49    13    0.464    297
        42    6.1    44    13    0.450    238
        43    4.0    34    13    0.424     89
        44    4.0    38    13    0.407     76
        45    8.0    61    13    0.508    614
        46    5.2    47    13    0.432    194
        47    3.7    33    13    0.389     66
```

As an initial step you can use a linear regression model and make provisions for a residual plot. The required SAS statements are

```
proc reg data=pines;
    model weight = height dbh age grav;
    output out=a p=pw r=rw;
proc plot data=a;
    plot rw*pw / vref=0;
run;
```

The results are shown in Output 6.2.

Output 6.2
PROC REG Output for the Linear Model

```
                        The SAS System                        1
Model: MODEL1
Dependent Variable: WEIGHT

                      Analysis of Variance

                            Sum of        Mean
        Source      DF     Squares       Square     F Value    Prob>F

        Model        4  6570094.5938  1642523.6485   124.059    0.0001
        Error       42   556075.95939   13239.90379
        C Total     46  7126170.5532

            Root MSE       115.06478     R-square      0.9220
            Dep Mean       369.34043     Adj R-sq      0.9145
            C.V.            31.15413

                      Parameter Estimates

                    Parameter      Standard     T for H0:
        Variable  DF   Estimate        Error   Parameter=0    Prob > |T|

        INTERCEP   1  -379.248220  206.69095392    -1.835        0.0736
        DBH        1   170.220326   16.23793314    10.483        0.0001
        HEIGHT     1     1.900155    3.01673726     0.630        0.5322
        AGE        1     8.145835    4.02036310     2.026        0.0491
        GRAV       1 -1192.868482  548.92714717    -2.173        0.0355
```

The model does fit rather well, and the coefficients have the expected signs. Surprisingly, however, the HEIGHT coefficient is not statistically significant. Furthermore, the significance of both the AGE and GRAV coefficients ($\alpha = 0.05$) indicate that the model using only the two-dimensional measurements is inadequate. Finally, the residual plot (see Output 6.3) shows a pattern which suggests a poorly specified model.

Output 6.3
Residual Plot,
Linear Model

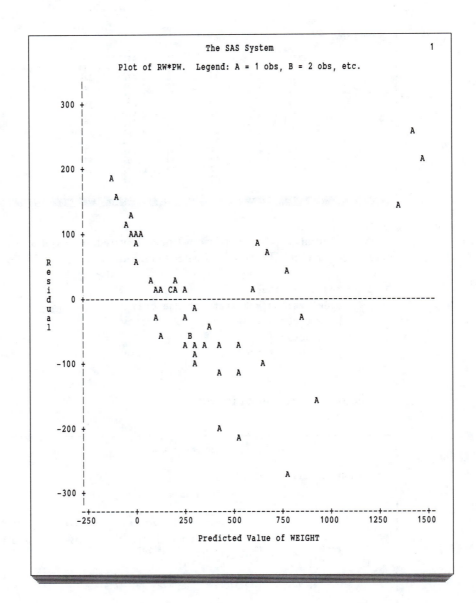

The pattern indicates the need for a curvilinear form such as, for example, a quadratic response function, as well as the possibility of heterogeneous variances. In this case, however, a multiplicative model is more suitable. The amount of lumber in a tree is a function of the volume of the trunk, which is in the shape of a cylinder. The volume of a cylinder is $\pi r^2 h$, where r is the radius and h the height of the cylinder. Thus, a multiplicative model for volume or weight using radius (or diameter) and height is appropriate. Furthermore, it is also reasonable to expect that age and gravity have a relative, or multiplicative effect. A log-linear model is used to estimate such a multiplicative model.

The log-linear model is implemented by obtaining the logarithms of the observed values in a DATA step:

```
data log; set pines;
    array x dbh -- weight;
    array l ldbh lheight lage lgrav lweight;
do over x;
    l = log(x);
end;
run;
```

The new variables, LDBH through LWEIGHT, are now available for use in the log-linear model. You can now use these variables with PROC REG and make provisions for the residual plot by creating a data set with PLW and RLW being the predicted and residual values for the log-linear model as follows:

```
proc reg data=log;
    model lweight = ldbh lheight lage lgrav ;
output out = b p=plw r=rlw;
proc plot data=b;
    plot rlw*plw / vref = 0;
run;
```

Output 6.4 shows the output from PROC REG.

Output 6.4
PROC REG Output for Log-Linear Model

```
                              The SAS System                              1
Model: MODEL1
Dependent Variable: LWEIGHT

                         Analysis of Variance

                            Sum of        Mean
    Source         DF      Squares       Square      F Value      Prob>F

    Model           4     36.58763      9.14691      572.856      0.0001
    Error          42      0.67062      0.01597
    C Total        46     37.25825

         Root MSE       0.12636     R-square       0.9820
         Dep Mean       5.49466     Adj R-sq       0.9803
         C.V.           2.29971

                         Parameter Estimates

                    Parameter      Standard     T for H0:
    Variable  DF     Estimate         Error    Parameter=0      Prob > |T|

    INTERCEP   1    -1.558233    0.56527317       -2.757          0.0086
    LDBH       1     2.144778    0.11910546       18.007          0.0001
    LHEIGHT    1     0.977846    0.16960799        5.765          0.0001
    LAGE       1    -0.155092    0.08050407       -1.927          0.0608
    LGRAV      1     0.107748    0.26746579        0.403          0.6891
```

Note that although R^2 and F statistics are not strictly comparable between the linear and log-linear models, it appears that the overall fit of this model is much better than that of the linear model. Furthermore, both the LDBH and LHEIGHT coefficients are highly significant, while neither of the other variables contributes significantly. Finally, the coefficients for LDBH and LHEIGHT are quite close to 2 and unity, respectively, which are the values you would expect with a model based on the cylindrical shape of the tree trunk.

Output 6.5
Estimating Tree
Weights: Residual
Plot, Log Model

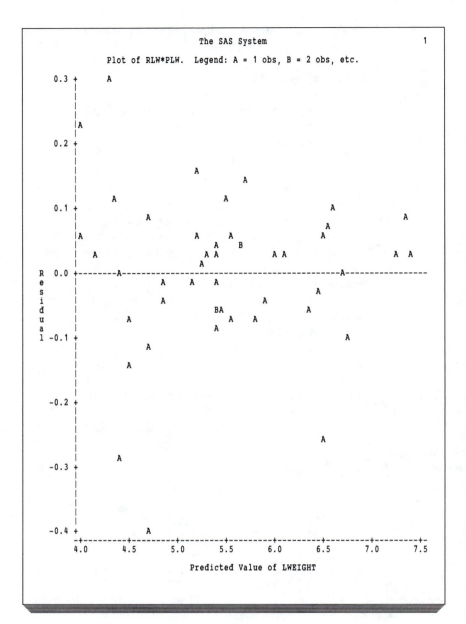

The residuals from this model (see Output 6.5) appear to show virtually no patterns suggesting specification errors. There are some suspiciously large residuals for some of the smaller values of the predicted values that may require further scrutiny. Of course, these residuals show *relative* errors and therefore do not necessarily correspond to large absolute residuals. You can use additional procedures for examining residuals as presented in Chapter 3, "Observations."

It may be of interest to see how well the log-linear model estimates actual weights rather than logarithms of weights. You can do this by taking antilogs of the predicted values from the log-linear model. This is done in a new DATA step:

```
data resid; set b;
    pmw = exp(plw);
    rmw = weight - pmw;
```

The variable PMW is the antilog of the predicted logarithm weights obtained by use of the EXP function, and RMW is the resulting residuals. Using the MEANS procedure to obtain the mean and sum of squares of these residuals, you obtain the following results:

```
mean residual = 3.970
sum of squares = 77,001
```

You can see that the sum of residuals is not zero, which illustrates the well known fact that estimated or predicted values obtained in this manner are biased. However, the residual sum of squares is smaller than that obtained by the linear model. Output 6.6 shows the plot of these residuals.

Output 6.6
Residual Plot:
Exponentiated Log
Residuals

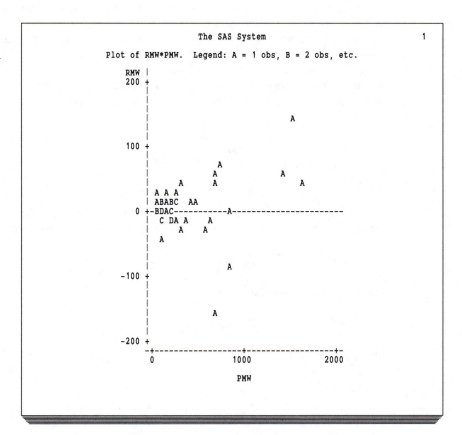

These residuals do not have the obvious specification error pattern exhibited by the residuals of the linear model. They do, however, show the typical pattern of multiplicative errors, where larger residuals are associated with larger values of the response variable.

6.3 Spline Models

In a review paper on spline models, Smith (1979) gives the following definition:

> Splines are generally defined to be piecewise polynomials of degree *n* whose function values and first (n-1) derivatives agree at points where they join. The abscissas of these joint points are called knots. Polynomials may be considered a special case of splines with no knots, and piecewise (sometimes also called grafted or segmented) polynomials with fewer than the maximum number of continuity restrictions may also be considered splines. The number and degrees of polynomial pieces and the number and position of knots may vary in different situations.

First consider splines with known knots, that is, splines for which the values of the independent variable are known for the joint points. Fitting spline models with known knots is much easier than with unknown knots, because with known knots you can use linear regression methods. Estimation of spline models with unknown knots requires the use of nonlinear methods, which are described in Chapter 7.

You can fit a spline of two straight lines with known knots to the fish growth at 29 degrees, as presented in Output 5.1. Judging from the plot in Output 5.3, the rate of increase is roughly constant until about AGE=80, at which point growth appears to stop abruptly. A linear spline with knot at AGE=80 would appear to be suitable for these data.

In order to perform a regression analysis, you need to write a linear regression equation to represent the spline model. Define a variable, AGEPLUS, as follows:

```
data spline; set temp29;
    ageplus = max (age - 80, 0);
run;
```

The MAX function returns the maximum of the two values specified in the argument. Next, represent the spline model with the regression equation

$$\text{LENGTH} = \beta_0 + \beta_1 * \text{AGE} + \beta_2 * \text{AGEPLUS} + \varepsilon$$

which defines the relationship

$$\text{LENGTH} = \beta_0 + \beta_1 * \text{AGE} + \varepsilon$$

for AGE<80, and

$$\text{LENGTH} = \beta_0 + \beta_1 \text{AGE} + \beta_2 (\text{AGE} - 80) + \varepsilon$$

or equivalently,

$$\text{LENGTH} = (\beta_0 - 80 * \beta_2) + (\beta_1 + \beta_2)\text{AGE} + \varepsilon$$

for AGE>80. Notice that both expressions give the same estimated LENGTH when AGE=80. In other words, the two line segments are joined at AGE=80. The SAS statements for performing the regression are

```
proc reg data=spline;
  model length = age ageplus;
run;
```

Results appear in Output 6.7.

Output 6.7
Linear Spline
Regression

```
                             The SAS System                              1

Model: MODEL1
Dependent Variable: LENGTH

                          Analysis of Variance

                        Sum of          Mean
     Source       DF    Squares        Square      F Value    Prob>F

     Model         2  38350272.549  19175136.275   3088.436    0.0001
     Error        18   111756.40333    6208.68907
     C Total      20  38462028.952

            Root MSE      78.79524     R-square      0.9971
            Dep Mean    3524.61905     Adj R-sq      0.9968
            C.V.           2.23557

                          Parameter Estimates

                     Parameter      Standard     T for H0:
     Variable   DF    Estimate        Error    Parameter=0   Prob > |T|

     INTERCEP    1  -327.618142   55.92915483     -5.858       0.0001
     AGE         1    60.175312    0.97297632     61.847       0.0001
     AGEPLUS     1   -58.863098    1.63526781    -35.996       0.0001
```

The fitted equation is

$$\widehat{\text{LENGTH}} = -327.62 + 60.18\ \text{AGE} - 58.86\ \text{AGEPLUS} \quad .$$

Therefore the fitted spline model for AGE<80 is

$$\widehat{\text{LENGTH}} = -327.62 + 60.18\ \text{AGE}$$

and

$$\widehat{\text{LENGTH}} = (-327.62 + 58.86*80) + (60.18 - 58.85)*\text{AGE}$$
$$= 4376.38 + 1.32*\text{AGE}$$

for AGE>80. Notice the small slope of 1.32 for AGE>80.

Although a formal test is not available, you can compare the fit of the linear spline to the fit of the fourth-degree polynomial used in Chapter 5. In Output 6.7, you see MS(ERROR)=6208 for the linear spline, while in Output 5.2 you see MS(ERROR)=13,202 for the fourth-degree polynomial, thus indicating a better fit for the spline function.

It is often useful to fit splines that have additional conditions imposed on their parameters. For example, you may wish to impose the condition on the fish growth spline that it is flat beyond AGE=80, that is, restrict the slope to be zero for AGE>80. From the general expression for the model for AGE>80, you see that the slope is $\beta_1 + \beta_2$. Thus, you would want to restrict $\beta_1 + \beta_2 = 0$. You can do this in the REG procedure with the following statements:

```
proc reg;
  model length = age ageplus;
  restrict age + ageplus = 0;
run;
```

Output 6.8
Linear Spline Regression with Zero Slope after 80

```
                              The SAS System                              1

Model: MODEL1
NOTE: Restrictions have been applied to parameter estimates.
Dependent Variable: LENGTH

                          Analysis of Variance

                            Sum of        Mean
        Source       DF    Squares       Square     F Value    Prob>F

        Model         1 38335595.263 38335595.263   5760.935    0.0001
        Error        19 126433.68946   6654.40471
        C Total      20 38462028.952

            Root MSE      81.57453     R-square     0.9967
            Dep Mean    3524.61905     Adj R-sq     0.9965
            C.V.           2.31442

                          Parameter Estimates

                       Parameter     Standard    T for H0:
        Variable  DF    Estimate       Error    Parameter=0   Prob > |T|

        INTERCEP   1  -358.018766   54.16287966    -6.610       0.0001
        AGE        1    61.075202    0.80467111    75.901       0.0001
        AGEPLUS    1   -61.075202    0.80467111   -75.901       0.0001
        RESTRICT  -1        11185  7531.3508254     1.485       0.1539
```

Results in Output 6.8 produce the fitted model

$$\widehat{LENGTH} = -358.02 + 61.08*AGE - 61.08*AGEPLUS \quad .$$

For AGE<80, you get

$$\widehat{LENGTH} = -358.02 + 61.08*AGE$$

and for AGE>80, you get

$$\widehat{LENGTH} = (-358.02 + 61.08*80), \text{ which equals } 4528.38.$$

This restricted spline model naturally has a larger SS(ERROR) than the unrestricted model (compare MS(ERROR)=6209 in Output 6.7 with MS(ERROR)=6654 in Output 6.8), but the difference is not very large because the slope for the unrestricted model is quite close to zero. The *t* test in Output 6.8 labeled RESTRICT under the variable list has value $t=1.485$ with significance probability $p=0.1539$. This is a test of the hypothesis $H_0: \beta_1 + \beta_2 = 0$. As pointed out earlier, $H_0: \beta_1 + \beta_2$ is the slope of the function for AGE>80. The *p* value of

0.1539 indicates that this slope is not significantly different from zero, so the model with flat response past AGE=80 seems appropriate.

Linear spline models are sometimes criticized because the abrupt change in trend going from one segment to the next does not represent what would naturally occur. The *true* change in trend should be smooth. In mathematical terms, this means the fitted function should have a continuous derivative at each value of the independent variable. This is not possible for linear splines, but it is possible for quadratic splines that are joined segments of parabolas.

The general equation for a quadratic spline function for the fish growth data is

$$\text{LENGTH} = \beta_0 + \beta_1 {}^*\text{AGE} + \beta_2 {}^*\text{AGEPLUS} + \beta_3 {}^*\text{AGE2} + \beta_4 {}^*\text{AGEPL2} + \varepsilon$$

where AGEPLUS is as defined in the linear spline and AGEPL2 is the square of AGEPLUS. Using these definitions, the equation for AGE<80 is

$$\text{LENGTH} = \beta_0 + \beta_1 {}^*\text{AGE} + \beta_3 {}^*\text{AGE2} + \varepsilon$$

and for AGE>80 the equation is

$$\text{LENGTH} = \beta_0 + \beta_1 {}^*\text{AGE} + \beta_2 {}^*(\text{AGE} - 80) + \beta_3 {}^*\text{AGE2} + \beta_4 {}^*(\text{AGE} - 80)^2 + \varepsilon \quad .$$

Collecting terms, this becomes

$$\text{LENGTH} = (\beta_0 - 80 {}^*\beta_2 + 80^2 {}^*\beta_4) + (\beta_1 + \beta_2 - 160 {}^*\beta_4) {}^*\text{AGE} + (\beta_3 + \beta_4) {}^*\text{AGE}^2 + \varepsilon \quad .$$

Checking for the continuity condition, the derivative of the function with respect to AGE (ignoring ε) for AGE<80 is

$$\beta_1 + 2\beta_3 {}^*\text{AGE}$$

and for AGE>80 the derivative is

$$(\beta_1 + \beta_2 - 160\beta_4) + 2(\beta_3 + \beta_4) {}^*\text{AGE} \quad .$$

Requiring the derivative to be continuous (in other words the quadratic spline function must be smooth) means the two derivative expressions must be equal at the knot (AGE=80). Setting them equal gives

$$(\beta_1 + \beta_2 - 160\beta_4) + 2 {}^*80(\beta_3 + \beta_4) = \beta_1 + 2 {}^*80\beta_3$$

which requires that $\beta_2 = 0$.

To fit the quadratic spline model to the fish growth data, you must first create the SAS variables AGESQ=AGE*AGE and AGEPLSQ=AGEPLUS*AGEPLUS in a DATA step and perform the regression:

```
data quad; set spline;
    agesq = age*age;
    ageplsq = ageplus*ageplus;
 proc reg data=quad;
   model length = age agesq ageplsq ageplus / p;
   restrict ageplus=0;
 run;
```

In this example, the RESTRICT statement produces results equivalent to leaving AGEPLUS out of the model. The advantage of using the RESTRICT statement is that you get a test for the effect of the restriction.

Output 6.9
Quadratic Spline with Continuous Derivative

```
                            The SAS System                              1

Model: MODEL1
NOTE: Restrictions have been applied to parameter estimates.
Dependent Variable: LENGTH

                        Analysis of Variance

                            Sum of        Mean
    Source          DF     Squares       Square     F Value      Prob>F

    Model            3   37822813.9  12607604.633    335.301      0.0001
    Error           17  639215.05193  37600.88541
    C Total         20  38462028.952

         Root MSE     193.90948     R-square     0.9834
         Dep Mean    3524.61905     Adj R-sq     0.9804
         C.V.           5.50157

                        Parameter Estimates

                  Parameter      Standard   T for H0:
    Variable  DF   Estimate         Error   Parameter=0    Prob > |T|

    INTERCEP   1  -987.158754  249.08298671    -3.963       0.0010
    AGE        1    99.008878    9.80225580    10.101        0.0001
    AGESQ      1    -0.445513    0.08286643    -5.376        0.0001
    AGEPLSQ    1     0.131968    0.14251631     0.926        0.3674
    AGEPLUS    1  -7.10543E-15   0.00000000     .            .
    RESTRICT  -1  -8617.752200 2296.8552650    -3.752        0.0016
```

Results in Output 6.9 show MS(ERROR)=37601, up from 6208 for the linear spline. This is an unacceptable increase in MS(ERROR) and should result in rejection of the quadratic spline model with a continuous derivative. This conclusion is supported by the test for the restriction required to assure continuous derivative which has a p value of 0.0016. Thus the quadratic spline, with conditions imposed to make the derivative continuous, is not a viable model.

The reason for the poorer fit is revealed by a residual plot, which you can get by adding the following interactive statement:

```
plot r.*age / vplots = 2;
run;
```

Output 6.10
Residual Plot for
Quadratic Spline
with Continuous
Derivative

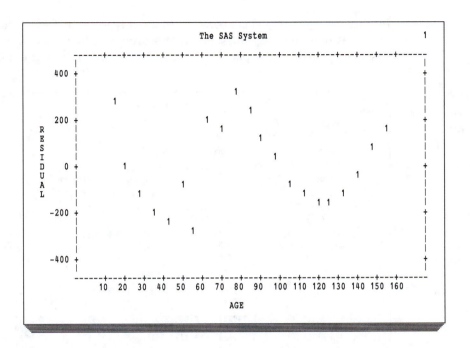

Output 6.10 shows a definite cycling of residuals, which is due to the requirement of a smooth transition of growth between the two segments, a condition that is not supported by the data.

6.4 Indicator Variables

The independent variables in a regression model are usally quantitative; that is, they have a defined scale of measurement. Occasionally, you may need to include qualitative or categorical variables in such a model. This can be accomplished by the use of indicator or dummy variables.

The example in Chapter 2 concerned a model for determining operating costs of airlines. It has been argued that long-haul airlines have lower operating costs than do short-haul airlines. Recall the variable TYPE shown in Output 2.1. This variable is an indicator (sometimes called dummy) variable that classifies airlines into two groups or classes. TYPE=0 defines the short-haul lines with average stage length of less than 1200 miles and TYPE=1 defines the long-haul lines that have average stage lengths of 1200 miles or longer.* Use PROC REG with the following statements:

```
proc reg;
    model cpm = utl spa alf type;
```

When TYPE=0, INTERCEP is the intercept for the model describing the short-haul lines. When TYPE=1, that is for the long-haul lines, the intercept is the sum of the INTERCEP and TYPE coefficients. The other coefficients are the same for both classes; hence, the TYPE coefficient simply estimates the difference

---

* This is an arbitrary definition used for this example.

in levels of operating costs between the two types of airlines regardless of the values of the other variables. In other words, you have estimated a model describing two parallel planes. The results appear in Output 6.11.

Output 6.11
Using an Indicator
Variable for an
Intercept Shift

```
                              The SAS System                              1

Model: MODEL1
Dependent Variable: CPM

                          Analysis of Variance

                              Sum of        Mean
         Source        DF     Squares      Square     F Value    Prob>F

         Model          4     6.04854     1.51214       8.676    0.0001
         Error         28     4.88013     0.17429
         C Total       32    10.92867

              Root MSE       0.41748     R-square      0.5535
              Dep Mean       3.10570     Adj R-sq      0.4897
              C.V.          13.44243

                          Parameter Estimates

                        Parameter      Standard    T for H0:
         Variable  DF     Estimate        Error    Parameter=0   Prob > |T|

         INTERCEP   1     7.748627     0.86312958      8.977      0.0001
         UTL        1    -0.139966     0.05620797     -2.490      0.0190
         SPA        1    -3.553836     1.12221061     -3.167      0.0037
         ALF        1    -6.236224     1.32043284     -4.723      0.0001
         TYPE       1     0.016729     0.18130634      0.092      0.9271
```

The positive coefficient for TYPE indicates higher costs for the long-haul lines. However, it is not statistically significant; hence, there is insufficient evidence of a difference in operating costs between the two types of airlines. The other coefficients are interpreted as before and have, in fact, quite similar values to those of the original model. This is to be expected with the insignificant TYPE coefficient.

The inclusion of the indicator variable only estimates a difference in the average operating cost, but it does not address the possibility that the relationships of cost to the various operating factors differ between types. Such a difference can be estimated by including in a model variables that are products of the indicator and continuous variables.

A simple example illustrates this principle. Assume the following model:

$$y = \beta_0 + \beta_1 x_1 + \beta_2 x_2 + \beta_3 x_1 x_2$$

where x_1 is a continuous variable, and x_2 is an indicator variable with values 0 and 1 identifying two classes.

Then, for the first class ($x_2 = 0$), the model equation is

$$y = \beta_0 + \beta_1 x_1$$

while for the other class ($x_2 = 1$), the model equation is

$$y = (\beta_0 + \beta_2) + (\beta_1 + \beta_3)x_1 \quad .$$

In other words, the slope of the regression of y on x_1 is β_1 for the first class and ($\beta_1 + \beta_3$) for the second class. Thus β_3 is the difference in the regression coefficient between the two classes. This coefficient is sometimes referred to as a slope shift coefficient, as it allows the slope coefficient to shift from one class to the next.

You can use this principle to estimate different regression coefficients for the two types of airlines for the three cost factors. You need to create three additional variables in a DATA step and then perform the regression:

```
data prod; set air;
    utltp = utl*type;
    spatp = spa*type;
    alftp = alf*type;
proc reg;
    model cpm = utl spa alf type utltp spatp alftp / vif;
    alldiff : test utltp,spatp,alftp;
run;
```

Three features of the model are of interest:

□ The TYPE variable must be included. Leaving this variable out is equivalent to imposing the arbitrary requirement that the intercept is the same for models describing both types of airlines.

□ The variance inflation factors are not necessary for the analysis, but they do show an important feature of the results of this type of model.

□ The TEST statement is used to test the null hypothesis that the three product coefficients are zero; that is, the effects of all three factors are the same for both types.

The results appear in Output 6.12.

Output 6.12
Using an Indicator Variable for Slope Shift

```
                              The SAS System                         1
Model: MODEL1
Dependent Variable: CPM

                          Analysis of Variance

                              Sum of         Mean
          Source      DF     Squares        Square      F Value    Prob>F

          Model        7     8.35794       1.19399       11.611     0.0001
          Error       25     2.57074       0.10283
          C Total     32    10.92867

              Root MSE       0.32067     R-square      0.7648
              Dep Mean       3.10570     Adj R-sq      0.6989
              C.V.          10.32523

                          Parameter Estimates

                        Parameter      Standard     T for H0:
          Variable  DF   Estimate         Error   Parameter=0   Prob > |T|

          INTERCEP   1   10.644365    1.50431265        7.076      0.0001
          UTL        1   -0.415894    0.07547880       -5.510      0.0001
          SPA        1   -6.054836    4.32444384       -1.400      0.1738
          ALF        1   -6.964992    2.09708992       -3.321      0.0028
          TYPE       1   -4.075799    1.72379750       -2.364      0.0261
          UTLTP      1    0.417513    0.09213361        4.532      0.0001
          SPATP      1    2.272941    4.41724924        0.515      0.6114
          ALFTP      1    0.611883    2.41187768        0.254      0.8018

                                        (continued on next page)
```

```
(continued from previous page)
                         Variance
       Variable  DF     Inflation

       INTERCEP   1    0.00000000
       UTL        1    3.72250309
       SPA        1   46.82543711
       ALF        1    6.13091228
       TYPE       1  232.92861273
       UTLTP      1   59.18560634
       SPATP      1  110.06339782
       ALFTP      1   95.46334774
```

```
                           The SAS System                              2

Dependent Variable: CPM
Test: ALLDIFF    Numerator:      0.7698   DF:    3   F value:   7.4862
                 Denominator:  0.102829   DF:   25   Prob>F:    0.0010
```

The overall model statistics show that the residual mean square has decreased from 0.174 to 0.103 and the R-SQUARE value has increased from 0.5535 to 0.7648. In other words, allowing different coefficients for the two types of airlines has clearly improved the fit of the model. The test for the three addititonal coefficients given at the bottom of the output ($p=0.0010$) indicates that the slope shifts as a whole significantly improve the fit of the model.

The statistics for the coefficients for the product variables show that among these only UTLTP is statistically significant ($p<0.05$). In other words, the coefficient for the utilization factor is the only one that can be shown to differ between the types.

In checking the statistics for the other coefficients, note that neither SPA nor its change or shift coefficient (SPATP) are statistically significant ($p=0.1738$ and 0.6114, respectively). This appears to contradict the results for the previous models where the coefficient for SPA does indeed appear to be needed in the model. This apparent contradiction arises from the fact that in this type of model, just as in polynomial models (see Chapter 5), it is not legitimate to test for lower order terms in the presence of higher order terms. In other words, if UTLTP is in the model, the test for UTL is not meaningful. One reason for this is the high degree of multicollinearity often found in models of this type. In this example, the multicollinearity is made worse by a large difference in the sizes of planes (SPA) used by the two types of airlines. Note that the variance inflation factors involving SPA and SPATP exceed 100.

For this reason, it is useful to reestimate the model omitting the two insignificant slope shift terms, STATP and ALFTP. The SAS statements are

```
proc reg data=prod;
     model cpm = utl spa alf type utltp;
     utltype1: test utl + utltp;
RUN;
```

Note that again the TYPE variable is kept in the model since it is a lower order term in the model that still includes one product term. The TEST statement is included to ascertain the significance of the effect of UTL for the TYPE=1 airlines. The results appear in Output 6.13.

Output 6.13
Final Equation for
Slope Shift

```
                                    The SAS System                              1

Model: MODEL1
Dependent Variable: CPM

                              Analysis of Variance

                              Sum of           Mean
          Source       DF     Squares         Square      F Value     Prob>F

          Model         5     8.33067        1.66613       17.315     0.0001
          Error        27     2.59800 -      0.09622
          C Total      32    10.92867

               Root MSE       0.31020      R-square      0.7623
               Dep Mean       3.10570      Adj R-sq      0.7183
               C.V.           9.98801

                              Parameter Estimates

                        Parameter      Standard     T for H0:
          Variable  DF   Estimate        Error     Parameter=0    Prob > |T|

          INTERCEP  1    10.141423     0.80789933     12.553       0.0001
          UTL       1    -0.420572     0.07116286     -5.910       0.0001
          SPA       1    -3.872952     0.83639693     -4.631       0.0001
          ALF       1    -6.409458     0.98175412     -6.529       0.0001
          TYPE      1    -3.533493     0.74133587     -4.766       0.0001
          UTLTP     1     0.422809     0.08681854      4.870       0.0001
```

```
                                    The SAS System                              2

Dependent Variable: CPM
Test: UTLTYPE1  Numerator:     0.0002   DF:    1   F value:    0.0019
                Denominator:   0.096222 DF:   27   Prob>F:     0.9653
```

The deletion of the two product variables has virtually no effect on the fit of the model. In this model all coefficients are highly significant.

This equation estimates that for the short-haul airlines a one unit (percent) change in utilization decreases cost by 0.42 cents. On the other hand, for the long-haul lines the corresponding effect is the sum of the coefficients for UTL and UTLTP; this estimate is $-0.420572+0.422809=0.002237$, or almost zero. A test that this effect is zero is performed by the TEST statement and it appears that utilization is not a cost factor for these lines.

The use of dummy variables is readily extended to more than one categorical variable and also to situations where such variables have more than two categories. However, for all but the simplest cases (such as the one presented here) this type of analysis is more easily performed by PROC GLM, which automatically generates the dummy variables. In addition, product variables can be specified directly with PROC GLM. The use of PROC GLM is presented in Chapter 4, "Details of the Linear Model: Understanding GLM Concepts," in *SAS System for Linear Models, Third Edition.*

6.5 Summary

The purpose of this chapter has been to show how PROC REG can be used to fit a wide variety of models that do not look linear. Using the logarithmic transformation on the dependent variable stabilizes the error variance, and using the logarithms of the independent variables provides a model whose coefficients are very useful in many applications. The use of specially coded variables allows the fitting of segmented regression or spline models that describe relationships where changes occur too abruptly to be fitted by polynomial models. Finally, indicator variables provide models that describe different relationships for different portions of the data.

Basically, PROC REG can be used to fit any model that is linear in the parameters. The models presented in this chapter are the most widely used special applications of linear regression, but many others can, of course, be developed. Because PROC REG has the most options for evaluating the results of a regression analysis, it should be the procedure of choice when possible. However, you should keep in mind that other SAS procedures are available when the use of PROC REG becomes awkward or produces numerically unstable results. Although PROC REG is quite useful for relatively simple models, the TRANSREG procedure should be considered for more complicated models.

Chapter 7 Nonlinear Models

7.1 Introduction

The expression *linear model* refers to a model that is linear in the parameters or that can be made linear by transformation (such as the log-linear model) or redefinition of variables (see the BOQ data in Chapter 4, "Multicollinearity: Detection and Remedial Measures"). It is apparent that such linear models need not be linear in terms of the variables. However, many relationships exist that cannot be described by linear models or adaptations of linear models. For example, the model

$$y = \beta e^{\gamma t} + \varepsilon$$

is not linear in its parameters. Specifically, the term $\beta e^{\gamma t}$ is not a linear function of γ. This particular nonlinear model, called the exponential growth or decay model, is used to represent increase (growth) or decrease (decay) over time (t) of many types of responses such as population size or radiation counts.

One major advantage of many nonlinear models over, say, polynomial models, is that the parameters represent meaningful physical quantities of the process described by the model. In the above model, the parameter β is the initial value of the response (when $t=0$) and the parameter γ is the rate of exponential growth (or decay). A positive value of γ indicates growth while a negative value indicates decay.

When a model is nonlinear in the parameters, the entire process of estimation and statistical inference is radically altered. This happens mainly because the normal equations that are solved to obtain least-squares parameter estimates are themselves nonlinear. Solutions of systems of nonlinear equations are not usually available in closed form, but must be obtained by numerical methods. For this reason, closed-form expressions for the partitioning of sums of squares and the consequently obtained statistics for making inferences on the parameters are also unavailable.

For most applications, the solutions to the normal equations are obtained by means of an iterative process. The process starts with some preliminary estimates of the parameters. These estimates are used to calculate a residual sum of squares and give an indication of which modifications of the parameters estimates may result in reducing the residual sum of squares. This process is repeated until it appears that no further modification of parameter estimates results in a reduction of the residual sum of squares.

The SAS procedure for analyzing nonlinear models is the NLIN procedure. PROC NLIN is introduced with an example of the simple exponential decay model in Section 7.2, "Estimating the Exponential Decay Model." Additional examples of the use of PROC NLIN include the logistic growth model (see Section 7.3, "Fitting a Growth Curve with the NLIN Procedure") and the estimation of spline functions when the knot is estimated from the data (see Section 7.4, "Fitting Splines with Unknown Knots").

These three models are relatively simple and the estimation of their parameters is relatively straightforward. This is certainly not true of all nonlinear models and for this reason PROC NLIN features a number of options for facilitating estimation for such models. Section 7.5, "Additional Comments on the NLIN Procedure," provides an overview of a number of these special options.*

7.2 Estimating the Exponential Decay Model

The SAS data set DECAY comes from an experiment to determine the radioactive decay of a substance. The variable COUNT represents the radiation count recorded at various times (TIME). Output 7.1 shows the data and the plot of COUNT versus TIME is given in Output 7.2. The decrease (decay) of COUNT with TIME is clearly evident.

Output 7.1
Decay Rate Data

```
                    The SAS System                        1

          OBS     TIME      COUNT

            1        0      383.0
            2       14      373.0
            3       43      348.0
            4       61      328.0
            5       69      324.0
            6       74      317.0
            7       86      307.0
            8       90      302.0
            9       92      298.0
           10      117      280.0
           11      133      268.0
           12      138      261.0
           13      165      244.0
           14      224      200.0
           15      236      197.0
           16      253      185.0
           17      265      180.0
           18      404      120.0
           19      434      112.5
```

---

* Nonlinear models may also be fitted using the MODEL Procedure in SAS/ETS software.

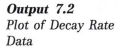

Output 7.2
Plot of Decay Rate
Data

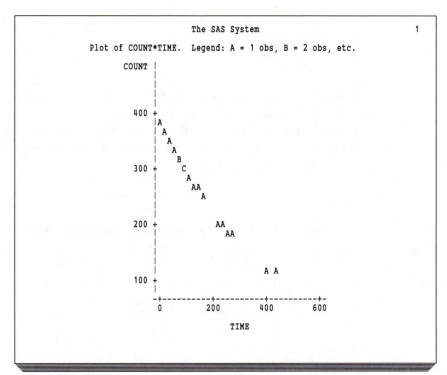

PROC NLIN is used for estimating the exponential decay model with the following statements:

```
proc nlin data=decay;
    parms b=380 c=-0.0026;
    model count = b*exp(c*time);
run;
```

You can see the differences between running PROC NLIN and PROC REG.

□ In PROC NLIN you must specify the complete model (except for the error) in the MODEL statement, whereas in PROC REG you need to list only the names of dependent and independent variables.

□ In PROC NLIN you must specify the names of the parameters in the PARMS statement because the MODEL statement includes both variables and parameters.

□ The PARMS statement is also used to provide starting values of the parameters that initiate the iterative estimation procedure. In this case, the starting values are specified as B=380 and C=−0.0026.

Providing good starting values is quite important because poor starting values can increase computing time and may even prevent finding correct estimates of the parameters. Starting values are usually educated guesses, although some preliminary calculations may be used for this purpose.

In this example, B is the expected COUNT at TIME=0, which should be close to the observed value of 383. The initial value for C is obtained by using the observed COUNT for a specific TIME and solving for C. Choose TIME=117, where COUNT=280, and solve

$$280 = 380*e^{117*C}$$

Taking logarithms makes this a linear equation, which is easily solved to obtain the initial value C=−0.0026.

Finding initial values is not always straightforward. For such cases, PROC NLIN provides a grid search that may be useful (see Section 7.5). The results from PROC NLIN appear in Output 7.3.

Output 7.3
Output from
PROC NLIN for
Decay Rate Data

```
                                The SAS System                            1
         Non-Linear Least Squares DUD Initialization    Dependent Variable COUNT
            DUD          B             C Sum of Squares
             -3    380.000000     -0.002600      991.103837
             -2    418.000000     -0.002600    15972.441615
             -1    380.000000     -0.002860      957.384346

         Non-Linear Least Squares Iterative Phase  Dependent Variable COUNT Method: DUD
            Iter         B             C Sum of Squares
              0    380.000000     -0.002860      957.384346
              1    390.348486     -0.002898      144.263953
              2    390.373398     -0.002892      143.072251
              3    390.337696     -0.002891      143.061410
              4    390.338405     -0.002891      143.061409
    NOTE: Convergence criterion met.


         Non-Linear Least Squares Summary Statistics    Dependent Variable COUNT

            Source            DF Sum of Squares    Mean Square

            Regression         2   1444456.1886    722228.0943
            Residual          17       143.0614         8.4154
            Uncorrected Total 19   1444599.2500

            (Corrected Total) 18    114296.2895


         Parameter    Estimate    Asymptotic              Asymptotic 95 %
                                   Std. Error          Confidence Interval
                                                       Lower         Upper
               B     390.3384055  1.4504201174   387.27830453  393.39850638
               C      -0.0028909  0.0000296844    -0.00295351   -0.00282825


                        Asymptotic Correlation Matrix

              Corr                    B                 C
         -------------------------------------------------
                B             1           -0.760299642
                C    -0.760299642                   1
```

The top portion of the output summarizes the iterative solution process. Under the heading Non-Linear Least Squares DUD Initialization you see the effort by the procedure to obtain improved starting values by increasing or decreasing the initial guesses by 10%. Increasing B by 10% to 418 produces an increase in the residual sum of squares from 991.1 to 15972.4. However, decreasing C from -0.00260 to -0.00286 reduces the residual sum of squares from 991.1 to 957.38.

In the next section, you see the Non-Linear Least Squares Iterative Phase. The DUD method is one of several available in PROC NLIN (see Section 7.5) used to produce a sequence of parameter estimates that yield ever decreasing residual sums of squares. The sequence converges when no further decrease appears possible. This occurs when the decrease in the residual sum of squares becomes sufficiently small, which in this case is in the ninth digit. The definition of sufficiently small can be altered by the CONVERGE= option in the PROC NLIN statement.

In the next section, you find the partitioning of the sum of squares that corresponds to the ANOVA portion of the PROC REG output. However, note that the partitioning starts with the uncorrected total sum of squares that is used in the REG procedure with the NOINT option in the MODEL statement. The reason for this is that in most nonlinear models there is no natural mean or intercept, hence the corrected sum of squares may have no meaning.

The regression and residual sums of squares and mean squares have the same interpretations as in PROC REG, although in nonlinear models the regression sum of squares is computed directly with the predicted values because there is no shortcut formula. Note, however, that the corrected total sum of squares is also provided in case you want to compute the equivalents of the usual F test or R-SQUARE. You should be aware that the resulting R-SQUARE may not have the usual interpretation (Kvalseth 1985). In the final portion of the output, there is information on the estimated coefficients. First, you see the parameter estimates, which provide the estimated model

$$\widehat{COUNT} = 390.34 * e^{-0.00289 * time} \quad .$$

The estimated initial count is 390.34 and the estimated exponential decay rate is -0.00289. This means that the expected count at time t is $e^{0.00289} = 0.997$ times the count at time $t-1$. In other words, the estimated rate of decay is $(1-0.997) = 0.003$, or approximately 0.3% per time period.

The estimated decay rate coefficient is used to get an estimated half-life, the time at which one half of the radiation has occurred. This is computed as $T2 = \ln(2)/C = 240$ time periods.

The standard errors of the estimated coefficients and the confidence intervals are *asymptotic*. This means that the formulas used for the computations are only approximately correct because they are based on mathematical theory that is valid only for very large sample sizes. So you can be approximately 95% confident that the true exponential decay rate is between -0.00295 and -0.00282.

You can create a data set with predicted and residual values for plotting and otherwise checking assumptions in the same way as with PROC REG. Use the following statements:

```
proc nlin data=decay;
     parms b=380 c=-0.0026;
     model count = b*exp(c*time);
output out=plot p=pct r=rct;
proc plot data=plot hpercent=50 vpercent=50;
     plot rct*time / vref=0;
     plot count*time='*' pct*time='+' / overlay;
proc univariate data=plot plot;
     var rct;
run;
```

Output 7.4
Predicted and
Residual Plots

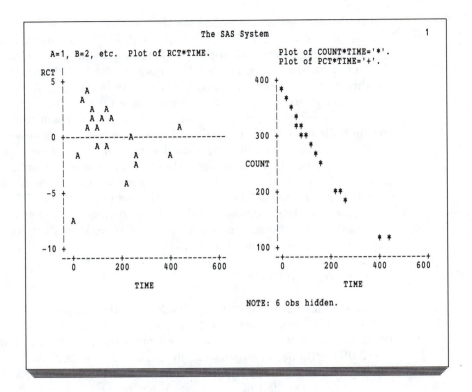

Output 7.5
Stem and Leaf and
Box Plots of
Residual

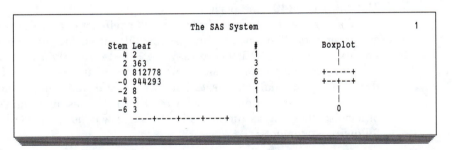

The resulting plots are given in Output 7.4 and the stem and leaf and box plots portion from PROC UNIVARIATE is given in Output 7.5. The residual plot indicates a problem with the observation at TIME=0, which appears to be due to an almost linear decay for the first three time periods, a phenomenon that is supported by the plot of actual and predicted values. The stem and leaf and box plots show a slight left skewness for the distribution of residuals that is not serious enough to cause difficulty.

Although most nonlinear models must be fitted by an iterative procedure such as PROC NLIN, some may be linearized and the linearized versions fitted by linear regression. The above decay model can be linearized by taking logarithms of the dependent variable and performing a linear regression using these values. In this example, the model

$$\log(COUNT) = \beta + \gamma(TIME) + \varepsilon$$

fits the decay model, with e^{β} being the estimated initial value and γ the decay constant.

You can do this using the following statements:

```
data logdecay; set decay;
     logcount = log(count);
proc reg data = logdecay;
     model logcount = time;
```

Output 7.6
Fitting a
Linearized
Nonlinear Model

```
                           The SAS System                            1

Model: MODEL1
Dependent Variable: LOGCOUNT

                        Analysis of Variance

                         Sum of         Mean
    Source      DF       Squares        Square     F Value     Prob>F

    Model        1       2.25695        2.25695    20390.869    0.0001
    Error       17       0.00188        0.00011
    C Total     18       2.25883

         Root MSE       0.01052      R-square      0.9992
         Dep Mean       5.52535      Adj R-sq      0.9991
         C.V.           0.19041

                        Parameter Estimates

                    Parameter      Standard     T for H0:
    Variable  DF    Estimate       Error        Parameter=0    Prob > |T|

    INTERCEP   1    5.968581       0.00393193    1517.979       0.0001
    TIME       1   -0.002906       0.00002035    -142.797       0.0001
```

The result in Output 7.6 provides estimates of initial value and decay constants of exp(5.9686) and -0.00291, which compare favorably with the values 390.3 and -0.00289 obtained by PROC NLIN in Output 7.3. The standard error of the linearized model estimate of the decay constant is 0.00002035 compared with the asymptotic standard error of 0.0000297 from PROC NLIN. The differences arise primarily in that the linearized estimates are not truly least-squares estimates because the log-linear models account for the standard deviation of residuals being proportional to the mean (see Section 6.1, "Introduction"). Since the residuals do not appear to have this feature (see Output 7.3 and Output 7.4), the log-linear model may not be appropriate.

7.3 Fitting a Growth Curve with the NLIN Procedure

A common application of nonlinear regression is fitting growth curves. This application is illustrated with the fish growth data from Chapter 5, "Polynomial Models," using the data for fish stored at 29 degrees. For convenience, the data are shown here in Output 7.8, with the fish length denoted as the variable LEN29.

Output 7.7

Fish Growth Data for Temperature of 29 Degrees

```
                        The SAS System                        1

               OBS     AGE     LEN29

                 1      14       590
                 2      21       910
                 3      28      1305
                 4      35      1730
                 5      42      2140
                 6      49      2725
                 7      56      2890
                 8      63      3685
                 9      70      3920
                10      77      4325
                11      84      4410
                12      91      4485
                13      98      4515
                14     105      4480
                15     112      4520
                16     119      4545
                17     126      4525
                18     133      4560
                19     140      4565
                20     147      4626
                21     154      4566
```

The relationship used here is known as the logistic growth curve. The general form of the equation for the logistic growth curve is

$$y = \frac{k}{1 + ((k - n_0)/n_0)e^{-rt}} + \varepsilon \quad .$$

This model has three parameters: k, n_0, and r. The parameter n_0 is the expected value of y at time $t=0$, k is the height of the horizontal asymptote (the expected value of y for very large t), and r is a measure of growth rate. The term ε is the random error and is assumed to have mean zero and variance σ^2.

You can fit the logistic model to the fish growth data with the following statements:

```
proc nlin data=fish;
   parms k=4500 no=500 r=1;
   model len29 = k/(1+((k-no)/no)*exp(-r*age));
run;
```

The starting values for the parameters in the PARMS statement are preliminary guesses based on knowledge of what the parameters stand for. The value $k=4500$ is selected because the values of LEN29 for large values of AGE are approximately 4500, and the value $n_0=500$ is selected because the value of LEN29 for early ages is around 500. Less is known about the value for r. Since growth is positive, (the values of LEN29 increase with age), r should be a small positive number. Because the starting values for k and n_0 appear to be quite good, a starting value of 1 should suffice for r.

Output 7.8
PROC NLIN
Output for Logistic
Growth Curve
Regression

```
                              The SAS System                              1

     Non-Linear Least Squares DUD Initialization    Dependent Variable LEN29
        DUD         K              N0                    R Sum of Squares
         -4    4500.000000    500.000000          1.000000      58440523
         -3    4950.000000    500.000000          1.000000      81127637
         -2    4500.000000    550.000000          1.000000      58440547
         -1    4500.000000    500.000000          1.100000      58440699

     Non-Linear Least Squares Iterative Phase  Dependent Variable LEN29 Method: DUD
        Iter        K              N0                    R Sum of Squares
          0    4500.000000    500.000000          1.000000      58440523
     WARNING: Step size shows no improvement.
     NOTE: Restarting DUD with smaller grid.

     Non-Linear Least Squares DUD Initialization    Dependent Variable LEN29
        DUD         K              N0                    R Sum of Squares
         -4    4500.000000    500.000000          1.000000      58440523
         -3    4950.000000    500.000000          1.000000      81127637
         -2    4500.000000    550.000000          1.000000      58440547
         -1    4500.000000    500.000000          1.100000      58440699

     Non-Linear Least Squares Iterative Phase  Dependent Variable LEN29 Method: DUD
        Iter        K              N0                    R Sum of Squares
          0    4500.000000    500.000000          1.000000      58440523
          1    4378.086775    443.774786          0.171507      35207809
          2    4372.267750    441.091107          0.127190      24052180
          3    4367.348933    436.165938          0.095041      12702482
          4    4359.644841    431.166571          0.045467       4870298
          5    4360.258342    426.317913          0.055991       1372618
          6    4361.003391    429.830844          0.056735       1346914
          7    4335.510367    282.420293          0.066732        971826
          8    4334.610519    276.870325          0.067579        968917
          9    4334.200974    274.763072          0.067218        960831
         10    4333.388682    270.644451          0.067087        957906
         11    4339.730915    276.532595          0.065847        950449
         12    4624.111267    215.434783          0.070510        276953
         13    4612.266267    271.190940          0.063952        180564
         14    4610.966539    260.467202          0.064696        178044
         15    4611.188641    258.147478          0.064854        177959
         16    4610.785797    258.036725          0.064872        177947
         17    4610.549469    257.762337          0.064970        177882
         18    4609.985447    257.033812          0.065023        177875
         19    4609.999742    257.176379          0.065012        177875
         20    4610.085431    257.154078          0.065013        177874
         21    4610.164862    257.184793          0.065007        177874
         22    4610.163625    257.183411          0.065008        177874
     NOTE: Convergence criterion met.


         Non-Linear Least Squares Summary Statistics    Dependent Variable LEN29

            Source            DF Sum of Squares    Mean Square

            Regression         3   299165882.76    99721960.92
            Residual          18      177874.24        9881.90
            Uncorrected Total 21   299343757.00

            (Corrected Total) 20    38462028.95
```

```
                              The SAS System                              2

        Parameter    Estimate    Asymptotic              Asymptotic 95 %
                                  Std. Error           Confidence Interval
                                                       Lower        Upper
            K      4610.163625  35.107594768    4536.4057923  4683.9214568
            N0      257.183411  28.178336235     197.9833142   316.3835072
            R         0.065008   0.002614803       0.0595141     0.0705010


                      Asymptotic Correlation Matrix

        Corr              K              N0              R
        ----------------------------------------------------------
            K             1       0.3785967261    -0.504830961
            N0   0.3785967261               1     -0.943422327
            R   -0.504830961    -0.943422327               1
```

Since no derivatives were specified, the DUD method is used to iterate toward the least-squares estimates of the parameters. The initial values of the parameters produce a residual sum of squares of 58440523. This is quickly reduced in the iterative process, ending in 22 steps with a residual sum of squares of 177874.

You should check to see if this is a reasonable value for the minimum residual sum of squares. To do this, compare the residual SS of 177874 from the PROC NLIN output with the residual SS of 211239 from the fourth-degree polynomial model fitted in Output 5.2. You see that the residual SS for the logistic fit is somewhat smaller than that for the fourth-degree polynomial fit. This indicates that the logistic model fits quite well, especially considering that the logistic model has only three parameters compared with five for the fourth-degree polynomial.

The final parameter estimates give the fitted model

$$\widehat{LEN29} = \frac{4610}{1 + ((4610 - 257)/257)e^{0.065^*AGE}}$$

$$= \frac{1}{0.00022 + 0.0037e^{-0.065^*AGE}}.$$

Asymptotic standard errors and corresponding confidence intervals for the parameters show that they are estimated with useful precision. The large negative correlation between n_0 and r indicates the presence of the nonlinear version of multicollinearity. This could indicate a family of curves with differing values of r and n_0 that all fit about as well as each other, meaning that parameter estimates are imprecise. However, the satisfactorily small standard errors indicate this is not the case.

You can examine the residuals from the fitted logistic growth curve as a further check on the fit of the model. Obtain a data set containing the residuals using the following statements:

```
proc nlin data=fish;
   parms k=4500 no=500 r=1;
   model len29 = k/(1+((k-no)/no)*exp(-r*age));
output out=plotdata p=plen29 r=rlen29;
run;
```

Plot the residuals with the following statements:

```
proc plot data=plotdata;
   plot rlen29*age;
run;
```

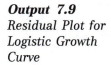

Output 7.9
Residual Plot for
Logistic Growth
Curve

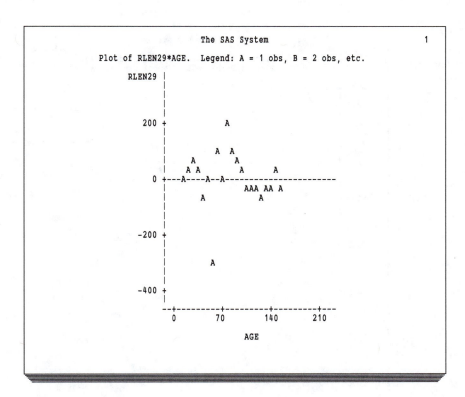

There is a large negative residual of about -300 corresponding to an age in the upper 60s, which is an apparent outlier. Also, there is a string of six negative residuals from ages 105 to 140. This indicates modest lack of fit in this region.

Now plot the fitted curve through the data with the following statements:

```
proc plot data=plotdata;
    plot len29*age='+' plen29*age='*' / overlay;
run;
```

Results in Output 7.10 agree with the residual analysis.

Output 7.10
Plot of Fitted Values for Logistic Growth Curve

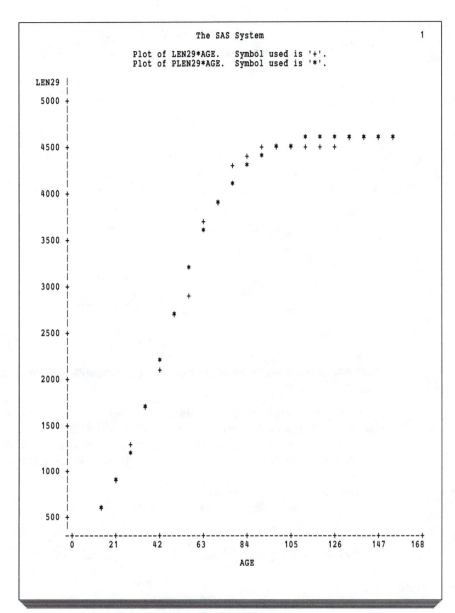

7.4 Fitting Splines with Unknown Knots

Section 6.3, "Spline Models," shows how PROC REG is used to fit a spline model when the knot is assumed known. Consider the more difficult problem of fitting the linear spline model with estimated knot. This cannot be done with linear regression methods, because now the knot is a parameter of the model.

As noted earlier, the spline model can be represented as

$$LEN29 = \beta_0 + \beta_1 {*}AGE + \beta_2 {*}AGEPL + \varepsilon$$

where AGEPL=AGE−KNOT if AGE≥KNOT and AGEPL=0 if AGE<KNOT. The variable AGEPL is equivalent to the variable AGEPLUS that was used when KNOT

was fixed at 80 (Section 6.3). You can use PROC NLIN to fit the model with
estimated knot, as follows:

```
proc nlin data=fish;
    parms b0=-328 b1=61 b2=-59 knot=80;
    agepl=max(age-knot, 0);
    model len29 = b0 +b1*age + b2*agepl;
run;
```

Starting values for the PARMS statement are those from the linear regression
model fitted with fixed KNOT=80 (Output 6.7).

Output 7.11
Estimating Linear
Spline with PROC
NLIN

```
                              The SAS System                                    1
        Non-Linear Least Squares DUD Initialization    Dependent Variable LEN29
DUD        B0              B1              B2             KNOT  Sum of Squares
   -5   -328.000000     61.000000      -59.000000      80.000000      224800
   -4   -360.800000     61.000000      -59.000000      80.000000      156340
   -3   -328.000000     67.100000      -59.000000      80.000000     8910313
   -2   -328.000000     61.000000      -64.900000      80.000000      483255
   -1   -328.000000     61.000000      -59.000000      88.000000     3507088

   Non-Linear Least Squares Iterative Phase  Dependent Variable LEN29 Method: DUD
Iter       B0              B1              B2             KNOT  Sum of Squares
   0   -360.800000     61.000000      -59.000000      80.000000      156340
   1   -349.721373     60.829590      -58.731908      78.795384      102001
   2   -352.782091     60.877643      -58.705344      78.716447      101935
   3   -361.181818     61.168831      -59.014286      78.474877      101359
   4   -361.181818     61.168831      -59.014286      78.485923      101355
   5   -361.181818     61.168831      -59.014286      78.485927      101355
NOTE: Convergence criterion met.


        Non-Linear Least Squares Summary Statistics    Dependent Variable LEN29

           Source            DF Sum of Squares    Mean Square

           Regression         3   299242402.46    99747467.49
           Residual          18      101354.54       5630.81
           Uncorrected Total 21   299343757.00

           (Corrected Total) 20    38462028.95

NOTE: The Jacobian is singular.


           Parameter   Estimate    Asymptotic          Asymptotic 95 %
                                    Std. Error        Confidence Interval
                                                     Lower          Upper
              B0    -361.1818182  0.0000000000  -361.18181818  -361.18181818
              B1      61.1688312  1.0303812321    59.00409483    63.33356751
              B2     -59.0142857  1.0185719415   -61.15421182   -56.87435961
            KNOT      78.4859268  1.0588299387    76.26142235    80.71043126


                      Asymptotic Correlation Matrix

Corr              B0              B1              B2             KNOT
----------------------------------------------------------------------------
        B0         .               .               .               .
        B1         .               1       -0.678333235    -0.904012857
        B2         .       -0.678333235            1        0.4462238065
      KNOT         .       -0.904012857    0.4462238065            1
```

Results in Output 7.11 provide the fitted model

$$\widehat{\text{LEN29}} = -361.18 + 61.17 * \text{AGE} - 59.01 * \text{AGEPL}$$

with the estimate of KNOT=78.49. The value of KNOT can be incorporated into the equation as

$$\widehat{\text{LEN29}} = -361.18 + 61.17 * \text{AGE} - 59.01 * \text{MAX}(\text{AGE} - 78.49, 0) \quad .$$

This provides the relationship

$$\widehat{\text{LEN29}} = -361.18 + 61.17 * \text{AGE}$$

for AGE<78.49 and

$$\widehat{\text{LEN29}} = 4631.69 + 2.16 * \text{AGE}$$

for AGE>78.49, which is very close to the fitted linear spline model obtained from Output 6.7 with the knot fixed at 80. The spline model with estimated knot has SS(ERROR)=101355 in Output 7.11 compared to 111756 for the model with the knot fixed at 80 in Output 6.7.

Some of the results from the NLIN procedure may not be valid for models like the one fitted here, because the partial derivative of the model with respect to one of the parameters (KNOT) is not continuous. In particular, the (asymptotic) correlation matrix, confidence intervals, and standard errors are not all correct. In this case, for example, the zero value for the asymptotic standard error of B0 is obviously not a logical result. In general, this discontinuity can disturb convergence of the iterative process and result in different final estimates depending on modest differences in specified starting values. You can see this in Output 7.12, which gives the parameter estimates portion of the PROC NLIN output when the starting value of KNOT is 78. The parameter estimates are identical, but the asymptotic standard errors and correlations are not. Because the curve has a discontinuity at the knot, the partial derivatives required for computing standard errors do not really exist at that point.

Output 7.12
Estimating Linear Spline with PROC NLIN:
Initial Value of KNOT=78

```
                                  The SAS System                              1

        Parameter      Estimate    Asymptotic          Asymptotic 95 %
                                    Std. Error       Confidence Interval
                                                       Lower        Upper
              B0    -361.1818182   60.410975655  -488.63708458  -233.72655178
              B1      61.1688312    1.214428976    58.60662510    63.73103724
              B2     -59.0142857    1.606538527   -62.40376575   -55.62480568
            KNOT      78.4859268    1.143490574    76.07338678    80.89846679


                        Asymptotic Correlation Matrix

        Corr               B0            B1            B2          KNOT
        -----------------------------------------------------------------
              B0             1   -0.914676808   0.6914306755   0.397403555
              B1  -0.914676808              1  -0.755928946   -0.594357912
              B2  0.6914306755  -0.755928946              1   0.0369095359
            KNOT  0.397403555   -0.594357912   0.0369095359              1
```

In Chapter 6, "Special Applications of Linear Models," it is noted that splines with discontinuous derivatives are not universally acceptable. However, the quadratic spline with continuous derivatives cannot be justified for the fish growth data. Another alternative is a spline joining a straight line to an exponential curve, which is demonstrated next. (See "Example 4: Segmented Model," in Chapter 29, "The NLIN Procedure," in the *SAS/STAT User's Guide, Version 6, Fourth Edition, Volume 2* for an example of fitting a spline model joining quadratic curve to a plateau.)

Recall that the exponential decay model fitted to the radioactive count data showed some lack of fit because the early decay was more linear than exponential. An alternative model has a straight line for time$<t_0$, and then an exponential decay curve for time$>t_0$. The equation for the curve for time$>t_0$ is

$$COUNT = B*exp(C*TIME) + \varepsilon \quad .$$

The curve passes through the point $(t_0, b*exp(c*t_0))$, and has slope $b*c*exp(c*t_0)$ at this point. The straight line for time $<t_0$ must also pass through this point and have the same slope at this point. The point-slope form for the equation of a line (ignoring ε) gives

$$COUNT = B*exp(C*t_0) + B*C*exp(C*t_0)*(time - t_0)$$

as the equation for time$<t_0$. Equivalently,

$$COUNT = B*exp(C*t_0)*(1 + C*(TIME - t_0)) \quad .$$

Fit this model with the following statements:

```
proc nlin data=decay;
  parms b=380 c=-.0028 t0=100;
    if time < t0 then do;
      model count = b*exp(c*t0)*(1 + c*(time - t0));
    end;
    else do;
  model count = b*exp(c*time);
    end;
run;
```

Results appear in Output 7.13.

Output 7.13
Spline Function
for Decay Data

```
                            The SAS System                              1

Non-Linear Least Squares DUD Initialization        Dependent Variable COUNT
   DUD          B                C                T0 Sum of Squares
    -4      380.000000        -0.002800        100.000000     1310.833907
    -3      418.000000        -0.002800        100.000000     7910.538109
    -2      380.000000        -0.003080        100.000000     4133.006880
    -1      380.000000        -0.002800        110.000000     1568.697784

Non-Linear Least Squares Iterative Phase  Dependent Variable COUNT Method: DUD
   Iter         B                C                T0 Sum of Squares
    0       380.000000        -0.002800        100.000000     1310.833907
    1       393.667891        -0.002952         76.775359       64.876787
    2       394.436824        -0.002951         78.484203       60.241648
    3       394.408078        -0.002950         78.446135       60.237924
    4       394.749760        -0.002956         81.612241       59.836973
    5       394.748213        -0.002956         81.649874       59.835147
    6       394.748093        -0.002956         81.648464       59.835090
    7       394.739471        -0.002956         81.638528       59.834942
    8       394.703263        -0.002955         81.331933       59.831905
    9       394.706564        -0.002955         81.361646       59.831821
   10       394.706600        -0.002955         81.361049       59.831820
   11       394.707776        -0.002955         81.362891       59.831819
```

(continued on next page)

```
(continued from previous page)
        12      394.710318      -0.002955      81.386511      59.831805
        13      394.709732      -0.002955      81.381464      59.831803
        14      394.709738      -0.002955      81.381270      59.831803
NOTE: Convergence criterion met.

    Non-Linear Least Squares Summary Statistics      Dependent Variable COUNT

       Source              DF  Sum of Squares      Mean Square

       Regression           3     1444539.4182      481513.1394
       Residual            16          59.8318           3.7395
       Uncorrected Total   19     1444599.2500

       (Corrected Total)   18      114296.2895


    Parameter     Estimate     Asymptotic              Asymptotic 95 %
                               Std. Error         Confidence Interval
                                                  Lower          Upper
         B      394.7097379   1.649912473    391.21209707   398.20737870
         C       -0.0029553   0.000027081     -0.00301270    -0.00289788
        T0       81.3812699  10.071198866     60.03138819   102.73115168


                Asymptotic Correlation Matrix

    Corr               B               C               T0
    -----------------------------------------------------------------
         B             1     -0.877254229    0.7821383192
         C  -0.877254229                1   -0.640861733
        T0  0.7821383192    -0.640861733               1
```

It is logical to use the same starting values for B and C that were used when fitting the standard exponential decay curve (see Output 7.3). Output 7.13 gives parameter estimates for the fitted model, along with SS(ERROR)=59.83. This is a reduction in SS(ERROR) from 143.06 for the standard exponential decay model shown in Output 7.3.

If you want a plot of residuals and predicted values, use the following statements:

```
proc nlin data=decay;
  parms b=380 c=-.0028 t0=100;
    if time < t0 then do;
      model count = b*exp(c*t0)*(1 + c*(time - t0));
    end;
    else do;
  model count = b*exp(c*time);
    end;
output out=plot p=pct r=rct;
proc plot data=plot vpercent=50 hpercent=50;
  plot rct*time ;
  plot count*time='*' pct*time='+' / overlay;
run;
```

Results appear in Output 7.14.

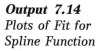

Output 7.14
Plots of Fit for
Spline Function

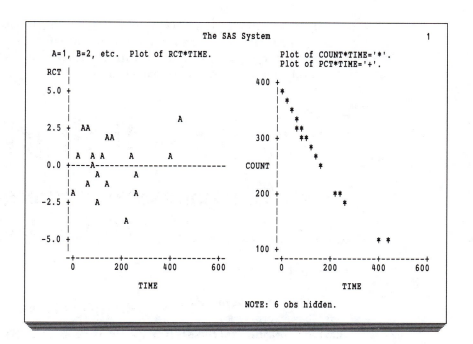

Output 7.14 displays no pattern in the residuals, and shows the fitted curve passing so closely through observed data that the observed and predicted points are identical on the line printer output.

7.5 Additional Comments on the NLIN Procedure

PROC NLIN works quite well with the rather simple models used in this chapter. For more complicated models, especially models having many parameters, estimation is not always so straightforward. PROC NLIN provides a number of options and special features to assist in more difficult applications. Some of the ones most frequently used are outlined here.

7.5.1 Estimation Algorithms

In all of the above examples, the SAS log carried a message similar to the following:

```
NOTE: DER.B not initialized or missing.
NOTE: DER.C not initialized or missing.
WARNING: Method changed to DUD because of missing first derivative.
```

DUD is an acronym for Doesn't Use Derivatives. Actually, all computational methods for finding minima of nonlinear functions require derivatives for determining what changes in the parameters result in reduction of the residual sum of squares. However, if derivatives are not provided in the PROC NLIN specifications, the DUD method estimates derivatives from the history of previous iterations. The negatively numbered iterations in the outputs are artificial iterations produced to provide the history needed for subsequent iterations.

PROC NLIN does provide for several other iterative methods that require the derivatives, and generally these methods are more efficient. The derivatives for these methods are the partial derivatives of the model function with respect to each of the parameters. For the decay model, these are

$$\frac{\partial \beta e^{\gamma t}}{\partial \beta} = e^{\gamma t}$$

and

$$\frac{\partial \beta e^{\gamma t}}{\partial_\gamma} = t\beta e^{\gamma t} \quad .$$

These derivatives are specified for PROC NLIN with DER statements:

```
proc nlin data = decay;
    parms b = 380 c = -.0026;
    model count = b*exp(c*time);
    der.b = exp(c*time);
    der.c = b*time*exp(c*time);
run;
```

Output 7.15

Results of the Gauss-Newton Method from PROC NLIN

```
                              The SAS System                          1

                     Non-Linear Least Squares Iterative Phase
                  Dependent Variable COUNT    Method: Gauss-Newton
          Iter            B                 C  Sum of Squares
           0        380.000000       -0.002600     991.103837
           1        390.155470       -0.002887     143.235814
           2        390.338730       -0.002891     143.061412
           3        390.337787       -0.002891     143.061405
           4        390.337794       -0.002891     143.061405
     NOTE: Convergence criterion met.


       Non-Linear Least Squares Summary Statistics    Dependent Variable COUNT

           Source            DF  Sum of Squares    Mean Square

           Regression         2    1444456.1886    722228.0943
           Residual          17        143.0614         8.4154
           Uncorrected Total 19    1444599.2500

           (Corrected Total) 18     114296.2895


         Parameter    Estimate    Asymptotic              Asymptotic 95 %
                                   Std. Error         Confidence Interval
                                                        Lower         Upper
              B    390.3377935   1.4505057553    387.27751190   393.39807511
              C     -0.0028909   0.0000296828     -0.00295351    -0.00282826


                       Asymptotic Correlation Matrix

                 Corr              B                  C
              -------------------------------------------------
                   B              1         -0.760327625
                   C     -0.760327625                  1
```

Output 7.15 gives the results of the Gauss-Newton method, which is the default method used if derivatives are provided. You can see the rapid convergence of the parameter estimates and residual sum of squares with this method. However, the final results are essentially indistinguishable from those obtained with the DUD method.

In addition to the DUD and Gauss-Newton methods, PROC NLIN provides for three alternative algorithms that may be implemented by using the appropriate METHOD= option in the PROC NLIN statement and supplying the partial derivatives of the model function with respect to the parameters. Depending on the shape of the residual sums of squares surface, one of these algorithms may work while others do not.

7.5.2 Other Methods

Difficulties with the estimation process increase much more rapidly with additional parameters in nonlinear regression than they do for linear regression models. For this reason, PROC NLIN provides a number of features, outlined below, to assist in providing estimates and other inferences that may be useful for more complicated models:

initial values   are required for starting the iterative solution process and are not always easily obtained. The NLIN procedure allows for the implementation of a grid search procedure that computes the residual sum of squares for a grid of potential parameter values, and then starts iterations at that combination of values giving the smallest residual sum of squares. A grid search is performed by specifying more than one initial value for one or more of the parameters in the PARMS statement, for example:

```
parms a = 190 to 220 by 10 ;
```

which fits the model with the four initial values 190, 200, 210, and 220. If multiple values are given for several parameters, PROC NLIN computes residual sums of squares for models with all possible combinations, so caution is advised.

convergence   is linked to choice of initial values. Occasionally the output of the iterative process indicates that convergence criterion has not been met. This means that a satisfactory least-squares solution has not been found. Since this is usually the result of a poor choice of initial values, a grid search can be useful in determining better initial values. Specifying a different solution algorithm or allowing more iterations can help. A number of options are available for modifying iterations, including the CONVERGE= or CONVERGEPARM= options, which are used to tune the differences in residual sum of squares or parameter estimates required to declare convergence.

local minima   can be problematic if the solution found by the iterative procedure is not the correct or global minimum residual sum of squares. Such an occurrence can result in an overly large residual sum of squares or unreasonable parameter estimates. One way to investigate this problem is to fit a polynomial model (for example with PROC

RSREG), which usually provides a reasonable approximation to many nonlinear functions and compare the resulting residual mean square with that of PROC NLIN. If the PROC NLIN residual mean square is considerably larger, there may be a problem with the estimated nonlinear model. Again, different starting values or estimation methods should be tried if the estimates are in doubt.

parameter estimates   can be restricted by using a BOUNDS statement. Implementation of BOUNDS statements may, however, invite finding local optima.

programming   can be used between the PARMS and MODEL
statements   statements. Programming statements, such as those used in the DATA step, can be used to simplify expressions and save computing time. For example, derivatives of exponential functions involve the same exponentials. Defining an exponential function once in a program step allows its repeated use without recomputation.

Specific instructions for using these various alternatives and options, together with other helpful hints, are found in the *SAS/STAT User's Guide,* as well as several interesting examples including iteratively reweighted least squares and maximum-likelihood estimation.

7.6 Summary

This chapter has provided some relatively simple examples of how PROC NLIN can be used to estimate nonlinear regression models. Additional options for dealing with more complicated models have been briefly noted but not explicitly illustrated.

Fitting nonlinear models is not always an easy task, especially for models containing as few as four or five parameters. Special strategies may need to be considered.

The spline model was relatively easy to fit, even though it had four parameters because three of the parameters were in linear form, and a closely related linear regression could be used to provide starting values. Therefore, if a nonlinear model contains a number of linear parameters, it may be possible to estimate the linear parameters using reasonable values of the nonlinear parameters to get starting values.

As a rule, if you need to fit a rather complicated model and you are not very familiar with nonlinear models in general and PROC NLIN in particular, try some simple examples first.

Example Code

Appendix

This appendix contains the raw data and DATA steps you need to produce the output in this book using Release 6.06 of the SAS System. The PROC statements and any additional DATA steps that you must use appear in the appropriate chapter in the context of the discussion.

This appendix is divided into sections that correspond to chapter numbers to help you quickly locate the example code you need. Each DATA step follows an introductory statement that identifies corresponding output.

Chapter 1

Use the following DATA step to produce Output 1.1.

```
data air;
input utl 1-4 .2 asl 5-8 .3 spa 9-12 .4 avs 13-15 .2
      alf 16-18 .3 cpm 19-22 .3 csm 23-26 .3;
type = (asl >= 1200);
cards;
 78717901375468591122581333
 95025153546483488227551111
 79113501920442412234109650
13303607339050139723570935
 84819631381470582236313750
 93811231481424466240411190
108015761361487535242512970
 83619123148465434271111770
 84315841607447439274312030
 88323773287473417278011590
 84214953597444400283311330
 96208401390425410284611660
 87113921148444447829061390
 84408711186438495295411461
 89109611236416476296214110
 68410081150413539297116000
 90008451390425409304411245
102016923007465381309611790
 82908771060437486314015280
```

```
80915283522432287330609♦9
9471408134547050433061662
7701236122142845533111507
9570863139042640533131343
8351031136542242233921431
7271416114543847634371636
7520975202539642634621476
9562189327946234935271230
7940949148840039436891452
7551164127042245237601700
1060278012824654253856163
1080151813564433623959143
6310823094340654140242176
5650821129040137847371791
;
```

Chapter 2

Use the following DATA step to produce Output 2.1 through Output 2.25.

```
data air;
input utl 1-4 .2 asl 5-8 .3 spa 9-12 .4 avs 13-15 .2
      alf 16-18 .3 cpm 19-22 .3 csm 23-26 .3;
type = (asl >= 1.200);
cards;
 7871790137546859122581333
 9502515354648348822751111
 7911350192044241223410965
 1330360733905013977235709
 8481963138147058223631375
 9381123148142446624041119
 1080157613614875352425129
 8361912314846543427111177
 8431584160744743927431203
 8832377328747341727801159
 8421495359744440028331133
 9620840139042541028461166
 8711392114844447829061390
 8440871111864384952954146
 8910961123641647629621411
 6841008115041353929711600
 9000845139042540930441245
 1020169230074653813096117
 8290877106043748631401528
 8091528352243228733060949
 9471408134547050433061662
 7701236122142845533111507
 9570863139042640533131343
 8351031136542242233921431
 7271416114543847634371636
 7520975202539642634621476
 9562189327946234935271230
```

```
       7940949148840039436891452
       7551164127042245237601700
      1060278012824654 2538561637
      1080151813564 4336239591432
       6310823094340654140242176
       5650821129040137847371791
      ;
      proc sort;
         by alf;
      run;
```

Chapter 3

Use the following DATA step to produce Output 3.1 through Output 3.7.

```
      data boq;
      input id $ occup checkin hours common wings cap rooms manh;
         drop id;
      cards;
      A 2 4 4 1.26 1 6 6 180.23
      B 3 1.58 40 1.25 1 5 5 182.61
      C 16.6 23.78 40 1 1 13 13 164.38
      D 7 2.37 168 1 1 7 8 284.55
      E 5.3 1.67 42.5 7.79 3 25 25 199.92
      F 16.5 8.25 168 1.12 2 19 19 267.38
      G 25.89 3 40 0 3 36 36 999.09
      H 44.42 159.75 168 .6 18 48 48 1103.24
      I 39.63 50.86 40 27.37 10 77 77 944.21
      J 31.92 40.08 168 5.52 6 47 47 931.84
      K 97.33 255.08 168 19 6 165 130 2268.06
      L 56.63 373.42 168 6.03 4 36 37 1489.5
      M 96.67 206.67 168 17.86 14 120 120 1891.7
      N 54.58 207.08 168 7.77 6 66 66 1387.82
      O 113.88 981 168 24.48 6 166 179 3559.92
      P 149.58 233.83 168 31.07 14 185 202 3115.29
      Q 134.32 145.82 168 25.99 12 192 192 2227.76
      R 188.74 937 168 45.44 26 237 237 4804.24
      S 110.24 410 168 20.05 12 115 115 2628.32
      T 96.83 677.33 168 20.31 10 302 210 1880.84
      U 102.33 288.83 168 21.01 14 131 131 3036.63
      V 274.92 695.25 168 46.63 58 363 363 5539.98
      W 811.08 714.33 168 22.76 17 242 242 3534.49
      X 384.5 1473.66 168 7.36 24 540 453 8266.77
      Y 95 368 168 30.26 9 292 196 1845.89
      ;
```

Use the following DATA step to produce Output 3.8 through Output 3.12.

```
      data irrig;
      input perc ratio inft lost advt ;
      cards;
      16.8 3.64 .343 21.27 .6991
      25.76 1.67 .343 21.27 .564
      14.73 2.34 .343 21.27 .750
```

```
12.71 3.78 .387 25.45 .680
14.56 3.73 .397 25.45 .701
13.16 2.71 .397 25.45 .747
9.06 4.97 .397 26.53 .772
14.46 3.17 .397 26.53 .436
17.16 2.32 .397 26.53 .596
9.52 6.86 .397 26.53 .840
13.72 3.69 .387 26.53 .600
12.96 3.35 .397 26.53 .760
19.04 2.39 .427 29.1 .600
18.03 2.82 .427 29.1 .730
34.83 .97 .427 29.1 .698
30.26 1.27 .427 29.1 .880
37.75 .77 .427 29.1 .582
26.26 1.87 .309 20.90 .836
30.60 1.27 .309 20.90 .685
33.75 1.15 .309 20.90 .519
25.75 2.25 .309 20.90 .841
29.05 1.51 .309 20.90 .800
;
```

Use the following DATA step to produce Output 3.13 through Output 3.17.

```
data diamonds;
input carats color $  clar $  price ;
 price = price / 1000;
csq = carats*carats;
cards;
1.9 H A 28473
1.35 F D 15297
1.46 G C  16596
1.03 G C 11372
1.66 E F 16321
.91 G F 4816
.68 G F 2324
1.92 D B 100411
1.25 D F 19757
1.36 E E 17432
.73 G E 3719
1.41 H A 19176
1.29 E A 36161
.5 H D 1918
.77 G E 3951
.79 G E 4131
.6 G E 2499
.63 G F 2324
.79 G E 4184
.53 I B 1976
.52 G E 2055
.54 G E 2134
1.02 D C 27264
1.02 G C 12684
```

```
1.06 F D 13181
.63 H D 2747
.52 I B 1976
1.23 E D 17958
1.24 E D 18095
.75 E E 5055
proc sort; by carats;
data _null_;  file print n=ps header=h;
do c= 21,45;
do r=6 to 20;
set diamonds;
put #r ac carats 4.2 +5 price 7.3 ;
end;end; return;
put _page_;
h:
put /// a20 'carats' +5 'price' +8  'carats' +5 'price';
```

Use the following DATA step to produce Output 3.18 through Output 3.21.

```
data consume;
input curr 1-3 .1 (ddep prices gnp)(4.1) wages 3.2
(income pop cons)(4.1)
yr 2. qtr 1.;
n=_n_;
idx=prices*pop; drop idx;
curr=100000*curr/idx;
ddep=100000*ddep/idx;
gnp=100000*gnp/idx;
wages=100*wages/prices;
income=100000*income/idx;
cons=100000*cons/idx;
cards;
251 920 8993180154270015401739511
253 929 9033258157276215471743512
257 939 9103328158280515541774513
260 959 9223369161285315611809514
263 972 9163395163286315671817521
265 980 9243391163286615731855522
268 990 9303456167291715811893523
272 999 9303577170301215881930524
2751001 9263642173306015941950531
2771007 9333675174307916001967532
2781008 9393658176306416071976533
2781010 9363608177298516151977534
2771015 9363607177299316212003541
2761018 9383604178299516282020542
2751032 9353647178302916362047543
2741046 9323734181310916432075544
2751060 9323862182320516502103551
2761067 9323944184328716572130552
2771072 9364025188334516652154553
2781073 9354088190340916732203554
```

```
2791077 935410619234301680223456l
2791080 947416219534831687225956 2
2801080 9544206198351916952291563
2811084 9624295202359317032326564
2821086 9694369203364517102367571
2821087 9804399204366017172384572
2831086 9874463206369517252433573
2831079 9914415208364017332452574
2821078 1005434720835791740246758l
2831093 1008438321035931746250658 2
2841106 1008451421237021754254558 3
2851122 1008466421738301762257058 4
2871133 1008474021939241769261259 l
2891141 1015486922140491777264859 2
2901146 1020484021939971784269059 3
2891136 1023490522440281792271759 4
2901123 1024503022641421798275160 l
2901114 1031504722641711805280160 2
2901119 1033504222274152181328066 03
2901120 1039503322941171821283960 4
2891127 1039503622941221828286561 l
2891137 1040514923242226183528896 12
2911143 1046524223243071843291961 3
2941155 1045537723744341851296561 4
2971160 1050547823844881858299862 l
3001162 1053557223945601864303262 2
3021158 1061564423946041872307262 3
3041164 1058572024346561879312062 4
3091176 1062577424447061885315863 l
3131185 1066584224647741892318863 2
3181195 1071594724748571900323863 3
3231206 1076605825149391907325963 4
3281211 1077617725150401913333664 l
3331218 1080628025351371919338164 2
3381236 1084638925652421926346464 3
3411249 1088645125853041933349964 4
3461254 1090662725954491938354465 l
3491263 1101675426155531944363565 2
3551277 1102690026356651951369865 3
3611298 1110708426658281957378565 4
3671319 1120725926860401962386566 l
3731332 1129736727161151967393366 2
3781323 1141748827462671973399866 3
3821320 1147762127763731979402666 4
3871330 1150766327963861984410967 l
3911352 1160775128264511989416267 2
3951391 1171791228565561995422467 3
4011410 1182816129167092001427467 4
4081426 1195835329668812005441268 l
4161451 1209858730070542010448568 2
4241483 1222876430472252016459168 3
4311503 1237892531173732021464468 4
4411527 1256908731375132025473669 l
```

```
448154212769248317765720304822692
452153712939428324780620354900693
460157713139522329786520414990694
;
```

Chapter 4

Use the following DATA step to produce Output 4.1 through Output 4.17.

```
data boq;
input id $ occup checkin hours common wings cap rooms manh;
if id = 'W' then delete;
cards;
A 2 4 4 1.26 1 6 6 180.23
B 3 1.58 40 1.25 1 5 5 182.61
C 16.6 23.78 40 1 1 13 13 164.38
D 7 2.37 168 1 1 7 8 284.55
E 5.3 1.67 42.5 7.79 3 25 25 199.92
F 16.5 8.25 168 1.12 2 19 19 267.38
G 25.89 3 40 0 3 36 36 999.09
H 44.42 159.75 168 .6 18 48 48 1103.24
I 39.63 50.86 40 27.37 10 77 77 944.21
J 31.92 40.08 168 5.52 6 47 47 931.84
K 97.33 255.08 168 19 6 165 130 2268.06
L 56.63 373.42 168 6.03 4 36 37 1489.5
M 96.67 206.67 168 17.86 14 120 120 1891.7
N 54.58 207.08 168 7.77 6 66 66 1387.82
O 113.88 981 168 24.48 6 166 179 3559.92
P 149.58 233.83 168 31.07 14 185 202 3115.29
Q 134.32 145.82 168 25.99 12 192 192 2227.76
R 188.74 937 168 45.44 26 237 237 4804.24
S 110.24 410 168 20.05 12 115 115 2628.32
T 96.83 677.33 168 20.31 10 302 210 1880.84
U 102.33 288.83 168 21.01 14 131 131 3036.63
V 274.92 695.25 168 46.63 58 363 363 5539.98
W 811.08 714.33 168 22.76 17 242 242 3534.49
X 384.5 1473.66 168 7.36 24 540 453 8266.77
Y 95 368 168 30.26 9 292 196 1845.89
;
```

Chapter 5

Use the following DATA step to produce Output 5.1 through Output 5.8.

```
data fish;
input age length aa ;
if age > 28 then age=age+1;
asq=age*age;
acub=age*asq; aqt=asq*asq;
if _n_ <= 21 then temp = 25;
```

```
if 22 <= _n_ <= 42 then temp = 27;
if 43 <= _n_ <= 63 then temp = 29;
if _n_ >= 64 then temp = 31;
tsq=temp*temp;
at=age*temp; asqt=asq*temp; atsq=age*tsq;
cards;
14 620 21 910 28 1315 34 1635 41 2120 48 2300 55 2600 62 2925
69 3110 76 3315 83 3535 90 3710 97 3935 104 4145 111 4465 118 4510
125 4530 132 4545 139 4570 146 4605 153 4600
14 625 21 820 28 1215 34 1515 41 2110 48 2320 55 2805 62 2940
69 3255 76 3620 83 4015 90 4235 97 4315 104 4435 111 4495 118 4475
125 4535 132 4520 139 4600 146 4600 153 4600
14 590 21 910 28 1305 34 1730 41 2140 48 2725 55 2890 62 3685
69 3920 76 4325 83 4410 90 4485 97 4515 104 4480  111 4520 118 4545
125 4525 132 4560 139 4565 146 4626 153 4566
14 590 21 910 28 1205 34 1605 41 1915 48 2035 55 2140 62 2520 69 2710
76 2870 83 3020 90 3025 97 3030 104 3025 111 3040 118 3177 125 3180
132 3180 139 3257 146 3166 153 3214
data _null_; set fish;
retain c1 7 c2 7 c3 7 c4 7;
file print header=h n=ps;
if temp=25 then do;
c1+1; put # c1 @19 age 5.  @29 length 5. ; end;
if temp=27 then do;
c2+1; put # c2 @39 length 5.; end;
if temp=29 then do;
c3+1; put # c3 @ 49 length 5.; end;
if temp = 31 then do;
c4+1; put # c4 @ 59 length 5.; end;
return;
h: put //
@ 20 'temp' +7 '25' +8 '27' +8 '29' +8 '31' //
@ 21 'age' ; return;
```

Use the following DATA step to produce Output 5.9 through Output 5.12.

```
data peanuts ;
 input length 30-32 .2   freq 36-38    space 42-44 .2   time 47-50 .2
unshl 53-56   damg 59-62 .2   exp 6 no 7-8 ;
if exp=2 then output ;      drop exp no;
cards ;
012s 1 1    2    2    2   125   130    40    720   117   550
012s 1 2    2    2    4   125   130    86   1620   217   460
012s 1 3    2    4    2   125   220    40    410   134   690
012s 1 4    2    4    4   125   220    86    850   229   310
012s 1 5    4    2    2   225   130    40    230   117   800
012s 1 6    4    2    4   225   130    86    520   117   400
012s 1 7    4    4    2   225   220    40    230   153   740
012s 1 8    4    4    4   225   220    86    580   128   380
012s 1 9    1    3    3   100   175    63   1600   221   360
012s 110    5    3    3   250   175    63    350   106   370
012s 111    3    1    3   175   100    63   1300   153   350
```

012s	112	3	5	3	175	250	63	500	116	400
012s	113	3	3	1	175	175	25	350	98	820
012s	114	3	3	5	175	175	100	1200	171	380
012s	115	3	3	3	175	175	63	430	150	580
012s	116	3	3	3	175	175	63	440	156	580
012s	117	3	3	3	175	175	63	440	145	520
012s	118	3	3	3	175	175	63	440	155	500
012s	119	3	3	3	175	175	63	440	151	570
012s	120	3	3	3	175	175	63	440	144	580
012s	2 1	2	2	2	125	130	63	925	149	823
012s	2 2	2	2	4	125	130	109	1800	240	315
012s	2 3	2	4	2	125	220	63	475	155	526
012s	2 4	2	4	4	125	220	109	1550	197	423
012s	2 5	4	2	2	225	130	63	400	84	902
012s	2 6	4	2	4	225	130	109	700	145	300
012s	2 7	4	4	2	225	220	63	225	97	741
012s	2 8	4	4	4	225	220	109	575	168	378
012s	2 9	1	3	3	100	175	86	1600	284	355
012s	210	5	3	3	250	175	86	350	168	372
012s	211	3	1	3	175	100	86	1300	154	354
012s	212	3	5	3	175	250	86	500	126	405
012s	213	3	3	1	175	175	48	350	100	816
012s	214	3	3	5	175	175	123	1200	195	380
012s	215	3	3	3	175	175	86	700	176	327
012s	216	3	3	3	175	175	86	625	177	438
012s	217	3	3	3	175	175	86	650	212	326
012s	218	3	3	3	175	175	86	650	200	357
012s	219	3	3	3	175	175	86	650	160	465
012s	220	3	3	3	175	175	86	650	176	402
012s	3 1	1	1	1	150	175	86	575	200	283
012s	3 2	1	1	2	150	175	100	925	248	217
012s	3 3	1	1	3	150	175	115	950	185	271
012s	3 4	1	2	1	150	220	86	475	201	388
012s	3 5	1	2	2	150	220	100	775	159	294
012s	3 6	1	2	3	150	220	115	775	200	249
012s	3 7	1	3	1	150	265	86	400	204	341
012s	3 8	1	3	2	150	265	100	650	205	227
012s	3 9	1	3	3	150	265	115	750	200	284
012s	310	2	1	1	200	175	86	350	176	368
012s	311	2	1	2	200	175	100	525	188	351
012s	312	2	1	3	200	175	115	650	150	321
012s	313	2	2	1	200	220	86	350	180	385
012s	314	2	2	2	200	220	100	450	185	451
012s	315	2	2	3	200	220	115	500	136	437
012s	316	2	3	1	200	265	86	300	180	461
012s	317	2	3	2	200	265	100	450	175	371
012s	318	2	3	3	200	265	115	525	171	298
012s	319	3	1	1	250	175	86	300	116	441
012s	320	3	1	2	250	175	100	425	151	220
012s	321	3	1	3	250	175	115	500	110	370
012s	322	3	2	1	250	220	86	275	129	369
012s	323	3	2	2	250	220	100	450	130	408
012s	324	3	2	3	250	220	115	425	120	354

```
012s 325      3      3      1    250    265     86    250    126    474
012s 326      3      3      2    250    265    100    400    124    438
012s 327      3      3      3    250    265    115    600    149    439
;
```

Chapter 6

Use the following DATA step to produce Output 6.1 through Output 6.6.

```
data pines;
input dbh   height   age   grav    weight;
cards;
 5.7    34     10    0.409     174
 8.1    68     17    0.501     745
 8.3    70     17    0.445     814
 7.0    54     17    0.442     408
 6.2    37     12    0.353     226
11.4    79     27    0.429    1675
11.6    70     26    0.497    1491
 4.5    37     12    0.380     121
 3.5    32     15    0.420      58
 6.2    45     15    0.449     278
 5.7    48     20    0.471     220
 6.0    57     20    0.447     342
 5.6    40     20    0.439     209
 4.0    44     27    0.394      84
 6.7    52     21    0.422     313
 4.0    38     27    0.496      60
12.1    74     27    0.476    1692
 4.5    37     12    0.382      74
 8.6    60     23    0.502     515
 9.3    63     18    0.458     766
 6.5    57     18    0.474     345
 5.6    46     12    0.413     210
 4.3    41     12    0.382     100
 4.5    42     12    0.457     122
 7.7    64     19    0.478     539
 8.8    70     22    0.496     815
 5.0    53     23    0.485     194
 5.4    61     23    0.488     280
 6.0    56     23    0.435     296
 7.4    52     14    0.474     462
 5.6    48     19    0.441     200
 5.5    50     19    0.506     229
 4.3    50     19    0.410     125
 4.2    31     10    0.412      84
 3.7    27     10    0.418      70
 6.1    39     10    0.470     224
 3.9    35     19    0.426      99
 5.2    48     13    0.436     200
 5.6    47     13    0.472     214
 7.8    69     13    0.470     712
```

```
6.1    49    13    0.464    297
6.1    44    13    0.450    238
4.0    34    13    0.424     89
4.0    38    13    0.407     76
8.0    61    13    0.508    614
5.2    47    13    0.432    194
3.7    33    13    0.389     66
;
```

Use the following DATA step to produce Output 6.7 through 6.10.

```
data temp29;
input age length @@ ;
if age > 28 then age=age+1;
asq=age*age;
if 43<= _n_ <= 63 then output;
cards;
14 620 21 910 28 1315 34 1635 41 2120 48 2300 55 2600 62 2925
69 3110 76 3315 83 3535 90 3710 97 3935 104 4145 111 4465 118 4510
125 4530 132 4545 139 4570 146 4605 153 4600
14 625 21 820 28 1215 34 1515 41 2110 48 2320 55 2805 62 2940
69 3255 76 3620 83 4015 90 4235 97 4315 104 4435 111 4495 118 4475
125 4535 132 4520 139 4600 146 4600 153 4600
14 590 21 910 28 1305 34 1730 41 2140 48 2725 55 2890 62 3685
69 3920 76 4325 83 4410 90 4485 97 4515 104 4480  111 4520 118 4545
125 4525 132 4560 139 4565 146 4626 153 4566
14 590 21 910 28 1205 34 1605 41 1915 48 2035 55 2140 62 2520 69 2710
76 2870 83 3020 90 3025 97 3030 104 3025 111 3040 118 3177 125 3180
132 3180 139 3257 146 3166 153 3214
;
```

Use the following DATA step to produce Output 6.11 through Output 6.13.

```
data air;
input utl 1-4 .2 asl 5-8 .3 spa 9-12 .4 avs 13-15 .2
      alf 16-18 .3 cpm 19-22 .3 csm 23-26 .3;
type=0; if asl>1.20 then type=1;
cards;
 78717901375468591225 81333
 95025153546483488227 51111
 79113501920442412234 10965
133036073390501397235 70935
 848196313814705822363 1375
 938112314814244662404 1119
108015761361487535242 51297
 836191231484654342711 1177
 843158416074474392743 1203
 883237732874734172780 1159
 842149535974444002833 1133
 962084013904254102846 1166
 871139211484444782906 1390
```

```
844087111864384952954146  1
891096112364164762962141  1
684100811504135392971160  0
900084513904254093044124  5
102016923007465381309611  79
829087710604374863140152  8
809152835224322873306094  9
947140813454705043306166  2
770123612214284553311150  7
957086313904264053313134  3
835103113654224223392143  1
727141611454384763437163  6
752097520253964263462147  6
956218932794623493527123  0
794094914884003943689145  2
755116412704224523760170  0
106027801282465425385616  37
108015181356443362395914  32
631082309434065414024217  6
565082112904013784737179  1
;
```

Chapter 7

Use the following DATA step to produce Output 7.1 through Output 7.6 and Output 7.13 through Output 7.15.

```
data decay;
input count time;
cards;
383 0
373 14
348 43
328 61
324 69
317 74
307 86
302 90
298 92
280 117
268 133
261 138
244 165
200 224
197 236
185 253
180 265
120 404
112.5 434
;
```

Use the following DATA step to produce Output 7.7 through Output 7.12.

```
data fish;
input age len29  aa ;
if age > 28 then age=age+1;
if 43<= _n_ <= 63 then output;
cards;
14 620 21 910 28 1315 34 1635 41 2120 48 2300 55 2600 62 2925
69 3110 76 3315 83 3535 90 3710 97 3935 104 4145 111 4465 118 4510
125 4530 132 4545 139 4570 146 4605 153 4600
14 625 21 820 28 1215 34 1515 41 2110 48 2320 55 2805 62 2940
69 3255 76 3620 83 4015 90 4235 97 4315 104 4435 111 4495 118 4475
125 4535 132 4520 139 4600 146 4600 153 4600
14 590 21 910 28 1305 34 1730 41 2140 48 2725 55 2890 62 3685
69 3920 76 4325 83 4410 90 4485 97 4515 104 4480  111 4520 118 4545
125 4525 132 4560 139 4565 146 4626 153 4566
14 590 21 910 28 1205 34 1605 41 1915 48 2035 55 2140 62 2520 69 2710
76 2870 83 3020 90 3025 97 3030 104 3025 111 3040 118 3177 125 3180
132 3180 139 3257 146 3166 153 3214
;
```

References

Allen, D.M. (1970), "Mean Square Error of Prediction as a Criterion for Selecting Variables," *Technometrics*, 13, 469-475.

Belsley, D.A. (1984), "Demeaning Conditions Through Centering," followed by comments by R.D. Cook et al., *The American Statistician*, 38, 73-93.

Belsley, D.A., Kuh, E., and Welsch, R.E. (1980), *Regression Diagnostics*, New York: John Wiley & Sons, Inc.

Berk, K.N. (1977), "Tolerance and Condition in Regression Computations," *Journal of the American Statistical Association*, 72, 863-866.

Brocklebank, J.C. and Dickey, D.A. (1986), *SAS System for Forecasting Time Series*, Cary, NC: SAS Institute Inc.

Dickens, J.W. and Mason, D.D. (1962), "A Peanut Sheller for Grading Samples: An Application in Statistical Design," *Transactions of the ASAE*, Volume 5, Number 1, 42-45.

Freund, R.J., Littell, R.C., and Spector, P.C. (1991), *SAS System for Linear Models, Third Edition*, Cary, NC: SAS Institute Inc.

Freund, R.J. and Minton, P.D. (1979), *Regression Methods*, New York: Marcel Dekker, Inc.

Fuller, W.A. (1978), *Introduction to Statistical Time Series*, New York: John Wiley & Sons, Inc.

Graybill, F. (1976), *Theory and Application of the Linear Model*, Boston: PWS and Kent Publishing Company, Inc.

Johnson, R.A. and Wichern, D.W. (1982), *Applied Multivariate Statistical Analysis*, Englewood Cliffs, NJ: Prentice Hall.

Kvalseth, T.O. (1985), "Cautionary Note about R^2," *The American Statistician*, 39, 279-286.

Mallows, C.P. (1973), "Some Comments on C(p)," *Technometrics*, 15, 661-675.

Montgomery, D.C. and Peck, E.A. (1982), *Introduction to Linear Regression Analysis*, New York: John Wiley & Sons, Inc.

Morrison, D.F. (1976), *Multivariate Statistical Methods, Second Edition*, New York: McGraw-Hill Book Co.

Myers, R.H. (1976), *Response Surface Methodology*, Blacksburg, Virginia: Virginia Polytechnic Institute and State University.

Myers, R.H. (1990), *Classical and Modern Regression with Applications, Second Edition*, Boston: PWS and Kent Publishing Company, Inc.

Neter, J., Wasserman, W., and Kutner, M.H. (1989), *Applied Linear Regression Models, Second Edition*, Homewood, IL: Richard D. Irwin Inc.

Rawlings, J.O. (1988), *Applied Regression Analysis: A Research Tool*, Pacific Grove, California: Wadsworth & Brooks/Cole.

SAS Institute Inc. (1988), *SAS/ETS User's Guide, Version 6, First Edition*, Cary, NC: SAS Institute Inc.

SAS Institute Inc. (1990), *SAS/IML Software: Usage and Reference, Version 6, First Edition*, Cary, NC: SAS Institute Inc.

SAS Institute Inc. (1990), *SAS Language and Procedures: Usage, Version 6, First Edition*, Cary, NC: SAS Institute Inc.

SAS Institute Inc. (1990), *SAS Language: Reference, Version 6, First Edition*, Cary, NC: SAS Institute Inc.

SAS Institute Inc. (1990), *SAS Procedures Guide, Version 6, Third Edition*, Cary, NC: SAS Institute Inc.

SAS Institute Inc. (1990), *SAS/STAT User's Guide, Version 6, Fourth Edition, Volume 2*, Cary, NC: SAS Institute Inc.

Searle, S.R. (1971), *Linear Models*, New York: John Wiley & Sons, Inc.

Smith, P.L. (1979), "Splines as a Useful and Convenient Statistical Tool," *The American Statistician*, 33, 57-62.

Steel, R.G.B. and Torrie, J. H. (1980), *Principles and Procedures of Statistics, Second Edition*, New York: McGraw-Hill Book Co.

Index

Your Turn

If you have comments or suggestions about SAS software or *SAS System for Regression, Second Edition*, please send them to us on a photocopy of this page.

Please return the photocopy to the Publications Division (for comments about this book) or the Technical Support Division (for suggestions about the software) at SAS Institute Inc., SAS Campus Drive, Cary, NC 27513.